NEW YORK CATHOLICS

Faith, Attitude & the Works!

Patrick McNamara

ORBIS BOOKS
Maryknoll, New York 10545

ORBIS BOOKS
Maryknoll, New York 10545

Fathers and Brothers
MARYKNOLL.

Founded in 1970, Orbis Books endeavors to publish works that enlighten the mind, nourish the spirit, and challenge the conscience. The publishing arm of the Maryknoll Fathers and Brothers, Orbis seeks to explore the global dimensions of the Christian faith and mission, to invite dialogue with diverse cultures and religious traditions, and to serve the cause of reconciliation and peace. The books published reflect the views of their authors and do not represent the official position of the Maryknoll Society. To learn more about Maryknoll and Orbis Books, please visit our website at www.maryknollsociety.org.

Copyright 2014 by Orbis Books
Published by Orbis Books, Box 302, Maryknoll, NY 10545-0302.
Design: Roberta Savage

Manufactured in the United States of America

Library of Congress Cataloging-in-Publication Data
McNamara, Patrick, 1968-
   New York Catholics : faith, attitude and the works! / by Patrick Mcnamara.
   pages cm
   Includes bibliographical references and index.
   ISBN 978-1-62698-071-6 (pbk.)
   1. Catholics--New York (State)--New York--Biography. I. Title.
F128.9.C3M39 2014
282.092'2747--dc23
                                        2014006050

To the loving memory of my father,
Thomas Warren McNamara (1931–1994),
And my mother,
Dolores Elizabeth Briordy McNamara (1931–2012),
Optimi Parentes

ACKNOWLEDGMENTS

First and foremost, I want to thank all the staff at Orbis. But my heartfelt thanks goes out in a special way to Mike Leach for his encouragement, support, and never-ending patience. He believed in me when I didn't always believe in myself. Thanks for everything, Mike!

I'm a fortunate person to have such a loving and supporting family. My wife, Virginia, never failed to encourage me in this project, and my daughter, Theresa, asked about it as well. I love you both! You both make me want to be a better person. A big thanks also goes out to my brothers, Tom, Jack, Rich, and Chris, who periodically asked me, "When are you finishing that book?" I hope they see some of themselves reflected in these pages.

There are so many new friends to thank, chief among them the people interviewed in the second part of this book. Thank you all for agreeing to be part of it. Each one of you has been an inspiration to me. I hope that I have accurately portrayed your story and your loving witness!

I have to thank the many archivists, scholars. and librarians who shared their knowledge with me, including Dr. Maria Mazzenga and W. John Shepherd at my alma mater, Catholic University; Dr. Tricia Pyne, Archdiocese of Baltimore Archives; Jac Treanor, Archdiocese of Chicago Archives; Rev. Rob Carbonneau, C.P., historian for the Passionists; Joe Coen, my former boss at the Diocese of Brooklyn Archives and longtime friend; Virginia Dowd, the Sister of St. Joseph Archives, Brentwood; Kate Feighery, archival manager, Archdiocese of New York; Msgr. Thomas J. Shelley, Professor Emeritus of Theology, Fordham University; Sister Loretta, F.H.M., the Franciscan Handmaids of Mary; Sister Constance Brennan, S.C., archivist, the Sisters of Charity; Sister Monica Wood, S.C., former librarian at St. Joseph's Seminary, Dunwoodie; Rev. Raymond A. Schroth, S.J., literary editor, *America* magazine.

There are also friends/inspirations, especially the following: Msgr. Sean G. Ogle; Dr. Paul A. Cimbala; Rev. Jack Replogle, S.J.; Rev. Thomas A. Lynch; Ellen Skerrett; Dave Cremin; Bob McNichol; Nora Saunders; Mary Whelan; Rob McCarthy; Msgr. Peter I. Vaccari; Sister Rose Pacatte, F.S.P.; Rev. George A. Pfundstein; Gene Halus; Kieran Doyle; Kevin Doyle; Rev. Robert E. Lauder; Bob Workman; Deb Linehan; Chris Flood; Rose Patrissi; Matt Bruner; Anne Ford; George Marsh; Alden V. Brown; Lenny Klie; Chip Rabus; Sean Mitchell; Jeff and Suzi Nauser; Inesa Lasher; Dan Oliva; Rev. Gerald R. Blaszczak, S.J.; Dr. Mark D. Naison; Doug Hart; Vincent Tennariello; Jeannie Stapleton Smith; Rev. Louis B. Pascoe, S.J.; Rev. Mark S. Massa, S.J.; Henry O'Neill; Curt Licitra; Al Van Damm; Pat Spellman; Nick O'Sullivan; Jeraldine Baichoo; Jim McEntee; Leonora Stein; Dr. Thomas M. Reilly, and many more too numerous to mention.

Any mistakes of course, fall squarely in my lap!

CONTENTS

INTRODUCTION

To love God and neighbor is not something abstract, but profoundly concrete.

—Pope Francis, address during visit at the homeless shelter, Dona Di Maria, May 21, 2013

I grew up in a neighborhood called Woodhaven on the southern end of Queens, right on the Brooklyn border. Its claim to fame is Niers, Queens' oldest bar, where *Goodfellas* was filmed. It was a great place to grow up, a community where everybody knew everyone else. In high school I branched out to Manhattan, where friends and I shopped for books, posters, records, rock jerseys, and camouflage pants. It was the eighties, and it was a great time to explore the city, which is just what we did.

After thirty years, I can say that every time there is like the first time. You could spend your whole life exploring these city streets and still be surprised decades later. I'm a Queens native, but I love all the boroughs. In short, I'm a New Yorker. I couldn't live anywhere else. It's an inherent part of who I am.

Another big part of my identity is my Catholicism. Growing up in a predominantly Irish, Italian, and German Catholic neighborhood, you defined yourself by your parish. In my case, it was St. Thomas the Apostle on Eighty-Seventh Street and Eighty-Eighth Avenue, a sizeable edifice with a Bavarian onion dome on top, reminiscent of its German founders. Life revolved around the church, the school, and especially CYO. You weren't from Woodhaven; you were from St. Thomas.

As an undergraduate at Fordham University I began to explore my New York Catholic roots. I read about how the Jesuits founded Fordham, I looked at old Catholic newspapers, and I took books out of the library on Catholic New York (and returned them!). I wrote my senior thesis on the *Brooklyn Tablet*, a paper my family received in the mail every Saturday. In graduate school I expanded my interest in the topic, and I was fortunate to work for ten years in the Diocese of Brooklyn Archives with a wonderful group of people. Every day I immersed myself in local Catholic history as a researcher and a writer.

New York Catholics are a special breed. We live in the craziest city in the world. There's little we haven't seen, and little surprises us. We're proud of our faith and our city, pardonably proud. We're surrounded by a rich heritage that few of us ever really take the time to explore: the hospitals and schools, the churches and the colleges, the statues and the stained-glass windows. We pass them every day, but do we really ponder their history and the work that went into these institutions?

As my friend Father Jim Martin says, take a look at the front doors of St. Patrick's Cathedral. On them you have a balustrade of saints and future saints. They invite us to explore the rich history that is Catholic New York: the men and women who built this local faith community we call New York. Their stories are ones we need to hear, as Catholics and New Yorkers.

On a Thursday afternoon in May 2011 I got a call from Mike Leach, who'd been reading my work and asked me if I'd consider doing a book on Catholic New Yorkers. I said yes (with an exclamation point) right away. It would be a book that cut right to the core of who I am. There were tough times along the way, including a fire that wiped out half my library—much of my archives on New York Catholicism—forcing my family and me to stay in a hotel until our house was repaired. Much of what you are now reading was written on a laptop in a hotel chair. That's what they call a labor of love. It's also the culmination of a lifelong interest, so I was determined to make it as true to the history and the flavor of New York Catholicism as I possibly could. The reader is the best judge of whether I have or not.

I loved writing about the people in this book, every single one of them, from St. Elizabeth Seton right on down to Father Mychal Judge. Some you may have heard of, like the two just mentioned. Others, like Mother Theodore Williams or Father John Drumgoole, may be less familiar. Each one, I think, tells us something about what it means to be a Catholic New Yorker.

So what *does* it mean to be a Catholic New Yorker?

I think it means, first of all, to know that you're part of something bigger than yourself, and I mean that in both the geographical and theological sense. New York City and the Catholic Church have much in common. Both have people from every corner of the earth. Queens alone has over a hundred nationalities speaking some 138 languages. Its churches have been described as a "second Pentecost." The church has survived all sorts of trials and tribulations, including the Reformation and the French Revolution. As one bishop said of the Catholic Church, "We're like the gas company. We've got our pipes in the ground, and we're not going anywhere."

There is also a distinctive charism to New York Catholicism: to welcome the newcomer. New Yorkers are a welcoming people (far more so than we're given credit for), and New York Catholics have been welcoming newcomers from all parts of the globe for as long as there's been a New York. From the Irish and Germans to the Vietnamese and Croatians, from the Italians and Polish to the Mexicans and the Nigerians, the whole world truly is here. It keeps the New York branch of Catholicism ever fresh and ever new. To quote a priest friend, "They don't call it New York for nothing."

The book you have in front of you is divided into two parts: historical figures and contemporary voices. In the first part, you'll meet a variety of people, some bishops, some priests, some laypeople, some religious. I chose them for their significance in delineating the history of Catholic New York, from its earliest days through the years of immigration, through the Gilded Age and the world wars and beyond. For example, John Hughes's story tells us an awful lot about the immigrant era, when so many Catholics came here in unprecedented numbers.

Can they say anything to us today? You bet they can! They remind of the need to reach out to society's least, to engage the larger culture in a fruitful and positive dialogue; they remind of what it really means to be Catholic in the original sense of the word: "universal."

I didn't want to write a book stuck completely in the past, lest I give the impression that nothing good was going on today. That's why I have a second part to this book: "Contemporary Voices." While I make no pretense to be a Catholic New York version of Studs Terkel, I did spend several months interviewing people involved in various ministries in this city. They range from the intellectual to the cultural, the pastoral, and the theological. Some work in a classroom, some on the streets and in the neighborhoods, and some on a computer screen. All are involved in making a difference in the life of this city and this church.

A word needs to be said about the criterion for choosing the following subjects, both historical and current. A few may be surprised about some of the choices, especially of figures that perhaps may not be noted for "regular" observation of their religious faith. But being Catholic is about more than observance of rules. Catholicism, as author Flannery O'Connor put it, is a "habit of being," a way of viewing and relating to both God and humanity. If such is the case, then all the people profiled herein qualify as Catholic, both with a big and a little "c."

In short, this book is meant to be a celebration of what it means to be a Catholic New Yorker. I hope you'll enjoy reading it as much as I enjoyed writing it. I hope it will inspire you to read more about these wonderful people, and I hope it will encourage you to further explore your own roots and heritage and celebrate that heritage. I firmly believe that when we celebrate one ethnic or religious group, we celebrate all.

Part 1

HISTORICAL VOICES

1

SIR THOMAS DONGAN

1634–1715

There was one common element in their religious beliefs that united them, and that was a detestation of Roman Catholicism, or as they would have said, "popery."
—THOMAS J. SHELLEY,
History of the Archdiocese of New York

Did you ever wonder where the name comes from? The "New" part is self-evident. It's a city that's always changing and reinventing itself. The "York" part comes from the English takeover of New Netherland in 1664, when both colony and city were renamed for King Charles II's brother James, Lord High Admiral and Duke of York. New York became a proprietorship—that is, James's personal property. While his authoritarian ways would spark controversy, so would his subsequent conversion to Roman Catholicism, heightening Protestant fears of papist influence at the highest levels of government.

In New York, these fears were exacerbated when James appointed Thomas Dongan as governor: Irishman, professional soldier, and Roman Catholic. Both among colonial New York's Dutch and English residents, anti-Catholicism was a potent element. As Thomas Shelley writes in his history of the New York archdiocese, "These Protestant colonists may not have been especially fervent church-goers, and they were themselves divided into rival denominations. Yet there was one common element in their religious beliefs that united them, and that was a detestation of Roman Catholicism, or as they would have said, 'popery.'"

Born in Kildare, Dongan belonged to Ireland's Catholic aristocracy. In the aftermath of the English Civil War (1642–1649) and the ascent of Oliver Cromwell, the Dongans fled to France, where Thomas joined the French army. A capable soldier, he rose to the rank of colonel, fighting the Spanish and the Dutch. After Charles II assumed the throne of England, he recalled all British subjects serving abroad in foreign armies. Dongan was appointed governor of Tangiers, then a British colony. It was in September 1682 when James appointed him governor of New York.

When Dongan arrived in New York, he brought his personal chaplain, an English Jesuit named Thomas Harvey. On August 26, 1683, Father Harvey celebrated the first Catholic Mass in New York City at Fort James, on the tip of Manhattan island. (Battery Park is named for the fort's guns.) More than a few Protestant eyebrows were raised at this sight, but Dongan was generally well received, due to his "knowledge, refinement, and modesty."

Soon Dongan convened the first assembly in New York history, which affirmed the basic political and personal rights of its citizens. The Charter of Liberties and Privileges granted religious freedom to all those professing "faith in God by Jesus Christ," thereby granting religious tolerance to Roman Catholics. In 1686 the charter was amended to include "all persons of what religion whatsoever." (The first Jewish New Yorkers had arrived in the 1650s from Spain.)

Dongan proved a capable governor. New York historians Edwin Burrows and Mike Wallace call him an "experienced imperial functionary." But, they note, his Catholicism "rankled" Protestants. So did his appointing Catholics to key government positions. In 1686, more Jesuits arrived, starting a school near what is now Wall Street. Nearly all the students at New York's first Catholic school were Protestant. (Apparently their parents appreciated the value of a good Jesuit education.)

The year 1688, however, was the turning point. James had succeeded his brother in 1685, the first Catholic monarch in over 150 years. At first, the English were willing to accept this as long as he produced no heir. But produce he did, and the Glorious Revolution led to his overthrow. By then, Dongan had left New York, but a Protestant uprising led by Jacob Leisler aimed to remove these "Popish Doggs and Divells" from power.

Soon Dongan's charter was revised to deny religious liberty "for any person of the Romish religion." Priests were banned from New York, and anyone aiding or harboring one was subject to fines and imprisonment. Catholics were banned from office and denied the vote, a state of affairs that wouldn't be changed until the Revolutionary Era. On the eve of the Revolution, one minister wrote that there was not the "least trace of popery" in New York.

Back in Ireland, Dongan succeeded his childless brother as the Earl of Limerick, but he died in a state of near-poverty in 1715. A pioneer of religious tolerance in early America, his plans ended in failure through no fault of his own. The times were simply against him. His plans for an open, inclusive New York would have to wait for another day. His name lives on not only in the Staten Island neighborhood of Dongan Hills, but also as the first significant Catholic New Yorker to make a difference in the life of a growing city.

2

Saint Elizabeth Ann Bayley Seton
1774–1821

Poor, deluded Mrs. Seton.

—A contemporary of Seton

Walking through downtown Manhattan, one comes across streets with names like Barclay, Delancey, and Duane: streets named for the families that dominated eighteenth-century New York. These were people whom Elizabeth Ann Bayley knew in her youth, back in the days when New York was a "walking city." At the time of her birth in 1774, what's now called Downtown composed the entire city, and one could walk it in twenty minutes.

Her father was an internationally renowned physician, and she moved

casually in the highest social circles. A relative of the Roosevelts, she knew many of the early republic's leading figures, including Washington, Hamilton, and John Jay. Betty Bayley, as her intimates called her, belonged to one of the city's first families, and she had numerous suitors, including a handsome young man named William Magee Seton, scion of another distinguished family.

William's father owned a shipping line and helped found the Bank of New York. He and Betty made an ideal couple: handsome, affluent, and very much in love. In 1794 they were married by an Episcopalian bishop. Over the years, five children arrived, and the future looked promising. In her spare time Mrs. Seton organized charitable work, raising funds for widows and orphans.

But soon the country experienced an economic downturn, and the young couple lost nearly everything. As William declared bankruptcy, his health took a turn for the worse. The Setons traveled to Italy in search of a healthier climate, but William died there of tuberculosis. Betty was a single parent stranded abroad. The experience proved to be the turning point of her life.

In Italy she had her first close encounter with Roman Catholicism. She found herself especially drawn to the Eucharist. She wrote, "How happy would we be, if we believed what these dear souls believe: that they possess God in the Sacrament, and that He remains in their churches and is carried to them when they are sick."

In addition to the Bible, which she had read since childhood, she also discovered spiritual classics associated with the Catholic tradition, especially *The Imitation of Christ* from the fourteenth century.

Back home, against all advice, Elizabeth decided to convert. But New York society, one historian notes, was "frankly bigoted." Episcopalianism was its unofficial religion. "Romans," on the other hand, "were the shiftless, scrubby immigrants who attended the shabby little church on Barclay Street." It was in that church, St. Peter's, in early 1805 that she was received into the Roman Catholic Church. A wealthy relative quickly disinherited her.

"Poor, deluded Mrs. Seton," as some called her, had many doors closed to her. To support herself and her children she opened a school in Manhattan. But these were tough times, and she considered relocating to Montreal. When a priest from Baltimore asked her to open a school there, she agreed. The site of the nation's first Catholic colony, Baltimore was a climate more congenial to converts like Elizabeth. This school proved a success.

Later she opened a school at Emmitsburg, just south of the Mason-Dixon Line. She enrolled her two sons at Mount St. Mary's, a nearby Catholic boys' school, and she taught her three daughters in a converted farmhouse. Over time, Elizabeth was increasingly interested in becoming a nun. (As a widow, such an option wasn't closed to her.)

Soon a group of like-minded women joined her, and they took religious vows. In 1809 Elizabeth was named Mother Superior. Their habits were the widow's garb that Mother Seton had worn: a black dress with a cape, and a cap tied under the chin. They called themselves the Sisters of Charity. They taught, conducted retreats, visited the sick, fed the poor, and tended the dying.

Barely five feet tall, Mother Seton was a tough woman. One biographer describes her as a "forceful personality." She didn't fear to challenge church leadership. Once, for example, she gave a young priest "a scolding he will remember" (in her own words), for delivering "a sermon so evidently lazy." He responded, "I didn't trouble myself much about it, Ma'am." She shot back, "Oh Sir! That awakens my anger. Do you remember a priest holds the honor of God on his lips? Do you not trouble yourself to spread his fire he wishes so enkindled? If you will not prepare and study when young, what when you are old? There is a Mother's lesson!"

"But prayer—"

"Yes, prayer and preparation, too!"

Her last years were difficult, as she lost two daughters while battling tuberculosis. In 1821 her last words to her Sisters and family were, "Be children of the Church, be children of the Church." Canonized in 1975, Elizabeth Ann Bayley Seton was the first American-born saint and the first founder of an American community for women religious.

During her lifetime, New York's population had expanded significantly, and so would its Catholic community. The Sisters of Charity would serve future generations of New Yorkers in the classroom and beyond. Today the

Seton name graces schools, colleges, hospitals, and health-care institutions worldwide. Statues, stained-glass windows, and prayer cards show her teaching children and tending the poor.

But, as James Martin notes, a saint is more than a statue, and idealizing them can lead us to overlook their relevance for today. Here we have a single mother, ostracized for her convictions, holding her family together through hard times. And she did something a parent should never have to do, bury her own children. This was a formidable woman indeed—as one biographer writes, "a New Yorker born and bred."

3

VENERABLE PIERRE TOUSSAINT
1766–1853

I saw how uncommon, how noble, was his character.
— A CONTEMPORARY OF TOUSSAINT

During New York's early years, not all men and women came here of their own free will. Among these was a young man named Pierre Toussaint, the household slave of one Jacques Berard, a wealthy French planter who barely escaped revolutionary Haiti with his life. While Pierre rarely discussed this experience, historians agree that Haiti was a time bomb waiting to explode. Decades of brutal exploitation resulted in a decade-long slave revolt. Monsieur Berard, his wife, and his slaves expected their stay in New York to be short, but events on the island precluded their return.

Nearly penniless, Jacques Berard sent Pierre to learn the hairdressing trade, intricate and detailed work in an age of elaborate hairstyles. He learned the profession quickly. One biographer notes that he became "the fashionable coiffeur of the day," whose clientele included the city's first families. Born on the family plantation, Pierre was intensely loyal to Berard. Fortunate enough to avoid the hellish existence of a field slave, he lived the relatively comfortable life of a domestic servant.

Through his earnings, Pierre almost singlehandedly supported the Berards. After Jacques's death, he looked after Madame Berard, who freed him shortly before her own death. (Slaves were by no means rare in New York City. As late as 1800, there were some twenty-five hundred.)* As a free person of color, Pierre was among New York's foremost black entrepreneurs. He bought a house in downtown Manhattan, investing in real estate and banks.

One of New York's most respected black citizens, contemporaries recalled his "innate sense of personal dignity," his "exquisite charity and consideration for others," and "tender compassion for all." One woman stated,

> I saw how uncommon, how noble, was his character. It is the whole
> which strikes me when thinking of him; his perfect Christian be-
> nevolence, displaying itself not alone in words, but in daily deeds; his
> entire faith, love, and charity; his remarkable tact, and refinement of
> feeling; his just appreciation of those around him; his perfect good
> taste in dress and furniture—he did not like anything gaudy and un-
> derstood the relative fitness of things.

Comfortably set, Pierre worked well into old age. "I have enough for myself," he once said, "but not enough for others." A benefactor of the city's Catholic Orphan Asylum, he and his wife raised several homeless African American children. He also tended the sick, sometimes at great risk. An early biographer writes,

> When the yellow fever prevailed in New York, by degrees Maiden
> Lane was almost wholly deserted, and almost every house in it

---

* Slavery was not banned in New York State until 1827.

closed. One poor woman, prostrated by the terrible disorder, remained there with little or no attendance, till Toussaint day by day came through the lone street, crossed the barricades, entered the deserted house where she lay, and performed the nameless offices of a nurse, fearlessly exposing himself to the contagion.

A daily communicant, for nearly sixty years Pierre attended morning Mass at St. Peter's Church on Barclay Street, New York's first Catholic church. During its early years, he also helped support St. Vincent de Paul, New York's first French parish. He also gave generously to causes such as the Catholic Orphan Asylum. Throughout his adult life, he was able to quote extensive passages from scripture and devotional works such as *The Imitation of Christ*.

Well-meaning but patronizing white Catholics would call Pierre a "Catholic Uncle Tom," but he wasn't naïve about racism in his city or his church. At least once he was refused admittance to a Catholic church. Although he rarely discussed slavery, he did purchase the freedom of several men and women. On a rare occasion when referring to the abolitionists, he commented, "They have never seen blood flow as I have."

But when Pierre died at eighty-seven in the summer of 1853, there were many "eyes glistening with emotion," one observer noted. In his sermon, Father William Quinn noted, "Though no relative is left to mourn for him, yet many present feel that they have lost one who always had wise counsel for the rich and words of encouragement for the poor. And all are grateful for having known him. . . . There were very few left among the clergy superior to him in devotion and zeal for the Church and for the glory of God; among laymen, none."

While Toussaint may not have directly challenged the larger injustices of the day, neither did he accept them passively. In his own quiet way, he showed that he was far from being the "Catholic Uncle Tom" that some well-meaning whites labeled him. As an example of holiness lived out quietly and consistently, he merits our consideration today. From slave to entrepreneur, a benefactor and friend of the poor, New York's Cardinal John J. O'Connor (who introduced his canonization cause) added, "If ever a man was truly free, it was Pierre Toussaint."

4

Peter Turner

1787–1862

Many of our Catholic histories read partly like pages of a ledger and partly like catalogues of bishops and priests.
—Charles Herbermann

In October 1895, at St. James Cathedral in downtown Brooklyn, Long Island's first Catholic church, a unique monument was formally dedicated to a person who played a key role in the church's founding seventy-three years earlier. The five-foot bronze bust didn't honor a bishop or a priest but an Irish immigrant named Peter Turner who was praised as a "pioneer Catholic layman." According to the *Brooklyn Eagle*, Turner did more than that; he "virtually founded" Catholicism on Long Island, long before a priest arrived.

When St. James was erected in 1822, Brooklyn was quite literally the frontier of New York Catholic life. Not one Catholic church, school, or building of any kind existed on Long Island. (At the time there were no more than a half dozen priests in the entire state of New York.)

But Catholic numbers, more specifically Irish Catholic immigrant numbers, were growing, especially after the founding of the Brooklyn Navy Yard. Among them was young Turner, who had emigrated from County Wexford as a teenager and settled on Fulton Street. By then, the neighborhood was known as Vinegar Hill, for a battle fought during the Irish Rebellion of 1798.

For Mass, Brooklyn Catholics took the Fulton Street Ferry to Manhattan, attending St. Peter's Church on Barclay Street. Tradition has it that Brooklyn's first Mass took place in 1820 at William Purcell's home on the corner of York and Gold Streets. As their numbers increased, they talked seriously about starting their own church. In January 1822, then, Peter Turner drew up a petition to the local bishop announcing their plans:

> [We] the Catholics of Brooklyn . . . want our children instructed in the principles of our Holy Religion; we want more convenience in hearing the Word of God ourselves. In fact, we want a Church, a Pastor,

and a place for Interment: all of which, with the assistance of Divine Providence . . . we have every reason to expect the cheerful assistance of the laity, as well as the Right Reverend Bishop and all his clergy.

This circular makes it clear that the laity, not the bishop or the clergy, took the lead here in starting Catholic life in Brooklyn. Meetings were held at Daniel Dempsey's home on Fulton Street. The Roman Catholic Society of Brooklyn was formed, with Turner as its first president. Land was purchased for a church, a school, and a cemetery, all of which were in place by the following year. (Not for another two years would a resident priest arrive, and his stay was short.)

In the years to come, as new churches rose across Long Island slowly but surely, Turner continued to play a leading role in Catholic life. In 1830 he was elected first president of the Roman Catholic Orphan Society of Brooklyn, an organization founded to care for disadvantaged youth. The following year, he was influential in persuading the Sisters of Charity to come to Brooklyn. Later he helped found the Emerald Association, whose annual ball has raised money for Catholic childcare on Long Island since 1839. Later in 1845 he was elected president of the Brooklyn Benevolent Society, another organization founded to provide for Brooklyn's orphans.

Also active in civic affairs, Turner served as health warden for the city of Brooklyn and was a member of the city's Poor Relief Committee. Peter Turner died at his home on Front Street on December 31, 1862, but the Turner family continued his legacy of service to the Catholic Church on Long Island. His son, John was among the first priests ordained for the Brooklyn Diocese. In 1857 he became rector of St. James Cathedral, the church his father had helped build, and vicar-general of the diocese.

In a 1916 article for the newly founded *Catholic Historical Review*, historian Charles Herbermann wrote, "Many of our Catholic histories read partly like pages of a ledger and partly like catalogues of bishops and priests." Two years later, Herbermann's colleague and friend Thomas Meehan added, "The layman, outside a few stock historic figures, is conspicuously absent." Turner's story shows that during the early years of the New York church, it was frequently the laity who paved the way for the growth of that church. Peter Turner was more than an interesting footnote in that history; he was an integral part of it, as much as the priests and bishops who often followed in his footsteps.

5

SERVANT OF GOD FATHER FELIX VARELA

1788–1853

A life of constant work and self-denial.
—A CONTEMPORARY OF VARELA

He came to New York in the winter of 1823, in the middle of a blizzard, with a price on his head, knowing little if any English. Until recently he had been among Latin America's most respected scholars. But after Father Felix Varela advocated liberty for his native Cuba, he was exiled for life. In time, however, he learned English well enough to author books and edit newspapers in both Spanish and English. The beloved pastor of a largely Irish parish, he took a leading role in governing the New York church.

Born in Cuba to a respected family, his grandfather was governor of Spanish Florida. Although he was expected to follow in the family profession, he rebelled, insisting that he would not "kill men, but save souls." He won, and he studied at Havana's College and Seminary of San Carlos. A brilliant student, he was ordained early at age twenty-three so that he could teach the younger students.

Within a decade the young priest was, in the words of one biographer, "Cuba's foremost philosopher and illustrious teacher." For Varela, Christians had a responsibility to bring about a free and just society based on gospel principles. The church, he believed, had to stand for freedom. As one future Cuban leader said, Varela "taught us to think."

He was elected as one of Cuba's delegates to the Spanish Cortes, an advisory assembly, in Madrid. A strong advocate of Cuban independence, he called for a dominion of independent colonies loosely affiliated with the mother country, Spain. The Spanish government responded by placing a death sentence on him, but he escaped to Gibraltar and from there to the United States aboard the *Draper C. Thorndike.*

Soon he founded New York City's first Spanish-language journal, *El Habanero*, where he continued to advocate Cuban independence. (Even this was dangerous business. In New York, several attempts would be made on Varela's life.) But he also practiced English, by translating agricultural manuals into Spanish. It was dull work, but it paid off. He wrote for and edited some of the city's first English-speaking Catholic newspapers as well.

If Varela spent the first half of his life advocating for the rights of the Cuban people, he spent the second half working for Irish immigrants who came to New York in ever-growing numbers. His natural sympathy for the oppressed seems to have played a role here, as many Irish immigrants came to the city with famine and poverty nipping at their heels.

A fellow priest described Varela as small and slight, "his dress thin and seedy, his face sharp and fleshless, with an olive complexion bordering on the Indian." Another priest noted, however, that although he was small and slight, he was nonetheless "a man of great decision of character and of indomitable courage in the defense of truth." His passion for justice and human rights won him the respect of his fellow immigrants.

In addition to being an author and an advocate, Father Varela was first and foremost a parish priest. When he came to New York, it was, one historian notes, "an immense, unwieldy, poverty-stricken missionary diocese." Two churches served twenty-five thousand Catholics. One author wrote of Varela's pastoral activity:

> The poor and the sick were the principal objects of his affection and care. He went to them at all times, he gave them all that he possessed—even the coat he had on, as he did on one occasion in winter, to a poor man who had been stripped in the street; and when the cholera was raging in New York in 1832, Father Varela may be said to have lived in the hospitals.

His housekeeper often yelled at him for giving away his goods. But Varela's was not a gloomy religion. During hard times, he told parishioners, "Never mind, go on, the sun shines for all without distinction." "True religion," he told them, "brings happiness." Prayers, he insisted, "are made to bring us consolation, not torture."

Editor, author and pastor, Varela rose to high leadership positions in New York. In 1837, he was named vicar-general of the Diocese of New York (a sort of second-in-command to the bishop). Many felt he may have been named a bishop himself had it not been for the Spanish government's strong opposition to any such move. But his greatest joy was being "the pastor of the Irish."

By the late 1840s, however, illness was getting the best of him, and he was forced to move to Florida, where he died in 1853. A contemporary notes,

> A life of constant work and self-denial . . . could terminate in but one result. Father Varela's health was undermined and ruined; and in 1846 he found himself prostrated, and unable to do the slightest work. He used to say, with a pleasant cheerful smile, half in jest and half in earnest, that he had three or four diseases at the same time, all struggling to break him down.

Long after his death, New Yorkers regarded him as a saint. In 1883, one priest wrote that former parishioners preserved locks of his hair and pieces of his cassock as relics, while some made an annual visit to his tomb in Florida.

Priest, teacher, philosopher, author, editor, jurist, Cuban nationalist: Felix Francisco Jose Maria de la Concepción Varela y Morales became all things to all people. He appears in Cuban history textbooks as well as on American stamps. Cuban Communists speak of him as a proto-Marxist. But as New York's Cardinal John J. O'Connor noted, everything Varela did was "founded in his identity as a Christian and a Catholic."

6

ARCHBISHOP JOHN JOSEPH HUGHES
1797–1864

He is always game.
—A CONTEMPORARY OF HUGHES

In the summer of 1817, when a young immigrant laborer stepped off a ship in Baltimore harbor, America's Catholic population was minuscule. Forty-seven years later, when that same immigrant died as New York's first archbishop, Catholicism was the country's largest denomination. During the years in between, immigration reached unprecedented levels, anti-Catholicism vehemently reasserted itself, the Irish assumed leadership roles in their church, and John Hughes ruled New York Catholics, writes one

historian, "like an Irish chieftain." But as a peer said, he did it "with feeling."

A fellow bishop described Hughes as "emphatically a self-made man." Born in 1797, his father owned a small farm in County Tyrone. From childhood he wanted to be a priest, but economic hardship forced him to leave school at an early age. At twenty he sailed for America. Over the next few years he worked as a day laborer in Pennsylvania and Maryland, doing construction jobs, digging in quarries, and gardening.

While he was working at a convent in Emmitsburg, Maryland, he met Mother Elizabeth Seton. Later as he worked on the grounds of nearby Mount St. Mary's Seminary, he rediscovered his vocation. But when he applied for admission, the president, Father John Dubois, rejected him. Mother Seton interceded for him, and he entered in 1820. Hughes always venerated her memory, but he never forgave Dubois.

Ordained in 1826, he was sent to Philadelphia. At St. Mary's, the city's most affluent parish, a struggle was taking place between the bishop and the trustees, who refused to relinquish control. Not long after being assigned there, Hughes told shocked parishioners that since *they* weren't observing *their* obligations, *he* wasn't interested in being their pastor, and he resigned on the spot. To put it simply, Hughes loved a good fight. One priest commented, "He is always *game*."

Through newspaper articles and public debates with Protestant ministers, he achieved national renown as a powerful Catholic spokesman. Bishop Henry Conwell of Philadelphia said, "Ah, that Hughes. We'll make him a bishop someday." It happened in 1838. He was sent to New York to assist Bishop John Dubois. At the time, his biographer writes,

> His personal appearance was striking and agreeable. He was about five feet nine inches in height, well formed, with a powerful frame, and, in early and middle life, an erect carriage. He had a remarkably large head, prominent features, a large but well-shaped Roman nose, a sharp resolute mouth, and brown hair. . . . Until age and disease had set their mark upon him he was a handsome man.

Frail and aging, Dubois was ill-equipped to lead a growing church, and Hughes took charge long before it was official. For over twenty-five years, he shaped Catholic life in New York like no bishop before him. Bishops preface their signature with a cross, but Hughes's opponents claimed that his was actually a dagger. Among the first to feel his wrath was the Public School Society, a Protestant organization running the city schools.

Public school days began with Protestant prayers, hymns, and Bible readings. Textbooks referred to Rome's "general corruption," and libraries carried books calling the Irish "drunken and depraved." Hughes argued that since the schools were essentially Protestant, Catholics should also receive public money. Appealing in vain to the usually pro-immigrant Democrats for help, he organized a political ticket that cost them votes at the polls. Catholic schools got no funding, but a bill was soon passed banning religion in public schools, thereby putting an end to the Public School Society.

As immigration from famine-stricken Ireland rose, hostility grew among native-born Protestants who resented their arrival. After they burned several Philadelphia churches, Hughes visited New York's mayor, who asked, "Are you afraid that some of your churches will be burned?" "No, sir," he replied, "but I am afraid some of yours will be burned. We can protect our own. I come to warn you for own good." Catholics citywide armed to protect their parishes. No churches were burned.

As the Catholic population increased rapidly, New York was named an archdiocese, and Hughes an archbishop. Many of today's parishes, schools, and charitable institutions have roots in his time. His statue stands on the grounds of Fordham University, which he founded in 1841 as St. John's College. In August 1858 he laid the cornerstone for a new cathedral uptown on Fifth Avenue and Fiftieth Street. Located far from what was then the city's center, it was called "Hughes's folly."

A champion of the common man, Hughes could also be domineering and high handed. When two Irish-born priests complained that he ignored canon law, he replied, "I will show you County Monaghan canon law. I will send you back to the bogs whence you came!" Undeniably charismatic, he was less gifted as an administrator. His own secretary recalled that he couldn't balance his books, his papers were always in disarray, and he "lacked all idea of order or system."

While recognized as a powerful advocate of the immigrant, he was frequently indifferent to non-Irish concerns. His relationship with the Germans, the archdiocese's second-largest ethnic group, was at best polite. For years he refused the Italians a parish because of a quarrel with one of their priests. During the 1863 Draft Riots, when largely Irish mobs victimized African Americans, his outrage was undeniably less powerful than it had been on other occasions.

John Hughes wasn't a diplomat, a scholar, or a bureaucrat. It's doubtful he had an ecumenical bone. But he did provide strong leadership for a young immigrant church that needed it, and his aggressive style suited a violently anti-Catholic era. Although New York has changed greatly over the years, his legacy continues in the schools he created, the religious orders he welcomed, the charities he began, and the parishes he founded. Perhaps his legacy is most visible in the cathedral he never saw completed, the symbol of Catholic arrival in America, St. Patrick's on Fifth Avenue, located in what is now the center of the world.

7

FATHER JOHANN STEPHAN RAFFEINER

1785–1861

The apostle to the Germans.

—BROOKLYN EAGLE

B y the mid-nineteenth century, New York City had a sizeable German community. After Berlin and Vienna, it was the world's third-largest

German city. Since the 1830s the Lower East Side was a bastion of German
American life. Yorkville would follow.
Many opted for Brooklyn: Williamsburg, Bushwick, and East New York.
Wherever they went they re-created
the villages they had known back
home, replete with shops, beer gardens, and high-steepled churches.

One of the most beautiful was
Most Holy Trinity, on the corner of
Montrose and Graham Avenues in
Williamsburg. Author Betty Smith
(born Elizabetha Sophia Wehner) was
baptized here. In *A Tree Grows in Brooklyn*, her protagonist Francie Nolan
calls it "the most beautiful church in Brooklyn. It was made of old gray stone
and had twin spires that rose cleanly into the sky, high above the tallest tenements. Inside, the high vaulted ceilings, narrow deepset stained-glass windows and elaborately carved altars made it a miniature cathedral." Stone was
imported from Wurzburg, stained-glass windows from Innsbruck, and people from Bavaria and Hesse. Together they created the church known as the
"German cathedral." The church was the brainchild of Father Johann Stephan
Raffeiner, one of the movers and shakers of German New York.

Born to a wealthy family in the Austrian Tyrol, he'd been interested in
the priesthood early on, and he studied in Rome. During the Napoleonic
Wars his seminary was closed, and Raffeiner opted for the medical field. As
a doctor he worked in a Roman hospital before serving as a surgeon with
the Austrian army. After the war, he continued practicing medicine (very
successfully) for a few years before going back to the seminary and being
ordained at age forty.

As a parish priest, Raffeiner was increasingly interested in the situation
of German-speaking Catholics immigrating to America in growing numbers. When an American bishop called for German-speaking priests, he
volunteered, coming to New York in 1833. The New York Germans, tired of
worshipping in basements, wanted their own church. "We do not want the
Irish over us," they said.

Raffeiner organized St. Nicholas Church on the Lower East Side. Soon it had some ten thousand people, many living in overcrowded buildings. Many missed the open country and the fresh air of home. Across the river, Williamsburg—a largely unsettled area with affordable housing—seemed a pleasant alternative to tenement life. Many of Raffeiner's parishioners were moving there.

In the summer of 1841, with his own money—he'd become independently wealthy from his medical practice—Raffeiner purchased the Meserole farm in Williamsburg. That October, the Church of the Most Holy Trinity opened, and he transferred there as the first pastor. He slept in the basement, which doubled as a schoolhouse. At the time, one parishioner recalled, there wasn't a single house within sight of the new church.

Seventy families, all German, composed the congregation. One Brooklyn historian writes, "The singing societies and the Turnvereins [gymnasiums] and dance halls and beer gardens . . . helped make life pleasant in the good old German way." In 1843 a German priest serving with Raffeiner described a typical Sunday as "work all day": morning confessions, Mass, afternoon catechism, evening prayers, and "pastoral conversation." One could reasonably hope, he suggested, for a congregation of "more than one thousand souls."

Not everyone welcomed them, however. Protestants calling themselves "Native Americans" joined a group, about which they pledged to reveal nothing—nothing, that is, but its deep hatred of Catholics. (They were called "Know-Nothings.") When Bill "the Butcher" Poole's* gang tried to burn local Catholic churches, Father Raffeiner stationed armed men around the parish grounds. The parish history has this to say: "In these stirring times the martial spirit of the old soldier-pastor of Holy Trinity came back to inspire his devoted flock to take measures to ensure the safety of their lives and property."

He started a school. In August 1853, four Sisters of St. Dominic from Bavaria stepped off the ship *Germania* in New York harbor. Their goal was Pennsylvania, but their escort never arrived. Father persuaded them to help him in Williamsburg. They were much needed. If priests were scarce in the 1850s, teaching nuns were scarcer.

---

* Portrayed by Daniel Day Lewis in Martin Scorsese's 2002 film *The Gangs of New York*.

That fall, the Dominican Sisters started teaching (in German) at Most Holy Trinity. Soon there were fifteen hundred students, all German, whose parents paid fifteen cents a week. By the time of Raffeiner's death in 1861, there were ten thousand parishioners and more coming. After the priest's death, the parish continued to expand impressively: a hospital, orphanage, home for seniors, even a daily newspaper (in German).

There was also a group for Civil War veterans, a dramatic society, a young men's club, and a parish library. The St. Joseph's Society provided for sick members and their families. On holy days, the Union Guard marched through the neighborhood while hymns like "Maria Meine Koenegin" ("Mary, My Queen") were sung. Long before the term "megachurch" was coined, Brooklyn's German Catholics lived it.

A parish's story involves more than just a building. It's about all the people like Johann Raffeiner who helped build and sustain it. It's about the hardships they endured to build a faith community, how they preserved that faith and handed it on to a new generation. Today, a new generation of immigrants does the same in Williamsburg, Brooklyn. (And trees still grow there.)

8

JEDEDIAH VINCENT HUNTINGTON

1815–1862

The first purely literary man Catholics in the United States can boast.

—ORESTES A. BROWNSON

Jedediah Huntington was a bit of a dilettante, and he could afford to be. Born to an old New York family, he was the son of a wealthy broker and the grandson of a Revolutionary War general. As a young man he *breathed* establishment. He attended the University of Pennsylvania, where he earned a medical degree he never used. Instead he opted to teach at St. Paul's, an Episcopalian school on Long Island, while he figured out what he wanted to do.

While there he studied for a divinity degree and was ordained an Episcopalian priest in 1841. For five years he served as rector of a church in Middlebury, Vermont, until he began to have doubts about his church's theological foundation, a concern brought on in part by the Oxford Movement and John Henry Newman's conversion to Roman Catholicism. After resigning his parish, Huntington and wife traveled to Europe, where they spent most of the next three years in Rome. As his biographer James J. Walsh notes, it proved to be "a step Romeward," and in 1849 both he and his wife were received into the Catholic Church.

Marriage banned him from continuing his ministry, so he moved back to his native New York to pursue a writing career. One of his poems expressed his love for the city:

> With much the soul that fetters and degrades,
> In thee, Manhatta! Yet are some things seen
> That lift to joy and love thy citizens;
> Refreshing as a dream of forest glades,
> Not seldom meets his eye when business jades
> In the brick desert of an oasis green.

Huntington was more successful as a novelist. Between 1849 and 1860 he wrote four novels dealing with Catholic themes in a contemporary setting. On the eve of the Civil War he was considered the premier American Catholic novelist of his time. He's largely forgotten now—and probably with good reason. But his books are important in that they deal firsthand with the topic of conversion to Catholicism and why people converted.

His first novel was perhaps his most successful. *Lady Alice* (1850) deals with an aristocratic English woman who visits Italy. While she's there, she wavers between Anglicanism and Roman Catholicism. The aesthetic appeal hits her first, when she visits the Duomo in Milan:

> No other cathedral of Italy impresses you with so profound a sense of religion as this. The vastness and dimness of the nave; the mighty shafts that sustain the groined roof; the grave color; the simplicity of the aisles, undisfigured by the numerous altars elsewhere seen; the grilled and gloomy choir, with its seven ever-burning lamps, and the crimson folds of the baldachino, half-screening the gorgeous windows of the Lady-chapel, are an impressive . . . [contrast] to the tawdry splendor too often observed in Italian churches.

Many did convert to Catholicism, some of the main reasons for which were its aesthetic appeal and sense of mystery, its rich tradition, its authoritative voice, and its balance between the individual and the communal. One non-Catholic observer wrote in the 1830s,

> The Catholics know and feel their power; they use all the senses, enlist them one and all into their service; their pictures, their sculptures, their music, and their architecture are all the most perfect they can obtain; and I have felt my heart throb with ecstasy, while I listened to the touching melody of their sublime chants—and oh, how many prostrate themselves before the altar, meted and subdued by the harmony; and imagine that feeling is the true worship of God.

Huntington's novels point to an important fact in both England and America during the years leading up to the Civil War. A notable number of antebellum Protestant men and women were converting to Catholicism.

Jedediah Vincent (he took the middle name upon converting) Huntington's life as a Catholic, however, wasn't always an easy one. A difficult character, and a bit pretentious, he tended to butt heads with fellow Catholics, and he moved from job to job: writer, editor, and back again. Walsh notes the "lack of refinement" he found among the Irish immigrants who composed much of his readership. (Huntington complained about the lack of a "sufficient Catholic reading public.")

Still, he was, according to Catholic author Orestes Brownson, "the first purely literary man Catholics in the United States can boast." His novels, all a variation on the theme of conversion to Catholicism, were well received both in England and the United States—although some critics accused him of impropriety in describing women's ankles, a risqué thing that appeared only in French novels. Huntington's goal was to create a fiction "imbued with Catholic faith and morality, so as to serve the interests of religion."

Never in strong health, Huntington died in 1862, and his literary reputation wasn't far behind. Other novelists would follow in his vein, creating works of Catholic fiction that continue to this day. He wasn't the best Catholic novelist in America. But he was the first, and for that he merits some degree of attention.

9

FATHER SYLVESTER MALONE

1821–1899

Would to heaven that all the faiths had men like you.

—A CONTEMPORARY OF MALONE

Williamsburg is a neighborhood that's reinvented itself numerous times through the years: from Hasidic to hipster, from Italian to Hispanic, from German to Polish, and sometimes back again. For a brief time in the 1850s, it was even its own city. When Sylvester Malone arrived there as a newly ordained twenty-three-year-old priest in the summer of 1844, little did he realize he would spend the next fifty-five years of his life there on South Third Street. At the start, some ten thousand people lived there; by the end, there were 350,000. And he had become one of its first citizens. Williamsburg's Jewish and Protestant citizens called him as "our Father Malone."

He never would have suspected such early on in his ministry, when the local firemen jeered at a priest in their midst or when Bill "the Butcher" Poole tried to burn his church. But he won people over by his patience, his charity, and his fundamental belief in the "brotherhood of man": Catholic, Protestant, and Jewish alike. It wasn't something Malone acquired in America; he brought it with him from Ireland. Born to an affluent family in County Meath, he grew up with ecumenism from an early age. At the time of his fiftieth anniversary as a priest, he wrote,

> My early life was toned by association with non-Catholics. The kindliest feeling was cultivated among people who followed different religious beliefs. . . . To this I lovingly turn as the school that has fitted me for the proper appreciation of what citizens owe each other in America, where religion is left as an individual interest with which no one has the right to interfere.

Malone was ecumenical long before Vatican II affirmed interfaith dialogue, and at a time when the phrase *Extra Ecclesiam Nulla Salus* was commonly invoked against heretics and atheists.

He first sailed for America in the spring of 1839, when an Irish-born bishop came looking for recruits to serve there. Ordained in 1844, he was assigned to St. Mary's Church in Williamsburg (which he renamed Saints Peter and Paul) on what is now South Third Street. It would be his one and only assignment as a priest—fifty years as pastor (surely a record). Within a few years, the neighborhood quickly changed. "We could not see at the time what the dreadful famine in Ireland in '47 and '48 would do in filling up the unoccupied spaces of the two great cities, New York and Brooklyn."

And the parish grew. At the time of Malone's twenty-fifth anniversary, an impressive Gothic church was in place, a dozen Sisters of St. Joseph ran a parochial school of some fifteen hundred children, and the parish was a center of community life. Malone said at the time, "When we came together in this parish a quarter of a century ago, we were not worth a cent financially. We had no lands, no edifices; but God has prospered us, and we have now a flourishing parish, and surrounding us are eleven other churches."

But Malone was by no means a typical inner-city pastor. At a time when most Irish Catholics were Democrat and proslavery, Malone was a Republican and an abolitionist. He is believed to have actually aided the Underground Railroad in his own parish. (Underground tunnels dating back decades were recently found underneath the church.) For Malone, slavery was "a blasphemous rebellion against the ordinance of God—to love one another—a radical injustice."

During the Civil War he showed his support for the Union by nailing a flag to the steeple of his church. It was believed to be to the first Brooklyn church of any kind to do so. In the years following the war Malone supported the cause of social activist Father Edward McGlynn, even incurring the wrath of his own bishop. (One of his former curates, assigned to start a nearby parish, wanted to name it St. Sylvester. The bishop refused, and it was named Transfiguration.)

Long before the word "progressive" came into fashion, Malone was all that and more. Almost a century before Vatican II he insisted that Christianity and anti-Semitism were incompatible. Speaking at a Williamsburg Purim Ball in 1870 he told a Jewish audience that the true spirit of Christianity "was opposed to ignorant prejudices," and he pledged himself to seeing that "persecution should not follow the Jewish race any longer."

For many years in Williamsburg, members of the Hebrew Benevolent Society were honored guests at St. Patrick's Day, and the Friendly Sons of St. Patrick attended the annual Purim Ball. One Brooklyn rabbi wrote that Malone "obliterated the lines of religious distinctions." In the pulpit Malone reminded his predominantly Irish parishioners that their own experience of religious persecution should make them sympathetic to their Jewish neighbors.

By the time of his death in 1899 Malone was one of Brooklyn's most beloved figures. The *Brooklyn Eagle's* obituary called him "everybody's friend. It made no difference to the venerable priest what the color, nationality, or creed was in matters of charity or good will. He had a heart for mankind." A Jewish friend wrote him, "Would to heaven that all the faiths had men like you; there would be less friction, less suffering, and more happiness."

10

SERVANT OF GOD
FATHER ISAAC THOMAS HECKER

1819–1888

I have found all that I have ever sought.
—ISAAC THOMAS HECKER

Early-nineteenth-century America was an exciting time, an age of reform. Known as "the era of the common man," it saw a movement toward greater democratization. It witnessed the rise of transcendentalism, the creation of utopian communities like Oneida and Brook Farm, the birth of the feminist movement, and the growth of abolitionism. In the area of religion, it was an era of intensive questioning and spiritual searching.

One of those seekers was a young New Yorker named Isaac Hecker, whose spiritual journey led him from politics to transcendentalism and Brook Farm, and ultimately to the Catholic Church—as well as to friendships with Henry David Thoreau and Ralph Waldo Emerson. Hecker concluded that Catholicism alone fully met the day's needs, spiritual and social, and as a priest he dedicated his life to the conversion of America.

Born in Manhattan to a German American family, Isaac Thomas Hecker was baptized Lutheran. His formal schooling was minimal, and he worked in the family bakery (Hecker Flour is still found on supermarket shelves). His early work in political organizing disillusioned him, and contact with reformer Orestes Brownson convinced him that true reform, social and political, needed a religious underpinning.

This was the beginning of his spiritual journey. In early 1842 he had what he described as a "vision" that left him "unconscious of anything but pure love and joy." It was a turning point in his life. At Brook Farm he mingled freely with some of the day's leading intellectuals, but he was spiritually unsatisfied; he turned to traditional Christianity for answers.

Through reading, travel, and conversation, Hecker concluded that Catholicism alone embraced "the full range of the Christian experience." It offered a unity that Protestantism lacked, and it balanced personal piety with social activism. In August 1844 he was baptized a Catholic. His conversion surprised friends. When Emerson asked Hecker if art and architecture had "turned his head," he replied, "No, but what caused all that."

Hecker had also decided to become a priest. In August 1845 he joined the Redemptorists, an order he admired for its pastoral bent. (The Jesuits he considered too academic.) He was ordained in October 1849. In a letter home he wrote, "All my seeking is now ended. . . . I have found all that I have ever sought."

Father Hecker was assigned to a team of priests who traveled the country preaching parish missions. These were weeklong events promoting repentance and renewal, composed of morning and evening lectures followed by confession. While these were primarily Catholic affairs, Hecker and his fellow missioners, all converts, wanted to extend their work to non-Catholics, as Hecker said, "to convert a certain class of persons among whom I found myself before my conversion."

In 1858 Hecker and four confreres left the Redemptorists to form the Missionary Society of St. Paul the Apostle, known as the Paulists. All converts, they were an impressive group: George Deshon was a West Pointer and friend of

Ulysses S. Grant; Clarence Walworth was considered the nation's finest Catholic preacher; Augustine Hewit, the grandson of a senator, was an accomplished writer; Francis Asbury Baker had been a prominent minister in Baltimore. Together they would evangelize America. Hecker wrote: "I feel like . . . adopting one word as our motto—CONQUER!"

During the 1850s, anti-Catholicism was widespread and powerful, and many Catholics took the defensive. Hecker aimed not merely to refute prejudice, but to persuade Protestants that they should convert. Instead of proceeding from doctrinal premises, Paulist preachers emphasized shared human experiences and the search for truth, arguing that Catholicism best met the needs of the soul and of society. Hecker wanted to convert Americans not for the church's sake, but for theirs.

He had no place for condemnation. In 1868 a minister described him as "a happy man—happy in his faith and in his work." A friend called him "one of those men whom you feel it is good to be with." But he also felt an urgency (and impatience) about his work. One Paulist described his "contempt for lazy devotion":

> Once, when upon a mission, a young priest just returned from Rome, where he had made his studies, expressed his desire to get back again to Italy as soon as possible, saying, "I find no time here to pray." Father Hecker felt indignant, for it did not seem to him that the young man was very much occupied. "Don't be such a baby," said he. "Look around and see how much work there is to be done here. Is it not better to make some return to God—here in your own country—for what He has done for you, rather than to be sucking your thumbs abroad! What kind of piety do you call that?"

Hecker was a workaholic, and he apparently suffered a nervous breakdown in the 1870s that affected his behavior. One observer noted his impatience with "opposition and contradiction," but also his "marvelous openness of heart."

Hecker never realized his dream of converting America. The defensiveness of church leaders frustrated him. As illness forced him to relinquish Paulist leadership, he disliked the move toward conventional parish work. A decade after his death in 1888, a cloud of suspicion rose over him as Pope Leo XIII condemned "heretical tendencies" in America. Although Hecker was not actually named, Leo warned against an "undue emphasis" on the

Holy Spirit's role in the life of the individual, a key component of Hecker's thought.

But time and Vatican II have vindicated Hecker, whose movement toward sainthood was recently initiated. He has much to say to modern seekers. Like them, he was politically conscious, explored world religions, took nothing for granted, and sought to fulfill basic human needs for truth, freedom, and love. In the age of what John Paul II called the "new evangelization," Hecker reminds Catholics not to write off the "unchurched," but emphasize shared experiences and common premises—in other words, meet them "where they're at" and travel with them on their journey.

11

LEVI SILLIMAN IVES

1797–1867

To extend to these little sufferers a helping hand.
  —LEVI SILLIMAN IVES

Some observers say that people come to New York to reinvent themselves, which is certainly the case for Levi Silliman Ives, a layman who worked in Catholic schools and orphanages during the Civil War era. At fifty-five he and his wife left North Carolina to start a new life. They gave up a lot: respectability, social standing, a solid livelihood—all for an uncertain future. Ives had been an Episcopal bishop in the antebellum South, a prestigious figure indeed, who converted to a despised religion, Roman Catholicism.

At Rome in 1852 Ives was received into the Catholic Church by Pope Pius IX, placing his episcopal ring at the pontiff's feet. It was the first time since the Reformation that a Protestant bishop converted. It was international news. The *New York Times* called it "a serious matter, independently of the merits of creed or conviction." What lay in store next was uncertain, only, Ives wrote, "peace of conscience and the salvation of his soul."

Born to a respectable New England family, he grew up in New York. After serving in the War of 1812 he studied for the ministry and was ordained in 1823, serving in New York and Pennsylvania. His wife, Rebecca, was the daughter of Bishop John Henry Hobart, founder of Hobart College, a man called "the very embodiment of American Epsicopalianism." Her godmother was Elizabeth Ann Seton, whom Bishop Hobart tried to dissuade from going Romeward. His star was rising. In May 1831, at thirty-four, he was elected bishop of North Carolina, a capable and popular figure.

This was the time of England's Oxford Movement, an attempt to re-affirm the Anglican Church's prophetic role. Soon the movement raised eyebrows, however, when its leading figure, John Henry Newman, became a Catholic. His decision was a shocker on both sides of the Atlantic. In America, many Episcopal clergy began to question the validity of Roman claims; among these was the bishop of North Carolina.

A historian of North Carolina Episcopalianism writes, "It was in 1848–'49 that the religious practices of Bishop Ives began to be at variance with the Church in which he held office." As Ives read more on Catholicism, he became increasingly uneasy about his own position. Finally, in late 1852, he took the leap, traveling to Rome. Later a General Convention of the Episcopal Church formally deposed him (even though he'd already resigned) for "abandoning that portion of the flock of Christ committed to his oversight, and binding himself under anathema to the anti-Christian doctrines and practices imposed by the Council of Trent upon all the Churches of the Roman Obedience."

One Episcopal historian suggests that Ives's "mind had been affected by the long attack of fever from which he had suffered."

The Catholic bishops felt a sense of responsibility toward Ives (who was almost one of them), and they gathered a collection for him. One historian notes they even discussed ordaining him a deacon (long before the permanent diaconate was restored) and sending him to North Carolina as a sort of vicar to oversee Catholic life, but nothing came of this. In New York, Archbishop John Hughes put him on the faculty of St. Joseph's Seminary in the Bronx (now Fordham University). Hughes didn't know what to make of

Ives; he tended to be wary of converts, especially the more prestigious ones. Ives's home on West 138th Street in Harlem became a meeting place for converts as well as Catholic intelligentsia. Besides Fordham, he also taught at Manhattan College and the College of Mount St. Vincent.

In charity work, however, Ives found his real niche as a Catholic. Soon after moving to New York he took charge of the local chapter of the St. Vincent De Paul Society, a lay organization created to help the poor. In 1863 he founded the Society for the Protection of Destitute Catholic Children, which opened the New York Catholic Protectory to care for homeless orphans. Its object was "to extend to these little sufferers a helping hand, to raise them from their state of degradation and misery and to place them in a condition where they may have a fair chance to work out for themselves a better destiny."

In quick time, the Manhattan facilities were overcrowded, and in 1865 a 114-acre farm was purchased in Westchester. Before Ives died at seventy in his Manhattanville home on October 13, 1867, his last words were, "Oh, how good God has been to me!" Bishops nationwide attended his funeral Mass. One Catholic paper declared, "His name should ever be held in benediction as the true friend of the poor and the suffering." An Episcopal historian commented, "His was a strange and eventful life."

12

BISHOP JOHN LOUGHLIN

1817–1891

To the non-Catholic inhabitants of the island, a "Romish Church" is no longer a thing of wonderment.
   —BROOKLYN EAGLE, 1877

In 1836 the city of Brooklyn was still obscure enough for the *U.S. Catholic Almanac* to list it as "Brookland" with no local repercussions. Decades later, a *Brooklyn Eagle* reporter discovering the error suggested there were probably Catholics around in Brooklyn at the time to notice. Back then Williamsburg's ten Catholic families took a ferry to Manhattan for Mass. All Brooklyn had two Catholic churches; Queens, Nassau, and Suffolk had none. Priests rode circuit across Long Island to places where "there was no railroad or talk of one."

Within a decade, however, things changed rapidly. New York was on its way to becoming one of the largest Catholic cities in the nation, due to immigration from revolutionary Germany and famine-stricken Ireland. By the early

1850s, in Brooklyn a third of all residents spoke with an Irish brogue or a German accent. The New York Archdiocese then covered all New York and northern New Jersey. In the summer of 1853 Long Island made a separate diocese with its seat in Brooklyn. The first bishop was a "smart bustling little man with piercing dark eyes": John Loughlin, a thirty-six-year-old Irish-born priest.

Born in County Down, he immigrated to New York as a child. After studying at seminaries in Canada and Baltimore, in 1840 he was ordained at Old St. Patrick's Cathedral on Mott Street. From the start he proved a capable administrator with a strong pastoral bent, ministering to the sick and reaching out to the city's African American community. By 1853 he was vicar-general of the archdiocese, second in command to Archbishop John Hughes, who clearly valued his ability and wanted him to lead the new diocese.

When Loughlin arrived, however, he wasn't entirely welcome. Dozens of anti-Catholic organizations, including the Know-Nothings, proliferated Long Island. (Williamsburg alone had about sixty such groups.) Riots between Catholic immigrants and Protestant natives (calling themselves "Native Americans") were all too common. One, John S. Orr, calling himself "the Angel Gabriel," addressed crowds on the Roman menace, wearing a gown and blowing a trumpet. He sang a song titled "We'll Chain the Pope to the Other Side of the River." Loughlin's approach to all this was to ignore it and do his job: build up the church on Long Island.

Through his five decades as bishop he brought priests and religious over from Ireland; he traveled from one end of the island to the other to administer sacraments; he ran the daily affairs of his growing diocese. Catholicism grew, and it overcame prejudices. One newspaper commented in 1877:

> Year after year develops the progress of Catholicity on Long Island. To the non-Catholic inhabitants of the island, a "Romish Church" is no longer a thing of wonderment, a Roman priest is no longer a stranger. Scarce a village from East New York to Sag Harbor, or from Glen Gove to Rockaway, is without a Church of the grand old faith. Hempstead, erst a village of zealous Protestantism and boasted anti-Romanishness, has now its beautiful cross-crowned Catholic spire.

Five years later, another local paper could say, "Brooklyn might well be called a Catholic city."

Through it all, Loughlin went about his work with a quiet exactness. He lived in a simple brownstone with the plate "Rev. J. Loughlin" on the front door. Every morning he took the trolley to the bank and the post office. (It was said that he "carried the chancery in his hat-band.") He was his own receptionist. The *Brooklyn Eagle* reported in 1889, "The Bishop has an aversion to two classes of persons—reporters and Jesuits." The difference was that he did interviews every now and then.

The main reason Loughlin didn't like Jesuits was that he felt they stole the best and brightest from his own diocese, men who have become Brooklyn priests. One exception he made was for the Vincentian Fathers, who named St. John's College (now university) in his honor. By the end of his episcopate they had named a parish, high school, college, church, and seminary for him, all on one city block (they even had a bust made of him).

In the summer of 1868 a unique ceremony took place in Brooklyn's Fort Greene section: the cornerstone laying for the Cathedral of the Immaculate Conception, a projected St. Patrick's–like edifice that would dominate the Brooklyn skyline. It would be the great work of local architect Patrick Keely, whose resumé would include some seven hundred churches, convents, and schools in North America. It was never completed (today it's the site of Bishop Loughlin Memorial High School).

Instead, Loughlin, known as "the good old man" by his priests, chose to use what money he had for other causes: caring for the elderly and the orphans, the sick and the poor, and ministering to immigrants. When he arrived in 1853, Catholics were a relatively scarce commodity on the island. By the end of his thirty-eight-year episcopate, a vast network of schools, churches, and social service organizations dotted its map from Red Hook to Blue Point. In thirty-eight years, 131 parishes, sixty-six parochial schools, twenty high schools, five hospitals, twenty-four orphanages, two colleges, and a seminary were erected. These became his real legacy, the "living stones" of Brooklyn Catholicism.

13

JOHN GILMARY SHEA

1824–1892

The hope and study of my life.
    —JOHN GILMARY SHEA

He seemed born to write history. In 1838, at age fourteen, John Shea wrote his first scholarly article on a Spanish cardinal for the *Children's Catholic Magazine*, edited by Father Felix Varela. Around that time he left school to work in the shipping business for a Spanish merchant. The Spanish he learned on the job served him well as a professional historian in later years when he wrote some 250 articles and books, mainly about Catholic America, the field to which he devoted his life. A peer wrote, "To bring home to his Catholic fellow-citizens first of all, and then to their non-Catholic neighbors, the claims of the Church in the discovery, the civilization and the building [of America], he labored day and night."

He's known as "the Father of American Catholic history." Previously American history was the domain of Protestants arguing that America was a Protestant nation. Standard histories and biographies resounded this theme, even public school textbooks. One geography book from the 1840s casually stated, "Superstition prevails not only at Rome but in all the states of Church. The inhabitants observe scrupulously all the ceremonies of religion omitting connected with form or etiquette, although apparently destitute of true devotion."

The son of a Columbia professor, John Dawson Shea (he adopted the name Gilmary, meaning "Mary's servant," as an adult) was born in Manhattan on July 22, 1824. He grew up in a cultured home that encouraged scholarship. Although he went to work at an early age, he returned to study law at Columbia before working briefly as a lawyer. But his heart was in history, writing for local magazines. In 1846 he was elected to the prestigious New-York Historical Society, the first of many honors received.

In the summer of 1848 Shea left law to join the Jesuits. His four years with them was crucial to developing his scholarly vocation. As part of his training he was sent to Canada, where he worked with Father Felix Martin, a leading Canadian historian who worked heavily in local archives. Shea learned from Martin the value of examining the original historical sources. Francis Parkman, the premier American historian of the nineteenth century, would later cite his debt to Shea's own work.

Over time, Shea concluded that his vocation wasn't to religious life, but as his biographer Peter Guilday writes, "To the end of his life he remained in spirit a son of Ignatius." In 1854 he married Sophie Savage, with whom he had two daughters. He supported his family through various writing and editing projects. At times, money was tight, and the Sheas would later relocate to more affordable Elizabeth, New Jersey.

Soon after leaving the Jesuits, Shea began delivering public lectures on church history. In 1852 his first book, *The Discovery and Exploration of the Mississippi Valley*, highlighted Catholic contributions to American history. It was the first book on American Catholic history, a success across the board. His style was accessible. Guilday notes that his second book, *History of the Catholic Missions* (1854), earned a place by "every Catholic fireside. Here was a volume which all could read and understand."

Historically speaking, Shea's work still holds merit, mainly for his pioneering role as well as his exacting research. (The American Catholic Historical Association annually awards the John Gilmary Shea prize for excellence in scholarship.) But he wrote nonetheless with a polemical purpose, to refute the charge that Catholics couldn't be good Americans. Shea wrote Cardinal

John McCloskey of New York, "As a loyal son of the Church I can rejoice at a stage where I can gather wisdom, the removing of scandal, and an answer to a reproach of Protestant scholars."

Who discovered America? he asked. Catholics. Who explored the Atlantic Coast? Catholics. Who explored the Mississippi first? Catholics. Writing in 1892, as Americans celebrated the four hundredth anniversary of Columbus's arrival, he wrote, "In this anniversary year, who can wipe these glorious names from the obelisk of fame?"

Shea encouraged the formation of Catholic historical societies to preserve key documents. There was a real need for it: "Every year in the houses and institutions of Catholics more historical material is destroyed than five historical societies will be able to collect in twenty years." He knew of many cases where important collections were destroyed. He noted, for example, that most of Archbishop John Hughes's papers had been destroyed by his relatives.

For all his loyalty to the institutional church, Shea still struggled to make ends meet. At one point he wrote New York archbishop Michael Corrigan asking if "there be any position in the Chancery Office, Calvary Cemetery Office or in any of the institutions where I could be sure of a modest salary." He did find work as editor of the *Catholic News*, the paper for the New York Archdiocese. But money continued to be an issue for Shea right to the end.

In 1883 the University of Notre Dame awarded Shea its first Laetare Medal to an outstanding layperson. Accepting the award, he said, "Love of the Church, love of my country, these indeed I have, and . . . I have labored animated by them." In 1886 he published the first of his four-volume *History of the Catholic Church in the United States*, "the hope and study of my life." In doing so, he sought to answer the question of "the progress of the Catholic element from the earliest days to its present." "Poet and artist," Shea wrote, "seek inspiration in Catholic annals, but they are studiously ignored by those who profess to give history. History!"

A genial companion and raconteur, Shea was indeed born to write history, and he died writing history. Before his death on July 22, 1892, he wrote, "It cannot be long before I drop the 'and' out of the Hail Mary and say: 'Pray for us now *at* the hour of our death.'" Shea's legacy lives on in the monographs he wrote (which are still used), the societies he founded, and the scholarship he promoted.

14

James Alphonsus McMaster
1820–1886

Ever intemperate.
—Brooklyn Eagle, 1886

Thomas Francis Meagher wasn't happy. James McMaster, editor of the *Free-man's Journal,* wrote an editorial critical of him. He asked McMaster for a retraction. Not getting one, he lay in wait at McMaster's Manhattan home, horsewhipping him. McMaster then shot Meagher in the face with his pocket revolver. The Irish American icon and future Civil War general suffered only powder burns, but both were arrested and fined five hundred dollars each.

Catholic journalism in 1850s America could be dangerous business.

Under McMaster, the *Freeman's Journal* became the most popular and influential Catholic periodical in mid-nineteenth-century America. One of the day's most controversial figures, McMaster locked horns with some prominent figures, including Abraham Lincoln, and occasionally he paid the price for it. One associate described his editorial approach simply: "He was a fighter."

Born in upstate New York, the son of Scots Irish immigrants, James McMaster was intended for the church early on. By age ten his father, a Presbyterian minister, had him reading Latin, Greek, and Hebrew. The family was said to have "unusual intelligence, deep piety, and great force of character," traits associated with James. One contemporary later wrote, "What a tremendously turbulent chief of a clan McMaster would have made in the time of the Stuarts, for he loved all lost causes, and was a rebel to the core of his heart."

James, however, decided against the ministry. After graduating from Union College he studied law at Columbia and practiced briefly. A turning point came when he found himself unable to defend a client he knew was guilty. By then he'd become an Episcopalian, entering New York's General Theological Seminary, which one alumnus called "a little Oxford on this side of the Atlantic."

There, like many of his classmates, he was influenced by the Oxford Movement. What started in 1833 under John Henry Newman as a way to reclaim Anglicanism's prophetic role led many to consider the claims of Roman Catholicism and "cross the Tiber." McMaster was one of these, and in 1845 he was received into the Catholic Church. From there he decided to study for the priesthood in Europe.

Tall and imposing, McMaster stood out in more ways than one. A forceful, opinionated character, his religious superiors encouraged him to pursue his skills as a writer back in America as a layman. Later he would marry. (His three children all entered religious life.) He always had a soft spot for the Redemptorists, but none for the Jesuits, whom he considered too liberal. Upon his conversion to Catholicism he took the middle name Alphonsus in honor of the Redemptorist founder.

In 1848 young McMaster took charge of the *Freeman's Journal*, founded in 1841 as an Irish American paper. With the help of Archbishop John Hughes, he turned it into a Catholic newspaper. (Interestingly, though, McMaster had a troubled relationship with the Irish; he claimed the "the Irish never respect a man till he appeals to their cowardice.") His approach to the paper was "intended to be practical, simple, ascetical, and edifying for such good people as are not overstocked with brains, or at least, not trained to following theological discussions."

There would be no place, he added, for "Namby-pambyism."

McMaster edited the paper for thirty-eight years. By the 1860s it achieved a nationwide readership, more than some more prominent papers. Generally speaking, Catholic papers in those days didn't last very long. Bishops, concentrating their resources on helping immigrants, had little money for a newspaper. A working-class Catholic population had neither the time nor money to support one. McMaster's paper (and it was unequivocally his paper) succeeded in large part due to the force of his contentious editorial personality.

He butted heads with Protestants as well as his fellow Catholics; he didn't care who. A biographer notes "his aversion to episcopal supervision and a determination to propound his own views . . . You were either with him or against him, and, especially if you were a Bishop, if you were against him, you were wrong."

Theologically, however, he was a strong champion of papal infallibility decades before its formal proclamation at the First Vatican Council in 1870. He was also a strong champion of Catholic education, habitually referring to public schools as "Godless schools."

One of McMaster's serious shortcomings was his own stark racism. Although a northerner he was strongly opposed to abolition, calling African Americans a "savage race." A staunch Democrat, he supported states' rights as well. During the war he attacked the Lincoln administration for what he considered its attacks on civil liberties. For a year during the war McMaster was imprisoned and the paper shut down. Far from breaking him, the experience actually empowered him. It was, a peer recounted, "an episode in life which he always considered glorious."

Following this episode, however, McMaster's influence waned. His writing became if anything more acerbic. "Fault-finding," recalled one associate, "was one of his weaknesses. He spared no one, high or low, who differed from him, and his invective was as bitter as an unlimited vocabulary could make it." One author writes that a new generation was "tired of McMaster's literary violence." By the end of his life, the paper lost both influence and readership.

At the time of McMaster's death in 1886 he was remembered as "ever intemperate and always arch-conservative." By his own admission, he was always "too hot and heavy," but over time he became even more irascible. One journalist recalled, "There could be no career for any man assisting to help in the conduct of Mr. McMaster's journal if he was too fully saturated in the gifts of the Holy Ghost." With the arrival of modern journalism, McMaster's "old-fashioned" acerbic personal style went by the wayside (at least for a while). He had his successors, as will be seen, but they carried no guns to work.

15

Father John Christopher Drumgoole
1816–1888

A quiet man who rarely raised his voice . . . but if someone hurt his children or spoke ill of them, he roused like a lion.
   —A contemporary of Drumgoole

"You would take any boy no matter what his reputation was for mischief—or worse?" the reporter asked Father John Drumgoole, chaplain of St. Vincent's Home for Boys in Manhattan.

"Oh, of course," the priest answered. "Some
of the worst cases—they called them 'terrors of
the city'—have been here, and they are holding
good jobs and would not go back to their old lives
for anything."

"You are more hopeful than some I have
talked with," the reporter noted.

"Oh, it's just that I look at it in a different
way," Drumgoole responded. "I think it really
is our fault that these boys are not better. Their
condition is due to our neglect."

The interview occurred in 1873, when some
forty thousand homeless children populated city streets. This was the Gilded
Age, when New York was becoming the financial and fashion capital of the
world. Underneath the gilding lay massive corruption, poverty, and crime.
While uptown mansions housed the city's elite, downtown some three hundred
thousand people were packed into a square mile in disease-ridden tenements.

These were the original "mean streets," and John Christopher Drumgoole
knew them well. He was a child of the slums. Both before and after becoming a
priest he dedicated his life to working with disadvantaged urban youth. By the
time of his death he founded what was then the largest childcare facility in the
United States, Mount Loretto, on Staten Island.

In 1824, at age eight, he had emigrated from County Longford, Ireland,
by himself. After his father's early death, his mother had gone ahead to New
York to find work. Meeting him at the Quarantine Dock on Staten Island,
she brought him to Mott Street, near the newly erected St. Patrick's Cathedral. Although he'd considered priesthood early, he had to work to help support the family. After working as a cobbler, John was appointed sexton of St.
Mary's Church on Grand Street, a parish factotum. Confiding his vocational
ambitions to his pastor, he was told that at twenty-five he was too old.

Soon he opened a Catholic bookstore across the street from the church.
At the parish he developed an informal outreach to homeless youth, "already
old in the knowledge of the worst side of life and with little information about
the better side." He created an impromptu shelter in the church basement,
started clubs and organizations to keep them away from gangs, and taught
them catechism. Still, he never abandoned the idea of becoming a priest.

By the 1860s Drumgoole had saved enough money to attend college at St. Francis Xavier on West Sixteenth Street, then "an unbuilt area but near a few fine houses and farms." By the end of the Civil War, his mother was in a comfortable enough position that he could pursue his longtime dream, entering Our Lady of the Angels Seminary in Niagara. On May 22, 1869, at age fifty-two, John C. Drumgoole finally realized his dream of becoming a priest.

He was sent to St. Mary's, his home parish. By then the problem of homeless children had gotten worse. In 1871 he was named chaplain of St. Vincent's Home on Warren Street, the "Newsboys' Home." Many boys who sold papers on city corners slept on the streets at night. Neither race nor religion were impediments to staying at St. Vincent's. "Here," Father Drumgoole said, "every child is welcome whatever his creed. No matter what their faith they are all hungry and they all get cold." Furthermore, he added, "There are no color bars in this home."

Drumgoole lived there. "If I don't make my home with them now and eat what they do and put up with their inconveniences," he wrote his archbishop, "I won't have much influence with them." He lived very simply. One biographer described him as a "quiet man who rarely raised his voice . . . but if someone hurt his children or spoke ill of them, he roused like a lion." He had no illusions about them. To a visiting English philanthropist, he described one particular boy, who told him,

> "Here you are with a really hard case, mister." But when I had him alone he dropped the swagger he had used with the boys. He looked very young and defenseless and he said, but sort of worried now, "If you really like hard cases, you'll like me." He certainly was one, too. He had been a juvenile Fagin with about twenty boys under him training to be pickpockets. He was scared now, for he knew the police were on to him. That was a few years ago, and now he has a nice job and wouldn't go back to the old life for anything. Pride—that's all—I gave him pride in himself.

"If only I had the means," he said, "I wouldn't be afraid to turn out one thousand reformed boys every year." In 1882 he bought the 138-acre Bennett farm on Staten Island for twenty-two thousand dollars, later adding additional property. He soon opened the Mission of the Immaculate Virgin, better known as Mount Loretto, for over a thousand boys and girls. Home to a towering church (used in 1972's *The Godfather*), vocational training, and many other services, the farm was then the largest in New York State. As one alumnus said, "Everything about the place was huge."

Drumgoole proved a capable fundraiser, creating a magazine titled *The Homeless Child*, published in five languages. Supporters included Saints Damien de Veuster and John Bosco, as well as Pope Leo XIII. (He turned down the title of monsignor because "it wouldn't help the boys.") But age and poor health caught up, and in March 1888, during the Great Blizzard, he died. An estimated one hundred thousand people showed up at the wake and funeral. A fellow priest said, "I think I can safely say that we can pray to him instead of for him." John C. Drumgoole died very much as he had lived, poor. Any money he raised or earned went to support those who really needed it. He himself could do on just a little.

16

FATHER EDWARD MCGLYNN

1837–1900

I began to ask myself, "Is there no remedy?"
    —EDWARD MCGLYNN

At the end of the Civil War, St. Stephen's Church on East Twenty-Eighth Street was the largest parish in the New York Archdiocese—and the poorest. For its new pastor, the biggest challenge wasn't running a school or refurbishing a church; it was helping his impoverished parishioners. As Father Edward McGlynn later wrote,

> I had begun to feel life made a burden by the never-ending procession of men, women, and children coming to my door begging not so much for alms as for employment. . . . I began to ask myself, "Is there no remedy? Is this God's order that the poor shall be constantly becoming poorer in all out large cities, the world over?"

"There is not much comfort," he later declared, "in the condescending advice to the slaves of poverty to remember that Christ proclaimed the poor blessed and bade them hope for a reward of eternal happiness." His views made him the country's best-known priest. They also got him excommunicated.

McGlynn himself didn't grow up in poverty. The son of a successful contractor, he grew up in Manhattan. At thirteen he was sent to the Urban College of the Propaganda, a Roman seminary where bishops sent promising students. In 1860 he was ordained and sent back to New York.

His first pastor, Thomas Farrell, was a strong influence, a confirmed liberal who supported abolitionism. At his death he left money to start an African American parish. (If the archdiocese failed to act swiftly enough, Farrell's will specified that the money be given to a Protestant church for the same purpose.)

McGlynn later joined an informal theological society of New York priests named the Accademia, which discussed everything from theology to politics. Long before Vatican II, they discussed celibacy, Mass in the vernacular, even women priests. (McGlynn defended celibacy as a gift to the church.) Other topics included poverty, slavery, and immigration.

McGlynn was one of its foremost members. An imposing figure, over six feet tall and two hundred pounds, he soon emerged as one of the era's most dynamic orators. Charles R. Morris writes, "In a day when platform oratory was popular entertainment, McGlynn was a thrilling speaker. Even on the page, his speeches ring with Martin Luther King–like cadences."

In the writings of political theorist Henry George, McGlynn found an answer. In his 1879 treatise *Progress and Poverty*, George laid out the "single tax theory." While the land was the people's "common property," in reality it was held by private landowners. By taxing the land out of their hands, George hoped to accomplish an equitable redistribution of society's goods. For conservatives, this bordered dangerously on the socialistic.

McGlynn called George "a man sent by God," and his program a way to do "God's will on earth as it is done in heaven." He campaigned actively for George, who ran for mayor of New York in 1886. But Archbishop Michael Corrigan considered George's theory a "civil disease bordering on madness," and he ordered McGlynn to desist. (The two men had been seminary classmates but not friends.)

George lost the election, but McGlynn's troubles weren't over, for he continued to advocate George's theories. Corrigan referred the case to the Vatican, and McGlynn was summoned there to explain himself. After refusing to go, he received notice of his formal excommunication. Over the next five years, he served as president of the Anti-Poverty Society, which advocated George's views and better working conditions. Christianity, he insisted, had to meet the real needs of the day if it was to survive.

A major theme of his speeches was "the Fatherhood of God and the Brotherhood of Man." In a speech titled "The Cross of a New Crusade," he declared, "It is by the doing of justice, by the inculcation of the spirit of equality, liberty, and fraternity on earth, that we shall prepare for the glorious millennial day when it shall be something more than a prayer and in great measure a reality—'Thy kingdom come, Thy will be done on earth as it is in heaven.'"

One journalist commented, "Never before have I heard the essentials of all religions promulgated at one time by one preacher, and in so eloquent a manner."

Pope Leo XIII, himself an advocate of social justice, was interested in McGlynn's case, and he had Archbishop Francesco Satolli, his representative to America, sound the priest out on the possibility of reconciliation. In December 1892, just before Christmas, the excommunication ban was lifted after McGlynn issued a public statement of his beliefs. (Scholars agree that Corrigan's handling of the situation cost him a cardinal's hat.)

After his reinstatement, McGlynn was assigned to an upstate parish, where Corrigan hoped he would make little trouble. There he died from health complications in 1900. A monument was erected in the Bronx's Woodlawn Cemetery, but because Woodlawn wasn't Catholic, his burial there was forbidden. So he was interred at Calvary Cemetery in Queens, where someone pinned a note to the grave, "To the Priest, as a Priest, and as a Defender of the Poor."

In his 1937 biography of McGlynn, Stephen Bell insisted that there was an "eternal relevancy" about the McGlynn story: "Each age must decide as best it can what is social justice and fraternal charity; what is religion, and what is politics. Hence do we need the McGlynns in Catholic crises, for they will risk making mistakes." Too many, Bell concludes, do little or nothing until it's too late. Such was the not the case with the man known as the *Soggarth Aroon*, Gaelic for "dear priest," who offered the poor something more than platitudes.

17

MARY ANNE SADLIER

1820–1903

The best-known Irish Catholic voice in American letters.
—MARJORIE HOWES, *Colonial Crossings*

New York has long been one of the world's great publishing capitals. In 1837, two immigrant brothers from Tipperary, Denis and James Sadlier, started a firm that would become the largest Catholic publishing house in North America. Eventually D. & J. Sadlier expanded northward, with James taking over Canadian operations. While he was there, he married Mary Anne Madden, a young woman from County Cavan with literary ambition who would produce dozens of books on Ireland and Irish America, work in the newspaper business, and turn herself into what one scholar calls "the best-known Irish Catholic voice in American letters."

The daughter of a wealthy merchant who encouraged her interest in writing, she published her first poems at age eighteen. In 1844 she emigrated from Ireland to Montreal. While raising a family of six (her daughter Anna would become a popular Catholic author in her own right), she produced novels, catechisms, and poetry. On the eve of the Civil War, they moved to New York. Their home on East Broadway became a Catholic literary salon where the best and brightest gathered: authors, novelists, philosophers, even bishops. Their summer home in Far Rockaway also became a gathering place for New York's Catholic intelligentsia.

Sadlier wrote for numerous Catholic papers, but she was best known for her novels. During the 1860s alone she wrote some fourteen novels, geared mainly toward an Irish American audience. *The Red Hand of Ulster* (1850) and *The Confederate Chieftains* (1860) dealt with early Irish history, the "almost innumerable multitude of saints and heroes, poets and sages." Irish American historian Charles Fanning calls these novels "practical fiction for the immigrant," something romantic and heroic to take their mind off everyday life.

The Blakes and the Flanagans (1850)—subtitled, "A Tale Illustrative of Irish-American Life"—focuses on two families, one succumbing to America's materialism, the other sticking to its Irish Catholic roots. One literary critic notes that Sadlier rewarded characters "who remain faithful to Irishness and Catholicism." Toward the end of *The Blakes,* the hero says, "I love America; it is, as it were, the land of my adoption, as well as my birth, but I cannot, or will not, forget Ireland."

Sadlier's novels, tending toward the sentimental and moralistic, haven't aged well. Their continued value is that they provide a unique insight into the everyday lives of nineteenth-century Irish Catholic New Yorkers; as one critic notes, they have "sociological value." In her 1861 novel *Bessy Conway; or, the Irish Girl in America*, a character in New York writes home to Ireland:

> They look more miserable here than the poor did at home. It would go to your heart to see the sights that I see every time I go outside the door. . . . And they tell me I only see a little of it after all, and that there's more misery hid away up in garrets and down in cellars than anybody living knows.

At the time, it was said that her novels "were read to pieces" by a largely immigrant Irish American community. Many books went into multiple editions, and one was even translated into German. Toward the end of her life (by which time she had moved back to Canada) the University of Notre Dame awarded her its prestigious Laetare medal (an honor given to outstanding laypersons), and Pope Leo XIII honored her for her literary work.

Thanks to her output, the name Sadlier became a byword in literature as well as publishing. While her literary reputation hasn't survived, Mary Anne Sadlier deserves to be remembered as "the first important Irish American female voice" and a major chronicler of the New York Catholic experience.

18

Sister Irene Fitzgibbon, S.C.

1823–1896

Can the citizens of New York ever repay the Sisters of Charity the debt they owe for the establishment of this great charity?

— New York World

The babies showed up at the front door of the house, in a variety of outfits and packages. Some were dressed in rags, some in fine clothing. Some had a dollar pinned to their blanket, all the mother could afford. Sometimes notes were left. One mother wrote,

> If in years to come I could hear that he has a home and some friends, I could die in peace. If I should not hear this, it would haunt me to the day of my death. Please, in God's names, remember the last request of a heart broken mother and be good to my dear little Charley.

Another wrote, "This little child has suffered since she was born. . . . My husband is dead and I have nobody to help me." One child was sent by a "wronged and heartbroken mother with no one to take an interest in her but God."

In the fall of 1869 a group of Catholic nuns rented a house on East Twelfth Street in Manhattan's Greenwich Village to care for the unwanted and the abandoned children of New York. Their leader was a determined, compassionate woman named Sister Mary Irene Fitzgibbon. Over the course of the following year, over a thousand infants were dropped at their doorstep. These Sisters of Charity, as they were known, were meeting a major social need of the day.

Described by her biographer as a "gritty and tough spirit," Catherine Rosamond Fitzgibbon was born in England to Irish parents. As a child her family came to America, settling in downtown Brooklyn. At St. James School, she studied under the Sisters of Charity. In 1849 she nearly died during one of the many cholera epidemics that swept nineteenth-century New York.

The illness proved to be a life-changing experience, and the following year she joined the Sisters of Charity, a "late vocation" at age twenty-seven. Catherine took the religious name Mary Irene. For nearly twenty years, she taught at St. Peter's School on Barclay Street, the first Catholic school in New York State. But she was increasingly drawn toward a different kind of apostolate than education.

In the years following the Civil War, it was estimated that some thirty thousand homeless children wandered the city streets. Some were unwanted pregnancies, most were the children of parents unable to provide for them. Stories of infanticide were common in the newspapers. One paper commented, "Day by day the papers tell of little human waifs thrown into areas, or left on doorsteps, or worse far, and more to be deplored, flung lifeless into vacant lots like garbage or refuse matter."

Stories like these touched the heart of Sister Irene, who decided to do something about it. She gave up her teaching position to start a home for the "countless numbers of abandoned babies" in the city. She asked permission from her religious superiors to start a home for these unwanted children. While alternatives did exist, these were woefully inadequate. At the almshouses on Blackwell's Island in the East River, many children often died from lack of care.

Care rooted in Christian charity would be the keystone of this new operation. In time, the *New York World* would write, "The infants were not merely abject numbers to her, but precious individuals who deserved complete dignity and loving care." The Sisters started with five dollars to their name. They ate their first meal on the floor using old newspapers for a tablecloth. At the front door, they placed a crib for mothers to leave their infants. A sign on the front door read, "The Home for Foundlings."

A report by state officials described the "home feeling" that was "cultivated with the utmost assiduity." The report continues,

> The foundlings exhibit toward the Sisters the confiding love of children toward their mothers; and are, in turn, met by an affection, spiritualized and strengthened by religion, which follows them through life, and, it is hoped, compensates them in a great degree, for the loss of natural maternal love.

The *New York World* asked, "Can the citizens of New York ever repay the Sisters of Charity the debt they owe for the establishment of this great charity?"

Sister Irene, her biographer writes, "was never happy . . . unless she was planning a new building or a new charity." Poor health caught up with her, and at age seventy-three she died of heart disease. Thousands turned out for her funeral. The *New York Herald* commented, "Never before in the history of New York has such a tribute been paid." The *New York Times* hailed her as "that great benefactor of humanity."

Today the New York Foundling is one of the city's oldest and most successful child welfare agencies. It continues its mission to society's least and smallest, to "abandon no one." Its work with society's "most vulnerable," reaching some thirteen thousand each year in New York and Puerto Rico, continues to be rooted in the determined compassion that motivated its foundress nearly 150 years ago. And it all began with five dollars, a crib, and an empty apartment building in the Village.

19

MOTHER MARY WALSH
1850–1922

I was beaten by life until she helped me get on my feet.
—A CONTEMPORARY OF WALSH

In the summer of 1876, in the slums of Manhattan, twenty-six-year-old Mary Walsh, an Irish domestic servant, was approached by a young girl desperate for help. The girl's mother was sick with fever and her father was in jail. Mary Walsh did something most people wouldn't do; she started begging on the streets for the girl's family. She nursed the mother back to health and helped the father find work when he got out of jail. In the process she lost her own job but found her life's work.

Later, working for a wealthy family, a poor man approached the back door begging for food. She gave him her own supper. "I knew that day," she said, "that thereafter I was to give whatever I had to those poorer than I." She would spend the rest of her doing exactly that, living barely about the poverty level.

While Mary Walsh had little education, she did have a natural sense of justice and a deep love for the poor. Orphaned in infancy, her grandmother raised her in Ireland. At nineteen Mary immigrated to America. She would stay for the next fifty years. New York, her biographer writes, "was always the point of her interest and affection."

In New York she was "a stranger alone in a city she did not know." It must have been frightening. Her first job was doing laundry for a wealthy family on the Upper East Side, where she got to know the Dominican Fathers at St. Vincent Ferrer Church. She considered joining a monastic community, but her spiritual director suggested a community where she could exercise her real calling: to help the poor.

Mary became a Third Order Dominican, a layperson who lives out a religious order's charism in her daily life (the first two orders are priests and sisters). With a friend she rented rooms near St. Vincent's, taking in laundry to finance her work with the poor. Later the two women moved to Hell's Kitchen, a largely immigrant community crowded in unhealthy and dangerous tenements. Together they looked after about twenty different families.

Many poor people feared hospitals, where the quality of care varied greatly, so Mary and her companions went to their homes. They cooked, cleaned, tended the sick, and eased the loneliness of the poor. "Just to let them talk," she once said, "helps them more than anything I could possibly say." She and her companions never discriminated on the basis of "color, or religion or lack of it."

"What a privilege," she insisted, "it is to work for the sick poor!" For Mary, they were "the children of God crucified on the Calvary of Life." For the children whom "Santa Claus had forgotten," she brought presents. One woman remembered Mary buying her a dress for her First Communion. One night she stayed all night in a bordello with a dying prostitute. When a policeman expressed his surprise at her being in such a place, she shot back, "Never forget, Mr. Clancy, that those poor people have souls, too."

A woman of medium height and plain features, Mary Walsh made a strong impression. People remembered her sincerity and enthusiasm, her strong will and generosity. One policeman said, "That woman is a saint, I do believe." A peer remembered, "She never stood for any nonsense; and when she thought someone was taking advantage of the poor, she could put him in his place." To those who suggested the poor didn't work enough, she shot back, "If you had an irregular starvation wage, and your wife was desperately sick and your children in need, what would you do?"

For thirty years, Mary Walsh and her companions lived and worked as a religious community without formal church approval. "They begged for the poor," one historian writes, "but not for themselves." She slept on wooden floors for many years before she ever had a bed of her own. In 1910, when Mary was sixty, they were accepted as "the Dominican Sisters of the Sick Poor." It was never a big community. By the time of her death, there were about two dozen Sisters.

They operated on their own labor and on donations. Mary called God her "banker." She told her Sisters, "Never mistrust my Banker." Once when she had bought dozens of blankets for the poor to the tune of eight hundred dollars, she came home to find a check for a thousand dollars from the millionaire Thomas Fortune Ryan in thanks for "favors received."

In time, the community would expand to the Midwest and Southwest. Mary's great ambition, albeit an unrealized one, was a free hospital for the poor. But, she said, "Never forget, hospital or no hospital, I want the poor to receive the same care as those who can afford to pay. If after my death I ever knew that one of God's poor was not treated as he should any member of our community, I would suffer indescribable pain."

In later years she suffered from angina pectoris. On her deathbed her last word was "Thanks." The *New York American* stated that her death would "bring heartfelt sorrow and mourning to thousands of the poor of the tenements of New York."

One woman said of Mary Walsh, "I was beaten by life until she helped me get on my feet." Another said, "I never met any other person who really loved his neighbor." At her funeral Mass, the priest observed, "Such love is seldom seen in this or any other era." A bishop commented, "I felt that I sat in the presence of one of God's saints." She came to New York with nothing, died with little more, but she made a difference in the lives of thousands. Mary Walsh's story is almost a retelling of the Beatitudes in a New York setting, and it's eminently worth retelling.

20

WILLIAM RUSSELL GRACE
1832–1904

A tool of the Romish Church.

—DEXTER HAWKINS, a Protestant New Yorker, writing
of Grace in 1880

In 1880, New York City elected its first Spanish-speaking mayor, an immigrant who arrived as a teen, who had made a fortune in Latin America. What made his election more problematic for some was that William Russell Grace was also the city's first Roman Catholic mayor. His election was a major breakthrough for New York Catholics, a highly significant voting bloc in urban politics. Grace's life was, according to biographer Marquis James, "a true-to-life Horatio Alger tale."

By the spring of 1846, Ireland was in the full throes of a famine that would ultimately leave a million men, women, and children dead from starvation. Death was in the air. One journalist described seeing

> Groups of families sitting or wandering on the highroad, with faltering steps, and dim, patient eyes. Sometimes I could see, in front of the cottages, little children leaning against a fence when the sun shone out—for they could not stand—their limbs fleshless, their bodies half-naked, their faces bloated—children that would never, it was plain, grow up to be men and women.

At fourteen, James writes, William Grace "decided that stricken Ireland was no place for him. He ran off to sea."

Born to a respectable Cork family, Grace had enough money to board a ship for New York City, where he worked in a variety of jobs. (He later wrote of feeling the "breath of opportunity" on his arrival.) For most of his two years there, he worked on the New York waterfront as a shipping clerk, an experience that would serve him well in years to come.

At sixteen, William Grace returned to his family in Ireland. In 1850, his entrepreneur father organized a colonization project for South America, where many Irish emigrants had already gone. Grace accompanied the party, and in Peru he entered the shipping business. Although the elder Grace soon returned to Ireland, the son worked his way up in the shipping industry. In 1854, at age twenty-two, he started W.R. Grace & Company as a shipping line.

He stayed in Peru another eleven years, making his company the first multinational company in Latin America. (It was said that he knew Spanish "as readily as English.") By thirty, Grace was a very wealthy man. When his business became big enough, Grace moved to New York in 1865 and ran it from there. (He maintained his Latin American interests; during the 1880s he helped refinance Peru's national debt.)

The Grace family (he married the daughter of a New England sea captain in 1860) initially settled in Brooklyn before moving permanently to Manhattan. At his downtown offices, Grace concentrated on his business endeavors. In politics, New York City historian William Bryk notes, Grace "was an independent Democrat who had never taken more than a layman's interest in politics."

By the year 1880, however, Grace's involvement had expanded considerably. During that year's presidential campaign, he took an active hand behind the scenes. Politics, James comments, seems to have ignited his "strain of idealism." At the time, New York politics were dominated by the machine known as Tammany Hall. That fall, "Honest John" Kelly, the Irish American kingmaker who headed Tammany, asked Grace to run for mayor. Grace said yes, adding, "But if elected, *I'll* be the mayor, you know."

As an Irish Catholic, Grace could count on the working people's vote. But anti-Catholicism was still fairly strong in the city. One Dexter Hawkins wrote to the *New York Times* that if elected, Grace would be little more than "a tool of the Romish Church," replacing public with parochial schools. One political orator declared:

> If Mr. Grace is a good Roman Catholic, he must, in the conscientious discharge of his duty, if elected Mayor, make this City subordinate to. . . . the Holy Father in Rome.

Grace won the election by a majority of 2,914 votes, a close win. Those who feared him as a tool of Tammany had nothing to worry about. A reform-minded executive, he proved, in the words of one recent historian, "an able and efficient mayor." When Kelly tried to influence his appointments, Grace heatedly replied: "No one can dictate to me, Mr. Kelly." In this, James aptly notes, he showed a rich man's "contempt for what the machines might do to him politically."

After a two-year term, Grace stepped down to concentrate on business. One journalist who initially opposed him said, "It is no small praise of a public man in this city to say that he has earned the cordial hatred of Tammany Hall." In 1884, reform-minded citizens asked him to run a second time, which he did, winning by ten thousand votes. His reelection was hailed as a "triumph for the forces of honest government."

Once again, when his term was over, Grace returned to private life, this time for good. A devout Catholic, every morning he attended Mass at St. Agnes Church in midtown. An active philanthropist, especially for Catholic causes, James writes that "his work for the Church was unending." His legacy lives on in Manhattan's Grace Institute, which he founded for immigrant women in 1897 and which continues to provide tuition-free training today for women in the workplace.

21

SAINT FRANCES XAVIER CABRINI

1850–1917

A woman of compassion.
> —MARY LOUISE SULLIVAN, *Mother Cabrini*

Her likeness is displayed at the Statue of Liberty, St. Patrick's Cathedral, the National Shrine in Washington, DC, and St. Peter's Basilica. Quite literally, Frances Xavier Cabrini, M.S.C., has made her mark on history. Less than twenty-nine years after her death, she became the first American citizen raised to sainthood. A few years later, she was named the "Italian Immigrant of the Century."

Born Maria Francesca Cabrini to a prosperous farming family in northern Italy, from an early age she wanted to be a missionary. With frail health she had trouble entering the convent. The first she applied to rejected her. Instead she became a teacher, and a good one. With blond hair and large blue eyes, less than five feet tall, students recalled her warm manner, "usually gentle yet firm."

After several years teaching, Francesca founded the Missionary Sisters of the Sacred Heart of Jesus, who taught school and ran orphanages. She took the name Frances Xavier, in honor of the great missionary saint. She hoped to work in the Far East, but soon was forced to look West, as thousands of Italians migrated to America for

work. In Piacenza, Bishop Giovanni Battista Scalabrini started a community of priests that would minister to them abroad.

In a meeting with Mother Cabrini, Scalabrini encouraged her to focus on the plight of the Italian immigrant in America—poor, uneducated, and exploited. He wrote, "I see that the pariahs among all emigrants are the Italians . . . that the most abandoned and therefore the least respected are our own countrymen. . . . What can be done to help them?"

As a "woman of compassion," she agreed to go. This decision was confirmed in a meeting with Pope Leo XIII, who told her to "look West and not East." In early 1889 Mother Francesca and six Sisters sailed on a steamship full of poor Italians whom they visited daily in stablelike quarters. One Sister recalled their arrival: "Finally, after twelve days of sickness and tribulation, we saw the beautiful Statue of Liberty at about four o'clock. Oh, how happy Mother was. I could read the joy on her face. She called us together to sing the 'Ave Maris Stella.'"

New York, Cabrini noted, was "swarming with people." They went right to the tenements. They visited homes, married couples in the church, had their children baptized, and prompted them to practice their faith regularly. They bought groceries and clothes for those in need. They helped the unemployed find work, got homeless children into homes, and legal aid for those needing it. They taught religious instruction to adults and children.

A shrewd businesswoman, Cabrini used any means available to raise funds. In her business dealings, she could be tough. In California she warned her Sisters that "fraud is the order of the day." In Chicago she dealt with "contractors used to cheating people." Of contracts, she said, "If it is not entirely clear don't accept it. I am tired of swindlers." A newspaper editor called her "a most rare, perhaps unique personality . . . How could it be possible to find in a nunnery a woman so broad-minded, of such fresh and clear culture, and an expert in events of yesterday and about men discussed in newspapers just that very day?"

Along the way, she faced prejudice. In New Orleans, a Dominican Sister said "that we are only taking care of a few dirty Italians." In New York, locals called them "guinea-pigs." The Italians, Mother Cabrini wrote, were "very much looked down upon by the English-speaking public . . . They cannot bear the sight of the Italians," while an Italian American journalist observed, "At that time the Italian Colony was in a deplorable state, exploited economically and morally by other Italians and by Protestants. The Italians were hated, treated like animals, persecuted worse than the Negro."

She had simplicity and humility, but she wasn't afraid to stand up to anyone. At one point, she got in an argument with New York's archbishop Michael Corrigan, who "grew red in the face" and told her to leave New York. Biographer Mary Louise Sullivan notes, "Cabrini responded by reminding the archbishop that she had been sent to America by Rome and would therefore remain." She remained, surviving Corrigan by fifteen years.

A member of her community recalled, "The love of God consumes her—it is evident on her face, in her words, in her dealings with others." But being superior wasn't easy, and Cabrini prayed for "the strength that is necessary to hide my sufferings so that I may be able to give comfort to the Sisters." She was no shrinking violet. One Sister wrote, "She could become quite angry and would raise her voice when upbraiding a sister in her native Italian."

By the time of her death on December 22, 1917, Mother Cabrini's community expanded nationwide, founding a far-reaching network of schools, orphanages, and hospitals. Historian Thomas Shelley writes, "They were active in the Italian community as teachers, nurses, social workers, and counselors even ministering to prisoners on death row in the prisons." Sullivan notes that immigrants "found a place where not only their language but their customs were understood and accepted."

In her official photo (later doctored to include a halo) she smiles placidly, with hands politely folded. One gets little sense of the fire that burned within, a sense that this tiny woman had a will of steel, what Sullivan calls "shrewd business sense," frankness, humility, and most of all compassion. This was no plaster statue, but a "multifaceted personality" whose "very being was afire with love of God and humankind."

22

FATHER NICHOLAS RUSSO
1845–1902

We had come to be their friends and look after their souls.
—NICHOLAS RUSSO

At the start of the twentieth century, Italian immigrants were arriving at Ellis Island at the rate of one hundred thousand a year. Many stayed in New York City, settling in an area that came to be known as Little Italy. Life was rough: large families were crowded into tenement apartments; men eked out a living on subsistence wages, and they faced prejudice from their neighbors. There were few places they could look for help.

One of them was the Catholic Church. Michael Corrigan, the archbishop of New York, made outreach a priority of his administration, founding Italian parishes throughout the metropolitan area for their benefit. He also assigned some of the best priests in the archdiocese to this work. After asking the New York Jesuits to start a new parish on the Lower East Side, Father Nicholas Russo, S.J., was picked to head it.

Born in Italy, Russo joined the Jesuits at seventeen and studied in France and the United States. After his ordination he was sent to Boston College as a philosophy professor. Over a period of eleven years he wrote two textbooks and served as acting president of the college. Between 1888 and 1890 he taught in New York and Washington before returning to a Manhattan parish, where he doubled as a speechwriter for Archbishop Corrigan.

Flexibility is a cornerstone of Jesuit life, the readiness to go anywhere and assume any task for what founder St. Ignatius Loyola called "God's greater glory." A respected professor and college president, Russo gave up a successful academic career to serve in the tenements. A biographer writes, "It must have been, humanly speaking, no small sacrifice . . . for he had held high positions in Boston and New York and his work had lain almost entirely among the better instructed and wealthy."

But Russo said he would gladly spend his life among his "poor Italians." He and his fellow Jesuit Aloysius Romano went right to work:

> We rented an old bar-room, turned ourselves into carpenters, cleaners, and decorators, made an altar and two confessionals, cleaned the walls, painted the inside doors, etc.—in a word gave the appearance of a chapel and put up a big sign on the outside, "Missione Italiana della Madonna di Loreto."

The chapel intentionally opened on August 16, 1891, the Feast of San Rocco. Getting the men to come to church was a challenge. The San Rocco Society participated, but, Russo commented, "I could not help looking with dread to the following Sunday."

Historian Mary Elizabeth Brown notes that Neapolitans, Sicilians, and Calabrians were living in what had once been an Irish neighborhood. They were mainly Catholic, but their fellow Catholics didn't always welcome them. The local pastor offered them the church basement for worship but later reneged. One old-timer, Bernard Lynch, wrote an article for a Catholic journal about what he considered the "Italian problem."

In an 1896 article for *The Woodstock Letters*, an in-house Jesuit magazine, Russo called Manhattan a "favorite place" for Italian immigrants. Their hope was to "find work here more easily, and thus better their condition." He estimated their local numbers at fifteen thousand. "Nearly all the southern provinces of Italy," he added, "are represented with their different dialects, customs, and manners." Most only understood their own dialect: "They *understand* good Italian fairly but cannot *speak* it."

There were numerous challenges, not all financial. There was local prejudice from nearby pastors. Russo was once denied use of the upper church at Old St. Patrick's Cathedral,* he wrote, "for reasons which a priest should feel ashamed to give." He occupied a small room in a tenement house. All in all, it was lonely, hard work, and he couldn't help believing that "things would not be in so bad a shape now . . . if they had been taken in hand in due time. . . . Look back to the first years of Italian immigration. Who was there to smooth their first difficulties, to warn them of the danger, to sympathize with their distressed condition, to turn their mind to heaven, and to remind them of their immortal soul?"

But the people's "own indifference" was a problem, too, and sometimes there was outright hostility. As Russo later recalled, "We were oftentimes received with the coldest indifference; not seldom avoided; at times greeted with insulting remarks. The word *pretaccio,* as we passed by, was one of the mildest."

Still, he felt sympathy for the men, who "work like slaves." Eventually, he added, "We had a nice little crowd" in the parish. His compassionate approach helped win over the people: "We spoke kindly to them; told them that we were not after their money; that we had come to be their friends and look after their souls; and finally begged them to send their children to us in the afternoon and come with them if possible."

To keep the young men involved in the parish, he started the St. Aloysius Club. Members produced plays that he composed. For those who only knew him as a professor, it was interesting to see how he would make himself "all to all." He also started devotions to the Sacred Heart, a traditional Jesuit devotion, which drew hundreds.

On April 1, 1902, he died at age fifty-six of pneumonia in his room. "There can be little doubt," one Jesuit wrote, "that he shortened his life by his constant labor for these poor people." By then, Our Lady of Loretto drew some three thousand every Sunday, and the school had nearly seven hundred students. Russo was remembered for his "zeal, patience, death to self, and charity." In his willingness to meet the needs of the day, without regard to personal comfort, Nicholas Russo proved a true Jesuit, giving without counting the cost.

---

* The original St. Patrick's Cathedral on Mulberry Street was built in 1809. The current cathedral on Fifth Avenue was completed in 1879.

23

GOVERNOR ALFRED EMANUEL SMITH

1873–1944

Rabble? That's me you're talking about.

—AL SMITH

He liked to say he "grew up with the Brooklyn Bridge" on the Lower East Side. As the first Catholic to run for president on a major party ticket, Al Smith's was the classic rags-to-riches story. It began in gaslight-era New York, when Trinity Church was the city's tallest building, and ended in the Empire State Building. Rising from clerk to CEO, Al Smith always considered himself an Irish Catholic kid from the Fourth Ward. He believed it was the best place in the world to grow up, a diverse community where everyone knew and looked out for each other.

An icon of Irish America, Smith was also Italian and German. For his family the neighborhood's centerpoint was St. James Church, founded fifty years earlier by Felix Varela. From cradle to grave, St. James met every need: religious, educational, and social. Although Al left the parish school early (after his father's death), he was active in the theater group, learning public speaking techniques that served him well in politics.

These were the days of Tammany Hall, the political machine that dominated New York for a century. Although popularly associated with forces of corruption, by Smith's time it was embracing reform. As a young man, Smith would work his way up from the Fulton Street Fish Market through minor offices into the State Assembly. Although his formal education was limited, he committed himself to learning the art of lawmaking, and he succeeded.

The Triangle Fire of 1911, in which 146 factory workers died, marked a turning point for Smith, from politician to advocate. As part of the investigative commission, what he saw changed his life: single mothers working 120 hours a week and children working eighteen hours a day. When one child was asked how long she had been working, she answered, "Ever since I was." Among other things, the commission helped ban child labor under age fourteen, made sprinklers mandatory in factories, and required seats for all, irrespective of gender or color.

Imbued with what one biographer calls "common sense and a belief in decency," Smith became an identifiable public figure, with his brown derby and cigar, his ability to captivate a crowd, and what a peer called "his 100 percent frankness." A biographer notes that "the stage was his to command." A friend said that "vitality goes out from him like a flood." From the assembly he aspired to the governorship. Beginning in 1918, he served four terms. Here he came into his own politically, as a champion of the common man and woman.

As governor he fought against discrimination, for workers' rights, and for decent housing. When a colleague complained about "rabble" moving into his community, Smith replied, "Rabble? That's me you're talking about." By 1924 he was emerging as a national leader in the Democratic Party during a Republican-dominated decade. (Taking credit for the era's prosperity, Republicans promised a "chicken in every pot.") Although Prohibition was the law of the land, Smith supported its repeal, and he unsuccessfully fought to have the Ku Klux Klan outlawed.

Anti-Catholicism was sweeping the nation at a level unseen since the days of the Know-Nothings. Oregon attempted to ban Catholic schools, and Florida's governor warned of a Vatican takeover. The Klan spread nationwide, stressing the Catholic "menace" to America. (At its height, national membership reached five million.) But nothing typified the era's religious hostility like the 1928 presidential campaign, when Alfred E. Smith dared run for the nation's highest office.

In Oklahoma, a minister said a vote for Smith was a vote against Christ. (When an opponent referred to papal encyclicals, Smith reputedly asked a priest friend, "What the hell is an encyclical?") Protestants envisioned the pope taking over the country. One journal predicted "a confessional box in the White House, and the secrets of the government whispered into the ear of a representative of the Vatican . . . [Smith] will be as a President what he has been as a governor, the pliant tool of the most Christless system of tyranny the world has ever known."

Although he received the largest popular vote of any Democratic candidate, he still lost by a wide margin. Most scholars agree that the religious factor (along with a decade of Republican prosperity) sealed Smith's fate.

His defeat was a serious blow to Catholics, reminded that they were still outsiders. The question still remained: Could Catholics be "real" Americans? Would their religious and political obligations conflict? It would be another three decades before John F. Kennedy answered that question definitively.

In the aftermath of the election, a jaded Smith moved away from politics, becoming president of the corporation that built the Empire State Building. In 1932 he attempted to win the Democratic nomination once more, but lost to Franklin D. Roosevelt. Some think he never quite forgave Roosevelt for this, and during the 1930s he opposed many of the president's measures. Smith called him "the kindest man that ever lived, but don't get in his way."

Yet through it all, Smith's biographer writes, "The greatest source of happiness in Al's life was his marriage." He died in 1944, not long after his wife's death. While doctors attributed the death to a heart condition and lung congestion, many believed he died of a broken heart. A Knight of St. Gregory and a papal chamberlain, he was buried at St. Patrick's Cathedral. An estimated two hundred thousand people filed past his coffin.

In the end, New Yorkers didn't remember an embittered ex-candidate. They remembered the kid from the Fourth Ward who rose from poverty to challenge notions of what a presidential candidate should be. They remembered the man who never forgot his roots, who fought for their rights. They remembered the man that Roosevelt himself once called "the happy warrior of the political battlefield."

24

THOMAS FRANCIS MEEHAN
1854–1942

I always found that he was riding high on his enthusiasms, always discovering something he had not known before.

—A CONTEMPORARY OF MEEHAN

On the evening of July 7, 1942, Thomas Francis Meehan passed away at his home on Greene Avenue in Brooklyn. He was eighty-eight years old. It seems he was working on an article about Catholics in New York City, a topic to which he had devoted his life as journalist and historian, when he slumped over his desk peacefully around nine o'clock at night. In some ways, it almost seemed a fitting end for one dedicated to chronicling the history of Catholic Gotham and passing it on to future generations. He died at his life's work.

Few were better qualified to do that work. By the time of Meehan's death, New York City had over four hundred Catholic churches, not to a mention a vast network of colleges and universities, schools, hospitals, and childcare institutions. During his long life he witnessed their birth and growth, and he liked nothing better than relating the story, either personally or on paper, of how they came to be.

He lived through the days when the Know-Nothings dominated national politics, through the Civil War and the building up of the nation and the church. His father, Patrick Meehan, edited one of the city's premier ethnic papers, the *Irish American*. Unlike many Irish New Yorkers, his childhood, writes his biographer, was marked by "culture, refinement, simplicity, and a wealth of literary attainments."

The oldest of eleven, Meehan was born in Brooklyn and grew up in Jersey City. He studied at St. Francis Xavier College, a Jesuit school in Manhattan (now Xavier High School). In those days, the line between high school and college was not clearly demarcated. He graduated with a bachelor's in 1873 and a master's the following year. Several of his classmates went on to the priesthood, and three became bishops. But Meehan's vocation lay elsewhere, in the field of writing.

After graduation, he went to work at his father's newspaper. For thirty years, he was the *Irish American*'s managing editor. He also wrote for several other newspapers and was New York correspondent for still others. He mostly covered current events of interest to the city's largely Catholic Irish community. But over time he became increasingly concerned with chronicling the city's Catholic history.

After his marriage to Molly O'Rourke in 1881 Meehan moved to Brooklyn, where he spent the rest of his life. Locally, in the 1890s, he helped organize the short-lived Brooklyn Catholic Historical Society, which attempted to preserve items of interest to the local community. Nationally, he held leadership roles in organizations like the American Catholic Historical Association and the U.S. Catholic Historical Society.

One of the accomplishments of which Meehan was most proud was his work with the *Catholic Encyclopedia*. It was Jesuit Father John J. Wynne, editor of the *Messenger of the Sacred Heart*, who came up with the idea at a time when encyclopedias were becoming all the rage. Wynne felt that their depictions of Catholicism veered toward the inaccurate and sometimes the unfair.

The *Catholic Encyclopedia* was to be "an international work or reference on the constitution, doctrine, discipline, and history of the Catholic Church." It was an international operation, with nearly fifteen hundred contributors from forty-three countries. Meehan was an assistant editor and wrote more articles than anyone else (over one hundred). One Protestant magazine called the encyclopedia, completed in 1914, the "greatest work undertaken for the advancement of Christian knowledge since the days of Trent."

In 1909 Meehan joined the editorial staff of the new Jesuit magazine *America*, where his friend Father Wynne was editor. He worked there for thirty-three years, writing mainly historical articles. A Jesuit from *America* said of Meehan, "I always found that he was riding high on his enthusiasms, always discovering something he had not known before . . . always being reminded of something that was 'awfully' interesting."

At home, Meehan led a comparatively quiet life, but sitting back in his chair in the back parlor of his Brooklyn home, with its high ceilings and tall windows, he came fully alive as he talked about the days when he met Archbishop John Hughes, and of Civil War–era New York.

At eighty-five, he was still making the hour-long commute from his Brooklyn home to America House in Manhattan. He liked to call himself the oldest Jesuit in the New York Province. At the time of his death, one Jesuit called Meehan "an integral part of the history of *America*." He was remembered as a "well full of tradition." If he had one fault, his coworkers remembered, it was "A cultured and inspiring fault. He loved to converse. Sometimes, in the stress of busy days the editors were not partial to talk. But it was hard to resist Mr. Meehan, for he was a very fascinating talker." New York and Brooklyn Catholic history were his favorite topics. He saw it as his vocation to pass down the story of the local church to the next generation. At times he grew frustrated with what he considered a lack of suitable enthusiasm on the part of his younger colleagues, but he literally went to his death telling the story he loved. Every historian should be so fortunate.

25

FATHER FRANCIS PATRICK DUFFY
1871–1932

Everyone in New York was a friend of Father Duffy.
—A NEW YORK POLICE OFFICER AT
FATHER DUFFY'S FUNERAL

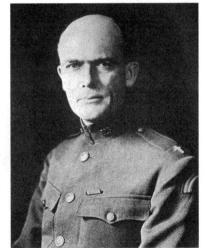

Millions pass his statue daily in Times Square, and many more have seen him featured in the 1940 James Cagney movie *The Fighting 69th*. Professor, pastor and soldier, apologist and ecumenist, Francis Duffy was, in his time, one historian writes, "the best-known priest in New York." A transplanted Canadian, he became the quintessential New Yorker: in love with the city, and living in the very heart of it.

Born on May 2, 1871, Francis Patrick Duffy grew up in the town of Cobourg, one of eleven children. His parents immigrated to Canada from Ireland. After Frank finished college in Toronto he secured a teaching job at the Jesuits' Xavier High School in Manhattan. A year later he began studies for the priesthood. He stayed in New York for the rest of his life.

Ordained in 1896 for the New York Archdiocese, he pursued graduate studies at Catholic University in Washington, DC. He then joined the faculty of St. Joseph's Seminary in Yonkers, teaching philosophy for fourteen years. One student called him an "Irish Socrates, not a lecturer, but a teacher who probed the mind of each student, sometimes in a disquieting fashion."

Although Duffy served briefly as a chaplain during the Spanish-American War, it was as a scholar that he first achieved national renown. He helped found the *New York Review*, perhaps the finest American Catholic theological journal of its time. For Duffy, a major challenge the church faced was "a certain intellectual sloth which masquerades as faith." The *Review* featured the latest theological advances worldwide and espoused the latest biblical scholarship.

This was the era of what is called the modernist movement, which Duffy's biographer Stephen Harris describes as "an attempt to reconcile historical Christianity with modern science and philosophy." But in higher ecclesiastical circles, theological innovation was increasingly seen as something subversive, a concession to a secularizing world. In 1907 Pope St. Pius X condemned modernism, and the *Review* operated under a cloud of suspicion. Within a few months, it ceased publication.

Duffy and his associates themselves operated under a cloud of suspicion, and soon they were reassigned from the seminary. Duffy was sent to the Bronx, to a converted storefront titled Our Saviour Church. In time he built a full-standing church, a school, and a day nursery for working parents. While he enjoyed the work (he loved being around people), he longed for a still more challenging task, what he called "a man's job."

In 1916 Father Duffy was appointed chaplain to the 69th New York Regiment (later renumbered the 165th U.S. Infantry), a predominantly Irish unit that saw hard fighting during the Civil War. When Duffy joined the regiment, Harris notes, "You could fill up a company with just O'Briens, O'Connors, O'Connells, O'Neills, and O'Reillys." As the United States entered the First World War, it earned hard-fought battle honors on the Western Front, in places like St. Mihiel and the Meuse-Argonne.

Duffy loved the character of the regiment, particularly its Irish Catholic character. He called the regiment his "parish—an itinerant parish." But he was no chauvinist, either ethnic or religious. He told the troops, Catholic and non-Catholic, "I come to you in soldiers' togs, with a message from the church. I want to be your friend, whatever your religion may be. I know many of you are leaving families behind you and will have many worries. Come to me with them and you will find me ready with a wide word and a merry one."

And he made an impression on the troops, who remembered him as a "salty personality, full of force and flavor." One soldier, after going to Duffy for confession, told his commanding officer, "You can put my name down for any old job out there. I'm all cleaned up and I don't give a damn what happens now."

The regiment celebrated St. Patrick's Day 1918 in the trenches singing traditional Irish songs. Through that summer and fall, he went "over the top" with his men. A newspaper reporter saw Duffy "covered with mud and grime . . . in the thick of the fighting, cheering on the living, administering the last rites of his church to the dying, filling the place of a stretcher bearer who had been struck down by a bullet, assisting the wounded, darting hither and yon, a ministering angel . . . For 117 hours he was under fire without rest."

Many felt he was pushing himself to a nervous breakdown, and he admitted, "I felt as if I were running on four tires and one cylinder." By 1918 he was, one historian writes, "the best-known American military chaplain of World War I." He would remain on active duty until 1920, when he became pastor of Holy Cross Church on West Forty-Second Street. Author Alexander Woolcott, a friend of Duffy's, wrote, "This city is too large for most of us, but not for Father Duffy. Not too large, I mean, for him to invest it with the homeliness of a neighborhood. When he walked down the street—any street—he was like a curé striding through his own village. Everybody knew him."

His friends included politicians and policemen, longshoremen and literary types. Duffy once said his secret was simple: "Being fond of people. Just people."

As New York's governor Alfred E. Smith ran for president on the Democratic ticket in 1928, a new wave of anti-Catholicism swept the country. How, many asked, could Smith be a loyal Catholic and a loyal American? Duffy helped write Smith's responses to the anti-Catholic charges thrown against him.

After his death of colitis in June 1932, Duffy's funeral at St. Patrick's Cathedral attracted some twenty-five thousand people. The story goes that a wealthy society matron tried to get past the crowd and was blocked by a police officer. "But," she said, "I was a friend of Father Duffy." The policeman replied, "Lady, everyone in New York was a friend of Father Duffy."

26

PATRICK FRANCIS SCANLAN
1894–1983

Catholic journalism with its sleeves rolled up.
—DEACON DON ZIRKEL

For some, the label "Brooklyn Irish Catholic" (BIC) is a point of pride; for others it evokes images of aggressive intolerance. Dorothy Day complained that BICs "went around with a chip on their shoulder being 'militant Catholics.'" Perhaps no single individual personified that image more than Patrick F. (Pat) Scanlan, longtime editor of the *Brooklyn Tablet*, once labeled a "one-man Anti-Defamation League."

From 1917 to 1968 Scanlan made the *Tablet* what one historian calls America's "most influential diocesan paper." Another historian writes that few papers "had the spice of the Brooklyn *Tablet*." Much of the paper's success had to do with Scanlan's editorial style: "Catholic journalism with its sleeves rolled up."

Born in Manhattan on October 7, 1894, Patrick Francis Scanlan was the son of a successful grocer. After studying at St. Joseph's University in Philadelphia, he followed his three brothers into the seminary (Monsignor Scanlan High School in the Bronx is named for his brother Arthur). There he decided his vocation lay elsewhere, and he took a teaching job on Staten Island before answering a call for a temporary managing editor at the *Tablet*, founded in 1908 as the official organ for the Brooklyn Diocese. The job lasted fifty years.

Although Scanlan had no journalistic experience, few Catholic editors in those days had any professional training. One of Scanlan's peers recalled, "We were basically looking for guys who had a real love of the faith and could write well." Another major requirement was a strong institutional loyalty. Scanlan's forceful writing style emerged early on. As world Protestantism celebrated its four hundredth anniversary in 1917, Scanlan wrote a letter to the *New York Times*, citing little reason to celebrate. Referring to a new Mormon temple in Brooklyn in 1918, Scanlan commented that he couldn't extend a welcome, because "the Church cannot take up cudgels with heretics."

Early on in his career Scanlan wrote, "Non-Catholics may not understand our attitude, but at least they must do us the justice to acknowledge that at least we have the courage of our convictions." For Scanlan, a major issue was anti-Catholicism, which reached a fever pitch in 1920s America with the resurgence of the Klan, and which included the vicious opposition to Al Smith's 1928 presidential campaign.

During this period, the Klan was no longer a southern thing; Klansmen defaced Coney Island churches and burned crosses in front of Queens convents. Scanlan dedicated much of his energy to fighting the Klan. Even in later years he still referred to opponents as "Klansmen." In 1923 he and his fellow Knights of Columbus even infiltrated a Klan meeting in Floral Park and broke it up. His approach to anti-Catholicism was simple: "Between the Church and a successful football team there is an analogy. Both have to fight."

His writing style attracted attention far beyond Catholic circles. Several times he was offered lucrative positions with the Hearst Corporation, which he always refused because he was "happier in the non-secular field." In his view, the secular press was anti-Catholic and money driven, whereas the Catholic press had a "sacred message to unfold." By the 1940s the *Tablet* had the largest circulation of any diocesan paper in the country, approximately four hundred thousand. Its influence matched that of national publications such as *Commonweal, America*, and *Our Sunday Visitor*.

Part of the reason for the paper's popularity far beyond Brooklyn circles was Scanlan's willingness to take on any issue: theological, political, intellectual, or cultural. During the 1930s Scanlan (who originally supported the New Deal) became a major opponent in Catholic circles of

President Franklin D. Roosevelt's economic policies, criticizing what he considered the growth of big government and excessive spending. A low point for the paper and editor came in the late 1930s with its insistence on defending the anti-Semitic demagogue Father Charles Coughlin, the Detroit radio priest.

Scanlan had a strong distrust of secular liberal intellectuals, whom he called "eggheads." He harbored his greatest venom, however, for Catholic liberal intellectuals, especially those connected with *Commonweal*, the "high-hat boys" who he felt "apologized for being Catholic." "Some of us," he said of the independent Catholic journal, "would like to see it more Catholic and if convenient, less high-brow." In 1945 he wrote, "A liberal Catholic paper—there is no such thing."

Perhaps Scanlan was most famous for opposing Communism, which he saw most manifest in the public schools and the labor unions. During the postwar years the *Tablet* became a virtual sounding board for anti-Communist groups and movements nationwide. In 1947 author John Gunther called it "one of the most fiercely reactionary Catholic papers in the country." (In 1950, Spain's Franco regime decorated Scanlan.) By 1950 Scanlan was the biggest supporter in the Catholic press of Joe McCarthy, whom he continued to praise long after the senator's demise.

By the 1960s, however, a new day was dawning. Scanlan didn't support presidential candidate John F. Kennedy, whom he considered too "high-brow." He liked Vatican II even less. He had an inherent distrust of *aggiornamento*; no windows, let alone doors, needed opening. When the council ended, Scanlan (at age seventy-one) was completely unequipped to deal with the changes of the sixties: political, theological, social, or cultural. As women religious expanded their commitment to social justice, Scanlan urged them to stay in the classroom. He warned against what he called a "theological cafeteria," where Catholics could choose their beliefs.

During the tumultuous summer of 1968 Scanlan retired from the paper to his Floral Park home. Before he did so, he quoted Hilaire Belloc in his last editorial: "For God's sake, never make apologies for the Catholic Church." His fiery, unapologetic approach to Catholic life was supplanted by a more dialogic, open form of Catholicism. Like James McMaster at the *Freeman's Journal* before him, the times had passed Scanlan by, but like McMaster, Scanlan too has had his successors.

27

MOTHER THEODORE WILLIAMS

1868–1931

God knows how many souls they reached.
—FATHER IGNATIUS LISSNER, S.M.A.

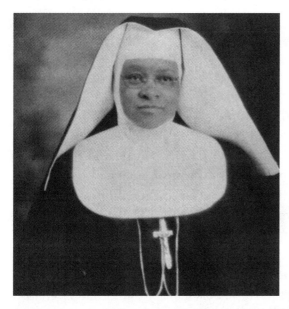

By the 1920s Harlem was the center for African American life in New York City. Many were migrants from the Jim Crow South, fleeing racism and poverty. Some consciously sought to create a center for black life and culture. Some came because they were asked. New York's archbishop Patrick J. Hayes requested Mother Theodore Williams, F.H.M., and her Sisters to come from Savannah and begin a daycare center for children of working parents. Today St. Benedict's Nursery on East 124th Street still fulfills this need.

There were three religious communities for African American women by the 1920s. The first, the Oblate Sisters of Providence, was founded in Baltimore in 1829. A decade later, the Sisters of the Holy Family were founded in New Orleans. In Georgia in 1916, a French priest named Ignatius Lissner and an ex-nun named Elizabeth Williams founded the Franciscan Handmaids of Mary.

During her lifetime, Elizabeth Barbara Williams had been associated with all three communities. Born in Baton Rouge, she was the oldest of nine in a Catholic family. (Her cousin John Plantevigne was one of America's first black priests.) About age nineteen, Elizabeth joined a contemplative community in Convent, Louisiana, an offshoot of the Holy Family Sisters. Taking the name Sister Seraphim, she stayed there until New Orleans' archbishop James Blenk dissolved the community in 1913.

The official reason given was the Mother Superior's death, but a more potent factor may have been southern racism. Many whites, Catholics included, found black women in habits a threat, and Blenk wasn't one to challenge such objections. It was he who banned Elizabeth's priest cousin from working in New Orleans, alleging "a negative reaction from whites." It was said that John Plantevigne died not long thereafter of a broken heart.

She transferred to the Oblates as Sister Mary Theodore but left in 1915. Although the reasons are unclear, her forceful personality may have played a role. From there she became a receptionist at a convent for white nuns in Washington, DC, but the Sisters didn't know her background. Still, she never gave up hope of returning to religious life, and she (literally) held on to her habit.

Elizabeth found a spiritual director in Father John Fenlon, a priest teaching at Catholic University. Fenlon liked her and encouraged her not to give up on her vocation. Around this time, Fenlon's friend Father Ignatius Lissner was visiting from Georgia, where religious and racial hatred had reached a fever pitch. Jewish businessman Leo Frank had just been lynched, the Klan was revived, and future senator Tom Watson was stirring up anti-Catholicism.

Lissner was particularly worried about a bill banning white teachers in black schools. A French-born missionary serving Georgia's black Catholics, Lissner founded several schools staffed by white Sisters. He now decided to pursue a longtime dream of starting a community for black women. Fenlon suggested that Lissner contact Williams. Lissner recalled she nearly bowled him over with enthusiasm. Although he thought her "a little headstrong," he "was satisfied that she had a vocation and could render a valuable service."

The feared bill never passed, and Lissner went ahead with his plans. In September 1916, after he purchased a house for the new community, Elizabeth arrived (with habit) and soon took vows as Mother Mary Theodore. She would be the superior. In a short time, a handful of young women gathered around her. They called themselves the Handmaids of the Most Pure Heart of Mary.

The response from the local community, black and white, was largely positive. But one exception came from white nuns. Lissner recalled,

As real southerners, they could not believe that a colored woman could make a real Religious Sister. . . . "It is a shame," they said. "Fr. Lissner will soon find out his mistake. He may give them the veil, but will that prevent them from stealing chickens and telling lies?"

Lissner, whose father was Jewish, was also subject to prejudice. The local bishop, a Civil War veteran who would later be buried with a Confederate flag, wrote privately that the priest had "all the objectionable traits of the race."

The Handmaids took over one school, while operating a laundry to support themselves. They begged in the markets along Savannah's waterfront. Mother Theodore held them together, "a woman of courage, strong faith, and an ability to bear many trials without discouragement." Although there was little future in Savannah, Lissner nonetheless observed, "God knows how many souls they reached" there.

Archbishop Hayes's request came at the right time. As Harlem's African American population grew, Hayes made outreach a priority. The Sisters first moved to East 131st Street. They began a school, one history notes, "out of the mutual regret of parents and Sisters to part with the children they have trained and loved in the Day Nursery."

As time went on, Lissner's influence declined, and Mother Theodore made the big decisions, including the move to New York. In 1929 she affiliated her community with the Franciscans. Today they are known as the Franciscan Handmaids of Mary. In Harlem, many of those they encountered were old friends. One Harlem woman commented that the neighborhood seemed "full of nothin' but Savannah people."

During the Great Depression, with few resources, Mother Theodore began a soup kitchen that ran most of the day, with people lined up three abreast for three blocks. Sisters begged for leftover food in downtown markets. Scraping off the rot, they boiled huge cauldrons of water with bones they gathered. They threw in the cleaned vegetables, and "soon a delicious soup was simmering."

By 1931, overworked and in poor health, Mother Theodore was dying of pneumonia. On the day of her death, July 14, a contemporary recalled, "It was a measure of the respect in which she was held that the entire block was quiet so that she would not be startled by any noise." Before she died she told the gathered Sisters it was time for them to carry on the work. It goes on today.

In the face of obstacles largely unimaginable today, Elizabeth Williams never gave up on her vocation, even when all seemed lost. Since her death, the Handmaids, although never a large group, have expanded their ministry back to the South and across to Africa. As they approach their centennial, they continue to bring God's love to the people of Harlem and beyond, in the spirit of their foundress.

28

SERVANT OF GOD
MONSIGNOR BERNARD JOHN QUINN
1888–1940

I love you, I am proud of every one of you, and I would willingly shed to the last drop my life's blood for the least among you.

—BERNARD QUINN

In June 1916 Brooklyn bishop Charles McDonnell asked his priests to consider volunteering for the rural South, which faced a serious priest shortage. One priest, a young man named Bernard Quinn, sympathized with the cause, but he felt that the real need lay closer to home. African Americans were migrating North in growing numbers, and they needed help, too. "What greater home mission have we," the young priest wrote, "than that of our Coloured brethren right here in our own diocese?"

Quinn asked to start a mission for black Catholics in Brooklyn, but McDonnell said he wasn't ready yet. As the United States entered the First World War, Quinn became an army chaplain in France. When he returned home, Quinn renewed his request, which the bishop approved this time. In early 1922, after much planning and organizing, St. Peter Claver Church opened in Bedford-Stuyvesant as Brooklyn's first black Catholic parish, with Father Quinn as pastor.

Interestingly, Bernard John Quinn was born on January 15, 1888, the day

Peter Claver was canonized. The son of Irish immigrants, he wanted to be a priest in his native Newark, but the diocesan seminary was overcrowded and wasn't taking any more candidates. Bernard applied to the Brooklyn Diocese. In 1906 he entered St. John's Seminary in Bedford-Stuyvesant. (Located on the same block were a church, grammar school, high school, college, and rectory.)

A well-rounded young man with a penchant for baseball, cigars, music, and jokes, Quinn made friends easily. On June 1, 1912, he was ordained a priest in Brooklyn. At St. Gregory's Church in Crown Heights, a wealthy Irish congregation included millionaire Thomas Fortune Ryan. While he was there, Father Quinn got to know some of the African American parishioners as well. He began to develop an interest in helping them. He also encountered Catholic racism.

During this decade, nearly two million blacks left the South to escape Jim Crow, many settling in Harlem and Bedford-Stuyvesant. While Quinn reached out to them, not all priests did. Monsignor John L. Belford, pastor of a prominent Bedford-Stuyvesant parish, was an outspoken character who complained to the bishop that African American newcomers had "invaded" his neighborhood and driven out the Irish. He would not allow them in his church or school.

As a chaplain, Quinn would encounter racism as well. After one battle, he saw a white army chaplain refuse to pray for a dying black soldier. Quinn prayed with the soldier and sent his belongings back home. While he was in France, the priest also read St. Thérèse of Lisieux's autobiography, which began his lifelong devotion to the "Little Flower." Back in New York he played a key role in promoting her devotion among New York Catholics.

In Brooklyn, Quinn was assigned to found a parish for black Catholics, which he called a "real answer to prayer." He began entirely from scratch, as he later recalled: "To tell the truth, I didn't know where to look to find the first colored Catholic. As I went about, whenever I met a colored man, I would stop and talk with him. But everyone I met turned out to be a Baptist or a Methodist."

Soon he learned of the Colored Catholic Club of Brooklyn, an independent group of laypeople who would form the nucleus of the parish. He raised enough money to buy a truck depot in Bedford-Stuyvesant. Within a few months it was converted into a worship space, and in February 1922 the bishop dedicated it. One parishioner recalled, "We used to meet in the unfinished basement of the church, and Father used to sit with us smoking his 'jackass rope,' a cigar from Jamaica, West Indies. You never felt you were talking to a priest, you know, scared and careful what you say."

New York had one other black parish, St. Benedict the Moor in Manhattan, founded in 1883. At St. Peter Claver, Quinn started devotions to Thérèse of Lisieux, who would be canonized in 1925. Her shrine attracted thousands of Catholics, black and white, citywide. Within five years, it was estimated that over two million New Yorkers had visited the parish. Soon a school opened, run by the Sisters of the Blessed Sacrament, a community dedicated to black ministry.

Father Quinn's plans extended beyond St. Peter's. He later started a second black parish in Queens, St. Benedict the Moor. In rural Suffolk County, he started an orphanage for African American children named Little Flower. (Klansmen would burn the original building.) Back in Brooklyn he created an outreach to black sailors. One project that never went far, however, was a religious community for African American men, the Oblate Missionary Brothers of Mary.

"I am an adopted son of the Negro race," Quinn liked to say. His affection for his parishioners ran deep. In his first pastoral letter, he wrote, "I love you, I am proud of every one of you, and I would willingly shed to the last drop my life's blood for the least among you." When Klansmen threatened his orphanage, he guarded the property with a shotgun. On many occasions he gave away his coat or hat to someone who needed it more (and in one case a pair of shoes).

In 1931 Quinn was named a monsignor, a title he saw as an honor to his parishioners, not himself. (He never used the title.) His assistant priests were men who requested to be sent to St. Peter's. These were enthusiastic young men who wanted to work in the African American community. Many went on to become inner-city pastors themselves.

Quinn's life, however, was cut short by cancer at age fifty-two in April 1940. One parishioner wrote, "No one, perhaps, will ever be able to fit into his shoes, for his style comes only in odd sizes." Some eight thousand attended his funeral. A pioneer in urban ministry and a candidate for sainthood, Quinn's legacy continues in the long line of inner-city pastors who dedicated their lives to the disadvantaged and the least.

29

Servant of God Dorothy Day

1897–1980

When you start asking, "Lord, what would you have me do?"
you always find yourself doing a lot more than you thought
you were going to do.
—Dorothy Day

On the rare occasions Dorothy Day had time to herself, she enjoyed the Metropolitan Opera's Saturday afternoon broadcast. A favorite was *La Bohème*, the story of Paris's romantic rebels. As a young woman in the 1910s, she herself was among Greenwich Village's pioneer Bohemians, an aspiring writer and activist who knew many of its leading social and literary figures, including Eugene O'Neill and John Reed, who authored an eyewitness account of the Russian Revolution.

Born in Brooklyn in 1897, her family moved to Oakland and later Chicago. At the University of Illinois, Day's growing interest in social and political issues led her to leave school and move to Manhattan. There she became a reporter for *The Call*, a socialist newspaper, covering labor strikes and antiwar demonstrations. She even met Russian revolutionary Leon Trotsky during his New York sojourn.

A self-conscious reformer, she saw little room for religion. Its day had passed, she felt, and it was time for "new prophets." (Baptized an Episcopalian, formal religious observance had little part in her childhood.) During World War I, as the government cracked down on political dissent, she was arrested during a protest for women's suffrage. Thirty days in jail—and cracked ribs—deepened her identification with the downtrodden.

Back in New York, she began an affair with journalist Lionel Moise, which led to an abortion she regretted. After their breakup, she entered a rebound marriage, but soon returned to Moise. All the while, Day's sense of vocation as a writer was growing. So was her interest in religion, particularly the Catholic Church, which she came to see as "the church of the immigrants, the church of the poor."

By the 1920s she was living on Staten Island with Forster Batterham, a botanist of English descent. After her abortion she doubted whether she could ever have children, and her subsequent pregnancy led to a religious awakening. "No human creature could receive or contain so vast a floor of love and joy as I often felt after the birth of my child," wrote Day. "With this came the need to worship, to adore."

She had her daughter, Tamar, baptized Catholic, and Day herself soon followed. But Forster was a committed atheist, and the move led to their separation. Day supported Tamar through her writing.

Looking to unite her social concerns with her faith, she found an answer in Peter Maurin, an eccentric Frenchman twenty years her senior, who was brimming with reform notions. He urged her to found a paper promoting Catholic social thought. As she protested about finances, he told her not to worry, just start. On May 1, 1933, the *Catholic Worker* was born, selling for a penny a copy. By December, one hundred thousand copies a month were printed.

They also began directly serving the poor on Manhattan's Lower East Side. Asked how that started, she said, "Well, if your brother's hungry, you feed him. You don't meet him at the door and say, 'Go be thou fed!'" Day and her coworkers lived in solidarity with society's outcasts, no easy task. In her diary, she confided, "The dirt, the garbage heaped in the gutters, the flies, the hopelessness of the human beings around me, all oppress me."

A strong spiritual life sustained her: the Liturgy of the Hours (the church's official prayers), the rosary, daily Mass, weekly confession, spiritual reading, and direction. "Without the sacraments of the church," Day wrote, "I certainly do not think that I could go on." In the 1950s she became a Benedictine Oblate (a layperson practicing the order's charism in daily life).

Surprisingly, given her identification with the poor, Day's favorite saint wasn't Francis of Assisi but Thérèse of Lisieux, whose "Little Way," an approach to holiness that concentrates on doing small things with great love, Day adopted. Former Catholic Worker Jim Forest writes,

> A visiting social worker asked Day how long the "clients" were permitted to stay. "We let them stay forever," Day answered with a fierce look in her eye. "They live with us, they die with us, and we give them a Christian burial. We pray for them after they are dead. Once they are taken in, they are members of the family. Or rather they were always members of the family. They are our brothers and sisters in Christ."

From the start, Day's movement attracted idealistic young people. Tom Cornell, a longtime Catholic Worker, learned about Dorothy in college. "Here," he said, "was the gospel being lived."

Not everyone liked what she was doing. Her pacifism (a position adopted long before her conversion) irked many, Catholics included. Conservatives considered her too left leaning, and her support of a Catholic cemetery workers' strike in 1949 didn't endear her with local church leaders.

But far from seeing Catholicism as limiting, Day considered it the source of her freedom. In 1950 she talked about meeting with Archbishop (future cardinal) James McIntyre of Los Angeles, an arch-conservative if there ever was one. These two didn't see eye to eye on lots of issues, yet in her diary, she talked about how the meeting "increased my devotion to the church and the hierarchy."

By the 1960s, the country was catching up with Dorothy Day as she marched for numerous causes: civil rights, world peace, workers' rights. And she still got arrested, no light matter. A coworker recalled an occasion when Day, then in her sixties, was subjected to degrading physical and sexual abuse from female guards who taunted her with obscenities as they strip searched her.

In 1972 Notre Dame awarded her its prestigious Laetare Medal for "comforting the afflicted and afflicting the comfortable." Toward the end of her life, she said, "When you start asking, 'Lord, what have you me do?' you always find yourself doing a lot more than you thought you were going to do."

After her death in 1980, historian David O'Brien called her "the most significant, interesting, and influential person in the history of American Catholicism." Robert Ellsberg, who edited Dorothy's diary, writes,

She challenges the reformers and social activists to maintain their love for the church and the gospel. She challenges conservatives to be attentive to the radical social dimensions of the gospel. She challenges both sides to resolve differences with mutual respect and love, for the benefit of the world.

Nothing irritated her more than pious comparisons. "Don't call me a saint," Dorothy famously remarked. "I don't want to be dismissed so easily." The day may soon come, however, when she won't have a say in the matter anymore.

30

BISHOP FRANCIS XAVIER FORD
1892–1952

To feel compassion.
    —BISHOP FORD'S EPISCOPAL MOTTO

In 1892, as America was preparing to celebrate the four hundredth anniversary of its discovery, Austin and Elizabeth Ford were preparing for their sixth child. When a son arrived on January 11, they considered naming him Christopher Columbus Ford. But Austin had just finished reading a biography of St. Francis Xavier (1506–1552), whom he had come to admire, so the baby boy was named for the great missionary saint whose unrealized ambition was to reach China.

A native New Yorker, Austin Ford published *The Irish World*. Born in Iowa, Elizabeth Anne Rellihan had moved east to write for the paper; within a year, she and Austin were married. Theirs was a comfortable, middle-class existence in Brooklyn. Young Frank had many career options ahead of him. When he was twelve, an Irish priest visited his parish to raise money for the missions, and talked about his work in China. The seeds of a vocation had been planted; Frank Ford decided he would be a Chinese missionary.

But back then there were few opportunities for American Catholics to engage directly in missionary work. (Until 1908, the Vatican officially listed the United States as mission territory.) Frank enrolled at Cathedral College, a Manhattan school for young men considering the priesthood. In 1912, during his sophomore year, an opportunity presented itself when Fathers James Walsh and Thomas Price came to Cathedral looking for young men to join their new community, Maryknoll.

A year earlier, the two priests founded America's first missionary order in Ossining, New York, on a hill named for the Blessed Mother. Frank Ford was their first applicant. Of slight build, with black hair and striking dark eyes, he was shy, but no shrinking violet. In 1918, a few months after his ordination, he was one of the first Maryknollers assigned to China, at Guandong in the south.

Like his fellow priests, he knew little of Chinese culture and traditions. He would learn on the job. More experienced European missioners predicted that the Americans wouldn't last a year. It was indeed hard work. They faced rough, slow travel through terrible heat and humidity replete with mosquitoes. There was political unrest. Locals mocked their attempts at Chinese. Still, Ford wrote,

> I'm only just now discovering the civilization of China and falling on love with it . . . To think that China was completely equipped with a literature and culture 3,000 years before our ancestors was a hard blow to an Irishman.

Too many Westerners, he noted, felt the Chinese were there to serve them. Later he would tell his own priests: "We come to China not to barbarians, but a civilization thousands of years older." Condescension, he insisted, had no place: "Our Lord never condescended; He never betrayed superiority in His dealing with others." For Ford, the encounter with the Chinese was to be one of "reverence, respect, and love, a meeting of brothers."

For many back home, there was glamour about the missions. But, Ford commented, "the routine is without glamour." There were warlords, bandits, and pirates. Communism under Mao Zedong was gaining ground, and there were antiforeign demonstrations. For many Chinese, conversion to Christianity was a hard thing. It meant adopting a religion closely associated with the Westerners exploiting their country.

In 1935, Father Ford was named a Bishop in China. He took as his episcopal motto *Condolere*, meaning "to have compassion." His mission program was years ahead of its time: lay catechists, native vocations, and women religious directly engaging in evangelization. Because sexes were strictly segregated, only women could reach out to other women. Hence it was they who preached the gospel. Women, Ford believed, offered the only "real progress for the Church in China."

As bishop, he lived in a simple farmhouse, in a tiny room with his books stacked on a chair. He rarely wore the trappings of office. Once when a new American missionary addressed him formally, he replied, "None of this 'Excellency' business." His one vice was a pipe, and a peer notes that his "consumption of tobacco was enormous. In his discussions his pipe was indicative of his mood."

In China the Maryknollers ran churches, schools, hospitals, and orphanages. Beginning in the 1930s, they labored under threat of Japanese occupation. During the Second World War, American officials advised Bishop Ford to leave, but he refused. Although they were tough years, he had high hopes for the postwar era. Sadly, he proved to be wrong, as the struggle for China now continued between Chiang Kai-Shek's Nationalists and Mao's Communists.

In the summer of 1949, the Communists won, and the future boded ill for religious groups. Again Ford was advised to leave but he refused to do so. He considered withdrawal equivalent to apostasy, a denial of the faith itself. He wanted to "minister to our people at the very moment they especially need spiritual aid to witness for Christ." If they were in danger, he wanted to be with them.

In December 1950, government troops arrested Bishop Ford. He was put on trial for subversion. Ironically, he was called an enemy of the poor. He was convicted as an American spy, but before his sentencing, his biographer writes, "he proclaimed his love of the Chinese people and his willingness to suffer, even to die, to show that love." On February 22, 1952, Francis Xavier Ford died in prison.

The ironic part was that Ford had worked hard for years to overcome the perception of missionaries as foreign agents. Love, he wrote, was "the bridge" that transcended cultural differences, and his work in China was a labor of love, a love that entailed a willingness to make the ultimate sacrifice.

31

SERVANT OF GOD
CATHERINE DE HUECK DOHERTY
1896–1985

You have to preach the gospel without compromise or shut up. One or the other.

—CATHERINE DE HUECK DOHERTY

When Catherine De Hueck first arrived in New York City, she recalled, "the actual sight was simply overwhelming." Then, she writes, she "did the strangest thing." Standing outside Grand Central Station, she "looked at the immensity of New York, and said out loud, 'You do not frighten me. . . . I'll conquer you.'" A nearby policeman said, "Atta girl!"

An impoverished Russian aristocrat, she took a variety of jobs: laundress, waitress, cashier at Macy's, personal trainer. It was a lonely time: "There is no greater loneliness than being in a crowd of people you don't know." At one restaurant, she soon discovered she was expected to provide additional services to male customers. She changed her uniform, threw it at her boss, and made it quite clear she was not there for their whims.

Born Catherine Kolyschkine in 1896, she grew up in the aristocratic privilege of czarist Russia. She traveled throughout Europe with her parents. At fifteen she was married to her cousin, Baron Boris De Hueck, an arranged marriage. During World War I, they both served in the army, he an officer and she a nurse. She was decorated for bravery under fire.

As Russia collapsed, they returned to St. Petersburg, where they found "nothing to eat." Forced to rummage through garbage cans, they were attacked as "aristocrats." They escaped from Russia, hiding along the way in pigsties. Westerners, she insisted, couldn't understand real starvation, "never having really experienced [food's] complete absence."

Finding refuge in England, she was received into the Catholic Church. Raised in the Russian Orthodox Church, she was taught by Catholic nuns at an early age. From there, she and Boris made their way to Canada, where the two would eventually divorce. In New York she sought work, not a cause. A lecture bureau asked her to speak on prerevolutionary Russia, with a handsome salary. Then, all of a sudden it seemed, she gave it up to go live with the poor in the middle of the Great Depression:

> During those days I was in the throes of hearing the Lord say, "Sell what you possess. . . . Come follow me," and I was running away from him. One night, while dancing with this man, I heard laughter, a very gentle and kind laughter. I heard what I thought was the voice of God laughing and saying: "You can't escape me, Catherine, you can't." I pleaded a headache and went home. Some new phase of my life was about to begin.

She began her work in Canada and came back to New York. Two things shocked her: the extent of white racism and living conditions in Harlem. At Columbia University she asked a professor why African Americans weren't discussed. He responded, "Oh, we don't study the Negro. We study American history." The United States, she wrote, "had this marvelous Constitution, but it doesn't apply to Negroes."

In Harlem, she found "a no-man's land of fear and doubt." Where was God in it all? she asked. In 1938 she founded Friendship House, an interracial apostolate dedicated to fighting segregation. Like her friend Dorothy Day's Catholic Worker movement, the "B.," as they called her, attracted idealistic young people nationwide. One volunteer recalled,

> White people, black people—talking, laughing, friendly, sipping coffee. How simple the solution all seemed then: the sooner we of differ-

ent races learned to work together, to pray together, to eat, to study, to laugh together, the sooner we'd be on the way to interracial justice.

Advocating civil rights could be as deadly as speaking out in revolutionary Russia. She was spit at and called a "nigger lover." At a Catholic women's group, she was berated for eating "with dirty niggers." When a woman told her, "You smell of the Negro," Catherine lost her temper: "And you stink of hell!" Once at a lecture in Savannah, she was nearly beaten to death by a group of white Catholic women.

"You have to preach the gospel," Catherine said, "without compromise or shut up. One or the other. I tried to preach it without compromise." She always ended her lectures the same way:

> Sooner or later, all of us are going to die. We will appear before God for judgment. The Lord will look at us and say, "I was naked and you didn't clothe me. I was hungry and you didn't give me anything to eat. I was thirsty and you didn't give me a drink. I was sick and you didn't nurse me. I was in prison and you didn't come to visit me." And we shall say, "Lord, when did I not do these things?" I would stop here, pause, and in a very loud voice say, *"When I was a Negro and you were a white American Catholic."* That's when the rotten eggs and tomatoes would start to fly!

One of her key supporters was New York's Cardinal Patrick J. Hayes, who was "always worried" about her. After she organized a study group at Friendship House, the local pastor visited her and said,

> "Listen to me, you Russian nitwit. What are you trying to do? Make them think they are loved just because they have become Catholics? You are giving them the raw gospel and it isn't getting you anywhere. Stop it!" I said, "Father, would you like to come with me to see the cardinal? If he orders me to stop, I will stop." "Oh, hell," he said. On the way out he slammed the door and smashed the glass in the window.

Later Catherine would remarry and move back to Canada, where she continued to be involved in apostolic work. But wherever she worked, she sought to actualize the gospel message in the present moment. As she once told a Fordham University Jesuit, "I have never read anywhere in the gospel where Christ says to wait twenty years before living the gospel. The Good News is for now."

32

GEORGE NAUMAN SHUSTER
1894–1977

To contribute to the efforts being made by all men and women of good will . . .

—COMMONWEAL, FIRST ISSUE, 1924

Since the 1820s New York has been home to many Catholic journals, but none quite like the *Commonweal*, founded in 1924. What made it unique was the fact that it was lay owned and operated. Michael Williams, the founder and first editor, believed there were enough internal publications sufficient for instructing Catholics. His idea was to found an independent Catholic magazine along the lines of the *Nation* and the *New Republic. Commonweal's* first editorial of November 12, 1924, announced its goal: "To contribute to the efforts being made by all men and women of good will, to bring peace upon earth, brotherhood among men, happiness to all peoples, and prosperity, good order, and the fruits of civilization—art, beauty, culture—to our own nation."

There was, and is, in *Commonweal's* pages no evidence of a narrow, separatist posture toward the larger culture, but a desire to engage in positive dialogue with that culture. That remains the magazine's legacy today, but in 1924 it was years ahead of its time.

A crucial figure in the journal's early years was George Nauman Shuster, a Columbia graduate student and part-time professor. A native midwesterner, Shuster had studied at Notre Dame and taught there before moving to New York to pursue a doctorate in English at Columbia. "I'll like that, really," his wife Doris said, "I've never been to New York at all, you know, and you are not educated until you have spent at least six months in New York. So education must not be neglected, must it?"

The Shusters stayed for thirty-five years. After serving as editor of *Commonweal*, George would go on to finish the doctorate at Columbia in 1940. By then, he was president of Hunter College, then the world's largest college for women. He would also do a stint as a government official in Germany before returning to his beloved Notre Dame in 1960. But it was in New York that he made a reputation as one of the outstanding layman of his generation. Above all, notes his biographer, Thomas Blantz, he had a commitment to the truth, whatever the cost.

At *Commonweal*, Shuster wrote articles, solicited authors and reviewers, wrote editorials, and above all challenged American Catholics to come out of their self-imposed shell and engage the larger culture. One of his earliest articles, written for the Jesuit magazine *America*, was titled, "Have We Any Scholars?" In it Shuster argued, "If we are honest, we must admit that during seventy-five years of almost feverish intellectual activity we have had no influence on the general culture of America." But, he argued, that could change.

Under Shuster's leadership, *Commonweal* became an organ for some of the best Catholic authors on both sides of the Atlantic. During the Great Depression it emerged as a champion of social thought, expounding the church's teachings on economic justice and supporting the New Deal of President Franklin D. Roosevelt, even against conservative Catholic critics like Father Charles Coughlin and the reactionary diocesan paper the *Brooklyn Tablet*.

If domestic issues caused division among American Catholics, no less did foreign affairs. Many if not most Catholics, seeing the Spanish Civil War as a fight against communism, supported General Francisco Franco's fascist regime. But there were exceptions. Dorothy Day at the *Catholic Worker* espoused pacifism, while George Shuster at *Commonweal* argued that neither side was without blame, and so neither could be endorsed in good conscience.

This stance cost the magazine a quarter of its subscription rate, and Shuster resigned rather than compromise his intellectual integrity. Years later, he recalled, as he was leaving the magazine, "It occurred to me that for Catholic New York the world outside the United States was either Communist or Fascism, and that therefore they had opted for Fascism."

During these same years, however, Shuster had been active in academia, publishing books on literature, religion, and foreign affairs, to name a few topics. He also taught English at several Catholic schools in the area, including St. Joseph's, a women's college in Brooklyn. He made quite an impression on his students, one of whom recalled, "Those of us who sat spellbound in your classes at St. Joseph's many years ago will never forget the warmth of your spirit, the depth of your humanity, the keenness of your sense of humor. Your very name carries inspiration for me as a teacher."

After leaving *Commonweal*, Shuster went to work at Columbia, where he earned his doctorate in 1940 at age forty-six. As president of Manhattan's Hunter College, a position Shuster held for twenty years, Blantz describes Shuster's tenure as a "grand success," a time that saw the expansion of the college and its curriculum as women took on larger roles in postwar American life. An expert on German life and culture (he authored three books on modern Germany), Shuster's tenure at Hunter was interrupted by a year serving in Bavaria as governor. Later he would be the American representative to UNESCO.

In 1960 George Shuster retired from Hunter and returned to Notre Dame at the request of the president, Father Theodore Hesburgh. (By then Doris didn't want to leave New York for South Bend.) He would serve as a special assistant to the president, promoting its expansion into the nation's preeminent Catholic university. He lived in South Bend until his death in 1977. By then, he had written nearly twenty books and some three hundred articles for various publications, academic and popular.

Author, editor, government official, college president, and teacher: George Shuster wore many hats in his time, and he wore all of them well. Through all of them, there was one consistent component: a commitment to excellence and a pursuit of the truth no matter where it led. A promoter of women's role in the public sphere, a champion of intellectual excellence, a thorough-going humanist and scholar, a believer in peace over partisanship, Shuster was years ahead of his time.

33

FRANK SHEED   MAISIE WARD
1897–1982   *1889–1975*

Real writers, not just worthy people with something to say.
   —FRANK SHEED

In the mid-twentieth century, there occurred a literary phenomenon known as the Catholic Revival, an international movement that saw some of the finest writers to embrace a Catholic pen, from Evelyn Waugh and G. K.

Chesterton to François Mauriac and Karl Adam. Catholic publishing was a booming industry, and nowhere more so than in New York, where Sheed and Ward produced some of the century's finest theological and literary output. This, along with the rise of the Catholic Worker movement and the liturgical movement, both of which addressed the spiritual dimensions of social activism, made it an exciting time to be Catholic.

Frank Sheed and Maisie Ward were nothing if not excited about being Catholic. He was a transplanted Australian and she a transplanted Victorian, daughter of a distinguished English Catholic family. He was the classic "scholarship boy," child of a broken home who made good academically, working his way through law school in Sydney. Long before laypeople were encouraged to actively promote their faith, the two met in England through the Catholic Evidence Guild, an organization devoted to street preaching, public debates, and disseminating Catholic literature.

Frank Sheed loved to argue, which drew him initially toward law. But as a young man he asked himself the question, "What am I arguing for?" Maisie, for her part, matched him, having been described as "the quintessential street corner preacher . . . part Major Barbara, part scholastic theologian." One relative asked at the time of their 1925 wedding, "Will she boss him or will they fight?" They did neither. Theirs became a love affair that lasted over fifty years.

If there was anything they loved more than arguing, it was good writing. Maisie came from a thoroughly literary and Catholic family, three generations of literary output with a religious bent. As her son Wilfrid wrote in his memoir, *Frank and Maisie*, "Religion was simply what the Wards did." Frank promised himself at sixteen that if he couldn't write like Shakespeare, he wouldn't write at all. Fortunately he didn't keep that promise.

In 1926, with money from her mother, Maisie and Frank started Sheed and Ward, a publishing house devoted to Catholic works. They published

Christopher Dawson's history, Jacques Maritain's philosophy, Karl Adam's theology, and Evelyn Waugh's novels. Wilfrid Sheed recalls of Frank, "Two of his boyhood heroes were Belloc and Chesterton, and now he was getting not just to meet them, but to publish them!" Relocating from London to New York in 1933 Sheed and Ward became a veritable "megaphone for the Catholic Revival of the mid-twentieth century."

They disproved the notion that Catholics weren't allowed to think. More than that, they published *good* writers. Frank, his son recalls, "wanted real writers, not just worthy people with something to say." One of Sheed and Ward's early discoveries was a young American priest named Fulton Sheen, who was sometimes less than careful with his sources. Of one Sheen manuscript Frank said, "I'll publish it if you'll agree to put the whole thing in quotation marks."

Frank and Maisie were also authors in their own right. Writing was in their blood, especially Maisie. Maisie would write some twenty-seven books. Many of their works are still in print, including Maisie's biography of G. K. Chesterton, which the *New Yorker* called "a great plum pudding of a book." Frank's *To Know Christ Jesus* has been hailed as "one of the most satisfying studies of the gospel ever made." For decades, his translation of St. Augustine's *Confessions* was the standard. Over time they became what their son called "an institution."

For everything she did, Maisie had "the enthusiasm of a teenager." Her son recalls that she "couldn't do anything she didn't believe in." Like her friend Dorothy Day, she had a strong love for the poor, and like Dorothy she tried her hand at starting communal farms. Unfortunately, they didn't work, but her commitment to social justice was no less real. For Maisie, the church "was not a living tradition . . . unless it physically lived and brought forth life." Her life was a balance of culture and compassion.

The decade leading up to Vatican II was the real heyday for Sheed and Ward, as they published some of the finest of the new theology. This included the writings of a young German priest named Hans Küng and a Dutch Dominican named Edward Schillebeecx. By then, Sheed and Ward had become an institution in promoting Catholic culture and thought.

Toward the end of their lives, in 1973, Frank and Maisie sold the publishing house, which had experienced something of a decline in the postconciliar years. Maisie died in 1975, and Frank seven years later. "When Frank died," his son wrote, "I was amazed at the number of people who wrote to say what an eye-opener Sheed and Ward had been."

Years ahead of its time, Sheed and Ward had developed into perhaps the premier Catholic publishing house of the mid-twentieth century, a key promoter of Catholic culture and thought at a time when many assumed Catholics didn't have it in them. Frank and Maisie proved them wrong.

34

FATHER THOMAS MERTON

1915–1968

"Don't act on impulses," I thought. "This is not rational. This is crazy."

—THOMAS MERTON

In 1936, twenty-year-old Tom Merton stepped off the dock into New York harbor with an overwhelming enthusiasm that's gripped many before and since: "New York, you are mine! I love you!" An expatriate returned home from England, he was glad to be back in "the big, wild city." He was here to finish his degree at Columbia University, and that decision proved to be a turning point in his life.

Much of his life had been spent traveling. The son of artists, a New Zealand father and a New York mother, he'd been born in France during the First World War. For much of his childhood he'd moved back and forth between Europe and America. Orphaned at sixteen, sent to an English boarding school, James Martin notes that this was a "lonely and aimless" time for the young man.

An excellent student, he won a scholarship to Cambridge University. But he spent little time in class, "breaking my neck trying to get everything out of life that you think you can get out of it when you are eighteen." The breaking point came when he fathered a child, at which point his guardian suggested a return to the States. Young Tom agreed wholeheartedly—thus the transfer to Columbia.

Merton liked Columbia's "genuine intellectual vitality." Commuting from his grandfather's Douglaston home, he took a more active role on campus than at Cambridge. He marched with other students at antifascist rallies, antiwar rallies, and peace strikes. He joined the Young Communist League under a pseudonym. He even tried the cross-country team, and he admitted he may have been more successful if he would have stopped smoking.

He was also searching for something more, what Basil Pennington calls "solid ground on which to stand." Studying medieval philosophy, with its arguments for God's existence, made an impression on him, as did reading the nineteenth-century Jesuit poet Gerard Manley Hopkins. At one point, reading an account of Hopkins's conversion, he began to think about his own. "Why don't you do it?" In his autobiography, *The Seven Storey Mountain,* Merton writes, "I stirred in the chair, I lit a cigarette, looked out the window at the rain, tried to shut the voice up. 'Don't act on impulses,' I thought. 'This is not rational. This is crazy.'"

He put the book down, put on his raincoat, and walked down Broadway to 121st Street, to Corpus Christi Church. He told the pastor, "Father, I want to become a Catholic." On November 16, 1938, Thomas James Merton was received into the Roman Catholic Church. He planned to write his dissertation on Hopkins.

Again, he was being drawn toward something more. If he was going to live his faith, Merton was going to live it all the way. He was going to become a priest. But he couldn't decide what kind of a priest to become. A Jesuit or a Dominican, teaching in schools? A Benedictine, living in a monastery? A Franciscan, ministering directly to the poor? A professor at Columbia, Dan Walsh, aided his discernment process, guiding him toward the Franciscans.

But when Tom Merton applied to the Franciscans in 1939 his application was rejected. (The main reason was his having fathered a child.) But he didn't rule out a priestly vocation altogether, even as he taught at the Franciscans' St. Bonaventure University in upstate New York. As Dan Walsh talked about a retreat he had made with Trappist monks in Kentucky, his interest was aroused.

Founded in seventeenth-century France, their goal is to live the monastic life more purely. In 1848 they established their first permanent American foundation, Our Lady of Gethsemani Abbey, near Bardstown, Kentucky. In the spring of 1941 Merton made an Easter retreat there. In *The Seven Storey Mountain,* he wrote,

> How did I ever get back out of there, into the world, after tasting the sweetness and kindness of the love with which you welcome those that come to stay in your house, even only for a few days, O Holy Queen of Heaven, and Mother of my Christ?

For the next few months, Tom Merton wrestled once more with the notion of a priestly vocation. "Are you sure you want to be a *Trappist*?" a Franciscan asked. "Father," Merton answered, "I want to give God everything." Although concerned that youthful indiscretion might cost him his vocation, the Trappists seem to have assured him that such was not the case.

On December 10, 1941, Thomas Merton entered the Abbey of Gethsemani. The Brother at the gatehouse, whom he had met during his retreat, asked if he was coming to stay this time. "Yes, Brother," he said, "if you'll pray for me." "That's what I've been doing," he said, "praying for you."

Merton had written poetry and tried his hand at novels, but when he entered the monastery, he assumed his writing days were over. Instead, the abbot of Gethsemani, Dom Frederic Dunne, recognized his ability and encouraged him to continue writing. Before his ordination in 1949 Dunne encouraged the young monk to trace his spiritual journey in writing. On October 4, 1948, *The Seven Storey Mountain* was released to popular and critical acclaim. The original hardcover edition sold over six hundred thousand copies.

Thomas Merton wrote many more books, and he has since emerged as one of America's great spiritual writers. Vain and petulant, occasionally cantankerous and self-pitying, he nonetheless fulfilled a deep-set need. In the midst of the spiritual restlessness that characterized postwar America, Merton helped many find their way. For some, this meant the monastic life, but for many more it meant (and continues to mean) coming to a closer relationship to God by cultivating an inner silence and listening to "that still small voice." This is no small task, especially for those living in a bustling, noisy city like the one that Tom Merton loved so much.

35

CARDINAL FRANCIS JOSEPH SPELLMAN

1889–1967

The powerhouse.

—A POPULAR NICKNAME FOR SPELLMAN

Upon its publication in 1963, Father Robert I. Gannon's biography of New York Cardinal Francis Spellman received positive accolades from the press and the public. Some modern scholars feel that it's still the best biography of Spellman. Yet some had reservations about the book. One priest-scholar feared it might serve as a how-to manual for future ambitious young clerics. In the wrong hands, this seemingly harmless book might do great damage.

An advisor to presidents and popes, for nearly thirty years Francis Joseph Spellman was the most powerful man in Catholic America, an ecclesiastical kingmaker and churchman extraordinaire. A successful archbishop, he was hailed as the "American Pope," a man whose influence extended far beyond New York's boundaries. As military vicar, he traveled overseas frequently, spouting a brand of uncritical patriotism that was old before its time.

Spellman's life and career *could* serve as a textbook for the ecclesiastically ambitious. No one practiced church politics better than this diminutive New Englander. As a young man he had the opportunity to attend Notre Dame, but he chose Fordham because he believed New York would be "an education in itself." When he decided on the priesthood he wasn't going to attend just any seminary. At his family's expense he enrolled in Rome's North American College, long known as a training ground for future bishops.

Indeed, most of his professors would become bishops, and he cultivated their friendship, which served him well later on. Yet after he was ordained for the Boston Archdiocese, Cardinal William H. O'Connell, himself a model of clerical ambition, took an immediate disliking to Spellman (why we don't know). For the young priest, there followed "a series of insignificant assignments," including newspaper proofreader and archdiocesan archivist. The future looked bleak for Father Spellman.

But eventually his overseas connections paid off, and in 1925 friends arranged for his assignment to Rome, where he befriended Cardinal Eugenio Pacelli, the future Pope Pius XII. In 1932, without having asked for one, Cardinal O'Connell was informed by Rome that he had a new auxiliary bishop in Spellman. (O'Connell caustically told Spellman, "Even if a bishop bought a bishopric, he is still a bishop." In his own diary, Spellman commented, "The same might be said for Cardinals.")

Working directly with O'Connell for the next seven years wasn't easy, but Spellman cultivated friendships with wealthy American Catholics like Joseph P. Kennedy, father of a future president. Through Kennedy, Spellman met President Franklin D. Roosevelt and other major political figures. When Cardinal Pacelli visited the United States in 1936, to O'Connell's surprise, Spellman served as his guide.

When New York cardinal Patrick Hayes died in September 1938, few expected Spellman to succeed him. But in February 1939 Cardinal Pacelli was elected Pope Pius XII. Two months later Spellman was named archbishop of New York. Monsignor James McIntyre, with whom Spellman had once butted heads, offered his resignation as chancellor. Spellman refused, saying, "Retaliation is a luxury I have never been able to afford." Recognizing McIntyre's ability, he had him made an auxiliary bishop. (McIntyre later became the first cardinal archbishop of Los Angeles.)

Soon after his appointment, Spellman was named Military Vicar of the Armed Forces, charged with overseeing ministry to Catholic military personnel. This role, Jesuit historian Gerald Fogarty notes, "launched him into national and international prominence." With his frequent trips overseas and his annual Christmas visit to the troops, he became the face of American Catholic patriotism from World War II through Vietnam.

As archbishop of New York he proved an administrative genius. Within a short time he cleared up a massive debt, launched school and church building campaigns, and strengthened the Catholic healthcare system. A political influence in New York circles, consulted by mayors, senators, and businessmen, his residence at 452 Madison Avenue was known as "the powerhouse," as was its chief resident.

He certainly made mistakes. In 1949, when poorly paid Catholic cemetery workers went on strike, he forced his own seminarians to act as strikebreakers, a move that cost him support among working-class Catholics. On another occasion he differed with Eleanor Roosevelt over aid to private schools, calling her anti-Catholic and an "unfit mother." Public opinion forced him to apologize. As a hardcore anti-Communist he backed the wrong horse in Senator Joseph McCarthy.

Still, the cardinal was capable of what one scholar calls "great pastoral sensitivity," especially in his outreach to New York's growing Puerto Rican community. Beginning in the 1950s, New York priests were sent to Ponce to study Spanish. Within a few years, one-quarter of all the archdiocese's parishes had developed an outreach to Spanish-speaking Catholics.

By the 1950s Spellman was at the height of his influence. His friend Pius XI was in power, and at home his opinion on any topic made the front-page news. During his visits to American troops, he echoed a sort of chauvinistic jingoism that was already almost out of style. Paraphrasing Stephen Decatur, he famously said, "My country, may it always be right. Right or wrong, my country!"

The 1960s proved difficult for Spellman. While he publicly supported Vatican II he was at heart a conservative who felt some of the changes too much to handle. He found it hard to deal with the rising counterculture, sexual revolution, political activism, and dissent within the church. By the time of his death in 1967 he was publicly attacked for his stance on Vietnam as protestors disrupted his Mass at St. Patrick's Cathedral.

In many ways, Spellman's death proved the end of an era, both for the church in America as well as New York. His kind of uncritical patriotism has gone out the window, never to return. Yet no ecclesiastical leader has ever exercised, nor maybe will ever exercise, the kind of unbridled influence that he did, both politically and religiously. He made New York the capital of Catholic America, but New York would need a different kind of leadership, more pastoral and less political, to steer it through the difficult years that lay ahead.

36

VENERABLE ARCHBISHOP FULTON JOHN SHEEN

1895–1979

Radio is like the Old Testament. . . . Television is like the New Testament.
—FULTON SHEEN

It was the golden age of television, and one of its shining stars was a Catholic bishop. In 1952 Fulton Sheen was placed in the same time slot as Milton Berle, "Mr. Television." Over the next five years, *Life Is Worth Living* won every major award and commanded an audience of thirty million. (Accepting an Emmy, Sheen thanked his writers Matthew, Mark, Luke, and John.) One critic called him the most influential Catholic bishop since before the Reformation.

For twenty years prior, Sheen had been a prominent radio personality, hosting *The Catholic Hour*. In his autobiography, *Treasure in Clay*, he wrote of his media career, "I was born in the electronic age. . . . Radio is like the Old Testament, for it is the hearing of the Word without the seeing. Television is like the New Testament, for the Word is seen as it becomes flash and dwells among us."

Growing up on an Illinois farm, a neighbor had told his father, "Newt, that oldest boy of yours, Fulton, will never be worth a damn. He's always got his nose in a book." Born May 8, 1895, he was named Peter but called Fulton (his mother's maiden name) throughout his life. From childhood, he knew two things: he hated farm life and he wanted to be a priest.

At St. Viator College in Bourbonnais, he joined the debating team. At one point, his coach said, "Sheen, you're absolutely the worst speaker I ever heard. Do you know what's wrong with you?" The young man replied, "I'm not natural." Biographer Thomas Reeves notes, "It was a lesson he never forgot."

Ordained in 1919, Father Sheen pursued doctoral studies at Belgium's University of Louvain. He shone brilliantly, earning the highest honors. Back in America he taught philosophy at Catholic University (he turned down offers from Columbia and Oxford). For a quarter century, he taught, conducted retreats, received converts into the church, and lectured worldwide. A student once commented, "I don't know how you do it." "Well," Sheen said with a flourish of his cape, "neither do I!"

In his lectures, in the pulpit, on radio, Sheen tried to make Catholic philosophy accessible to modern audiences. He told an interviewer, "Bring big ideas down to the level of second-year high. . . . No idea is too abstract for anyone to understand." As a professor, he aimed to "answer the errors of modern philosophy." On radio and later television, he tried to do the same thing.

Even before he appeared on television screens, Sheen was considered undeniably dynamic. Watching him preach at St. Patrick's Cathedral in 1940, actress Loretta Young noted, "He had tremendous acting ability and a God-given sincerity." In 1949 journalist Gladys Baker called him the "name priest in America . . . By members of all faiths, Monsignor Sheen is considered the most electric orator of our times."

In 1950 Monsignor Fulton J. Sheen was named national director of the Society for the Propagation of the Faith, a fundraising organization for the missions worldwide. There, a peer noted, he put in "ten times as much work as any businessman on Madison Avenue." Sheen loved New York. One priest friend recalled, "Mention New York and the big expressive eyes gleamed."

In 1951 Sheen was named a bishop to assist New York's cardinal Francis Spellman. In his memoir he admitted praying to become a bishop. Reeves notes that he saw "no conflict between his personal ambition and his passion for souls." Sheen explained it away as a "holy ambition," but still it was ambition. (Lore has it that when Spellman was named archbishop in 1939, Sheen took to bed for three days in despair.)

Perhaps the most memorable portion of Sheen's life was his television career. He appeared before his audience resplendent in cassock and cape, with silver hair and dark eyes shining on black-and-white screens nationwide. Charles Morris suggests that he "may have been the finest popular lecturer ever to appear on television": "He was elegant, elevated, relaxed, often very funny. Only Jack Benny could top Sheen's ability to hold back a punch line—ten seconds, sometimes even longer—gazing calmly at the camera the entire time.

"All at the same time," Morris concludes, "he managed to be religious, undogmatic, humane, and unthreatening. Week after week, the performances were simply brilliant."

The show ended abruptly after he butted heads with Spellman over mission money, and Sheen lost. He continued at the society until 1966, when he was named bishop of Rochester, New York, at age seventy-one.

The Second Vatican Council had just ended, and Sheen sincerely tried to implement it. But this was a difficult time in the church and a difficult time for Sheen. Critics suggested that his best days were past, that he was not suited to running a diocese, that he was more suited to big ideas than small details. In October 1969 he submitted his resignation. Named an honorary archbishop, he went into semiretirement.

In his later years, Sheen, suffering from heart disease, was largely confined to his Manhattan apartment. Occasionally he preached at various events. The most dramatic moment in a dramatic life occurred in St. Patrick's Cathedral in 1979, two months before his death. There Pope John Paul II embraced Sheen, saying, "You have written and spoken well of the Lord Jesus, and you are a loyal son of the church." Sheen broke down in tears, and so did the rest of the cathedral.

Fulton John Sheen was admittedly ambitious, undeniably vain, and he loved the limelight. At the same time he possessed a deeply generous heart with a sincere love of humanity. Seeking to use his talents in the interest of humanity, he succeeded, for his books, radio programs, and television shows have inspired countless thousands. They still do today. There's a good chance we may never see his like again.

37

FATHER JOHN CORRIDAN

1911–1984

A homegrown reformer . . . with ample toughness to match the boys of the waterfront.
  —JAMES T. FISHER, *On the Irish Waterfront*

On the Waterfront (1954) was Marlon Brando's breakthrough role. But for Oscar-winning screenwriter Budd Schulberg, the real hero was Karl Malden's character, Father Barry, the priest who stirs up the fight against waterfront corruption. He based the Barry character on a real priest who spent the better part of a decade doing  just that, Father John M. Corridan, a Jesuit from Manhattan's West Side.

At the end of the Second World War, New York was the world's busiest port. Its two most influential figures were "King Joe" Ryan, president of the International Longshoremen's Association (ILA), and businessman William J. McCormack, aka "Mr. Big," whom historian James Fisher calls "arguably the most powerful Catholic in New York." They controlled the port through kickbacks, payoffs, murder, and the shape-up, where hundreds of men waited for work. Those picked paid a fee, while the rest had to take high-interest loans.

For a decade, Jesuits involved in the labor movement had tried to make a breakthrough. Beginning in 1946, a tall, balding, chain-smoking priest named John Michael Corridan became a key player in the struggle. Fisher calls him a "homegrown reformer . . . with ample toughness to match the boys of the waterfront."

The son of a policeman, Corridan grew up on the West Side where one either became "a priest or a hood." After graduating from the Jesuits' Regis High School, he worked on Wall Street while attending night school. At twenty-one he joined the Jesuits. After his ordination, Corridan became interested in conditions on his native West Side, especially after reading up on the 1945 longshoremen's strike.

In 1946 he was assigned to the Xavier Labor Institute, a program attached to St. Francis Xavier Church on West Sixteenth Street. Jesuits offered courses to workingmen in labor-management relations, parliamentary procedure, and Catholic social teaching. They fought Communists and supported unionization. But the waterfront was a tough nut to crack. Many unions hadn't held elections in decades.

Corridan created a database of waterfront conditions, interviewed longshoremen, and helped journalists trying to expose corruption. He spoke to various groups, stressing "the right to a living wage" and "to decent working conditions." One Jesuit remembered him as "a forceful speaker" who "blended a deeply analytical intelligence with street smarts": "I suppose some people would smirk at the thought of Christ in the shape-up. It is about as absurd as the fact that he carried carpenter's tools in His hands and earned His bread by the sweat of His brow."

Corridan helped journalist Malcolm Johnson with his Pulitzer-winning series "Crime on the Waterfront," which led to the establishment of a Waterfront Crime Commission. Corridan started an independent longshoremen's paper and even debated Joe Ryan on television. When Budd Schulberg started research for the movie screenplay, Johnson sent him to Corridan.

Schulberg was immediately impressed by Corridan's language, combining "the gritty language of longshoremen with mob talk, the statistical trends of a trained economist, and the teachings of Christ." He later felt "the closest thing I ever came to feeling what true Christianity was all about." In this meeting, he felt, was the real birth of *On the Waterfront.*

Admittedly, Schulberg said, the priest had chosen a "dangerous road to Christian service." He was not only fighting mobsters and racketeers but some highly prominent figures with a wide reach in city circles. McCormack had very close connections with the New York Archdiocese (his son became a bishop), and he received several important papal honors.

By 1951 Corridan devoted himself full time to the waterfront. He served as an advisor, as well as a "a clearinghouse and a coordinator." Testifying before the Crime Commission enhanced his public image. He wanted Joe Ryan ousted from union leadership so that the "ILA mob" would be replaced by "a genuine trade union."

As Charles Morris notes, Corridan won several battles, but Ryan and McCormack won the war. Pro-Ryan forces won the 1954 union election, and Corridan was finished on the waterfront. He said, "I've lost, I believe the city and the people of New York have been lost. The mobsters won. They're still on the docks." Soon Corridan was assigned to teach college. Until his death he engaged in a series of unsatisfying ministries. It's not clear he ever overcame his "failure" to clean up the waterfront.

But his work lives on. *On the Waterfront* captured nearly every major award. For playing Corridan, Karl Malden received an Oscar nomination. His famous speech in the "hole" combined various speeches. Standing over Kayo Dugan's corpse, a longshoreman killed before he could testify, Malden is told to go back to his church. "Boys," he shouts, "*this* is my church! And if you don't think Christ is down here on the waterfront, you've got another guess comin'!" The rest is pure Corridan:

> You want to know what's wrong with our waterfront? It's the love of a lousy buck. It's makin' the love of the lousy buck, the cushy job, more important than the love of man! It's forgettin' that every fellow down here is your brother in Christ! But remember, Christ is always with you. Christ is in the shape-up. He's in the hatch. He's in the union hall. He's kneeling right here beside Dugan. And He's sayin' with all of you, if you do it to the least of mine, you do it to me! And what they did to Joey, and what they did to Dugan, they're doin' to you. . . . All of you! And only you, only you with God's help, have the power to knock 'em out for good.

Malden borrowed the priest's hat and coat for the movie, with one condition. "Karl," Corridan said, "please don't make me holier than thou. Just make me a human being."

38

Servant of God
Cardinal Terence James Cooke
1921–1983

Kindness goes about doing good. We do this not just sometimes but always with a sense of mission.
—TERENCE COOKE

Urban decay, race riots, white flight, antiwar protests: 1968 was one of the most tumultuous years in American history. Its most tragic event occurred on April 4, when Martin Luther King Jr. was assassinated. Riots erupted nationwide. That night Terence J. Cooke, the newly installed archbishop of New York, went to Harlem to make a plea for peace. None of his predecessors began their tenure on a more eventful day, nor at a more troubling time in church history. Men and women exited religious life in growing numbers. Schools, convents, and churches closed in areas that had been heavily Catholic for generations. Debates increased over a variety of topics: war and peace, sex and love, authority and dissent. Through it all, Terence James Cooke displayed what one bishop called "habitual, unruffled calm."

He took the same approach throughout his life, whether as parish priest, social worker, baseball coach, administrator, bishop, or cardinal. At every stage, a peer noted, "He never changed. He was always the same, always gentle." A capable administrator, he was also a man of great humility whose sainthood cause is under way.

He was the third child of Irish immigrants. Born in Manhattan, he grew up in the Throgs Neck section of the Bronx. From an early age he was interested in becoming a priest. He and his brother Joe attended Cathedral Preparatory Seminary, a high school for young men considering the priesthood. During his high school years, Terry Cooke worked at a furniture store on 146th Street in the Bronx and volunteered with the growing Puerto Rican community.

After studying at St. Joseph's Seminary in Yonkers, Cooke was ordained a priest on December 1, 1945, at St. Patrick's Cathedral. Immediately he was assigned to graduate school for social work. For five years he worked in Catholic Charities as a social worker. For the young priest, social work was an extension of his priestly ministry: "We are not in the work for what we can get out of it. We are in the work to become saints, serving Christ in others."

For Cooke, a key to his ministry, whether as priest or cardinal, was kindness. But his was not a simplistic understanding of the word:

> Kindness should flow from a deep interior life, the real love of God. . . . When we are kind, as apostles of charity, we radiate goodness and joy. Kindness goes about doing good. We do this not just sometimes but always with a sense of mission.

Assigned as an administrator to his alma mater, St. Joseph's Seminary, Cooke showed his administrative ability. He proved to be, according to Father Benedict Groeschel and Pastor Terence Weber, "an excellent fiscal organizer." It was here that Cardinal Francis Spellman of New York began to realize the priest's capability.

Soon Spellman made him his personal secretary. He proved to be one of the most capable administrators in the New York Archdiocese. One bishop said he had the makings of a Wall Street CEO. By 1965 he was vicar-general, the cardinal's right-hand man, and an auxiliary bishop. But whenever someone suggested that Cooke might succeed Spellman, he said, "You're crazy."

Cooke considered Spellman almost a second father. A larger-than-life figure, the cardinal in his later years was a lonely old man, and Cooke knew it. He would turned down dinner invitations if it meant Spellman had to eat alone. The affection was returned, yet no one was more shocked than Cooke to discover he was named Spellman's successor. A very private man, it was one of the few times he wept openly.

The reason, he told a friend, was that "nobody knows the situation better than I. It's going to be terrible, But that's what 'Fiat Voluntas Tua' means."* The days of church dedications were over, and the age of consolidation had begun. By levying a tax on all parishes, he kept the poorer ones going. The parish school enrollment declined by half, but only 10 percent of the schools closed. By the time of his death, the archdiocese was on a firm financial footing, several hundred million dollars in the black.

As he moved through all this, Terence Cooke harbored a terrible secret: he was battling cancer. (A confirmed workaholic, stress played a factor.) First diagnosed in 1965, he was in remission for nearly ten years. He went from morning radiation treatments to a full day's work without a hint of complaint. To a fellow bishop he confided, "If I had not done it, and let everybody know

---

* Latin for "Thy will be done," Cooke's motto as archbishop.

what I had, I would have been a lame duck as archbishop. I never would have been able to get done those things I had to get done."

Finally, in August 1983, Cooke publicly announced that he had terminal cancer. Two months later he was dead. As Thomas Shelley notes, "His faith and courage made a deep impression on many New Yorkers."

Critics liked to note Cooke's faults. He avoided controversy, he disliked criticism from the press, and he wasn't a theological innovator. But he had a great ability to get people of different backgrounds to work together. He also held the New York church together during a difficult era, preparing the way for future growth. And most of all, throughout his tenure as archbishop, but especially in his last days, he was a sign of hope.

As a seminarian, Cooke wrote, "I only want to be a parish priest." As high as he rose, he never stood on his office. Although a cardinal is, technically speaking, a "prince of the church," he preferred to think of himself as "someone who was there to be a brother to all." For his innate humility and decency, his compassion and kindness, Weber and Groeschel conclude, "It cannot be denied that, in the eyes of many, Terence Cooke was a prince among men."

39

Monsignor Bryan Karvelis

1930–2005

This is gospel poverty. . . . This is what I want.
—Bryan Karvelis

When Father John Fagan started Transfiguration Church in South Williamsburg in the summer of 1874 he celebrated the first Mass in a carpenter's shop. By the turn of the century, there was a thriving parish with a large school in what was then a thoroughly Irish Catholic neighborhood. But Williamsburg never stays one way for too long, and within a few years Jewish immigrants from the Lower East Side were making the neighborhood their home, too. By the 1940s, Puerto Rican immigrants were coming in larger numbers, looking for work in Williamsburg's numerous factories.

A new day was dawning for Transfiguration. Most of the old-time Irish congregants
had moved away, and the parish was becoming increasingly Hispanic. In the summer
of 1956, a clean-cut freshly ordained priest
named Bryan Karvelis arrived at the rectory,
having just been assigned there. Little did he
know it would be his one and only assignment as a priest, or that it would last nearly
fifty years, or that he would transform the
face of urban ministry in the process.

A native Brooklynite, Karvelis was inter-
ested in priesthood early on. At fourteen he entered Cathedral Prep Seminary on Atlantic Avenue. As a major seminarian, he spent a summer on the
Lower East Side working with Dorothy Day, an experience that affected him
deeply. "I saw the cockroaches on the walls," he recalled in an interview, "and
the people from the Bowery coming in, and I thought, 'This is gospel poverty.
This is what I don't see elsewhere. This is what I want.'"

By the time Father Karvelis came to South Williamsburg, it was already
experiencing a downturn. Poverty and unemployment, drugs and gangs
were major problems. Tensions between Puerto Ricans and Hasidic Jews ran
high. Public housing couldn't meet the needs of a growing neighborhood.
The public school system, which had few Puerto Ricans on the local school
board, was called an "absolute disaster." By the late 1960s Williamsburg was
described as "a sewer where poverty breeds an anaesthetized agony."

Karvelis was an organizational dynamo. He offered teens an alternative
to gangs. Clubs named Romans and Corinthians wore special jackets and
met in the parish youth center. He founded the South Third Street Block Association to clean streets. The South Side Mission reached out to the sick and
the elderly. He organized boycotts, community meetings, and marches, and
advocated for better housing. In 1969 a reporter wrote, "Father Bryan Karvelis has been trying to relate the things that are in the gospel with the things
that happen on the streets of Williamsburg."

At the same time Karvelis was a deeply contemplative man. He was
strongly devoted to Charles de Foucauld, a nineteenth-century French her-
mit who set up small faith communities called fraternities in the North Af-

rican desert. During the 1960s Karvelis created groups of fifteen to twenty men and women who gathered weekly to study scripture and reflect on how it applied to their community. Within a few years Transfiguration had some twenty fraternities. In 1968 Karvelis bought property in Tarrytown for a retreat house, which he named Tabor (the mountain where the transfiguration took place).

By then, he had moved out of the five-story rectory on Marcy Avenue for an apartment, living under the same conditions as his parishioners. By the 1970s the number of Latino immigrants in the parish was growing, Dominicans and Mexicans replacing the Puerto Ricans of earlier days. Immigrants from Guatemala, El Salvador, and Honduras came in short order. He decided to turn the rectory into a home for them.

"It seemed outrageous," he later said, "that we had this huge rectory building, and so many homeless immigrants needed help." Later Karvelis would turn the convent into Casa Betsaida, a hospice for AIDS victims. By the early 1990s, there were somewhere close to one hundred people living on the grounds of the parish facilities, many illegals among them. "No person," Karvelis contended, "is illegal in the eyes of God."

In 1986 he was named a monsignor, a title he never used. Karvelis wasn't one to stand on ceremony. One reporter visiting the parish wrote of him, "Wearing a navy plaid shirt, navy sweat jacket, and black corduroys, he looks more like an aging laborer than a cleric." He became so fluent in Spanish, an observer noted, "that he sometimes stumbled when speaking English." When he needed a kidney transplant, one of the men in the rectory donated his. Karvelis commented, "Now I say my flesh and blood is Hispanic. I have a Puerto Rican kidney. That is the result of the kingdom of God moving among us. It is pure gift."

When asked how he was, Karvelis always replied, "En la lucha" (in the struggle). Beginning in 2000 he would be hospitalized twenty times over the next five years. Diagnosed with lymphoma, Bryan Karvelis died on October 18, 2005. He was beginning his fiftieth year as pastor of Tranfiguration. Richard John Neuhaus, who worked in Williamsburg as a Lutheran pastor, called him "the dean of inner-city ministries," who "lived with and for the poor until the end." Brooklyn city councilman Victor Robles earlier said of him, "He symbolizes what the priesthood is, not just the Mass and the clothing, but he shows he's God's servant. He reaches out to everyone."

40

CARDINAL JOHN JOSEPH O'CONNOR

1920–2000

A very human person.
—A CONTEMPORARY OF O'CONNOR

His phone rang early Monday morning in Scranton. It was Archbishop Pio Laghi, the pope's representative to America. During their conversation, Laghi said, "By the way, the Holy Father has appointed you archbishop of New York."

"Come on," John O'Connor responded, "are you kidding?"

"I'm not kidding," Laghi answered.

So began the career of New York Catholicism's most colorful leader since John Hughes.

"I'm called the 'controversial archbishop of New York' whenever I'm introduced," he once said with a grin. Even a decade after his death, his name alone can still engender a debate. But O'Connor biographer Terry Golway notes that while he was called outspoken, he was actually quite soft-spoken. This ecclesiastical celebrity who engaged easily in national and global debates lived a simple life. His move to New York involved some clothing, a few duffle bags, and a truckload of books.

John Joseph O'Connor never forgot where he came from, a row house in Philadelphia. "My father," he frequently noted, "was a union man." Thomas O'Connor originally hoped his son would join the union, but he supported Jack's vocation. The formation program at St. Charles Seminary, Overbrook, was quite strict, and O'Connor admitted wanting to quit many times along the way, but he kept his eye on the priesthood.

In his first seven years of priesthood, Father O'Connor taught high school, served as a hospital chaplain, ran a radio program, and began a center for developmentally disabled children. During the Korean War he was appointed a navy chaplain, a job for which he initially had little enthusiasm. During Vietnam he served with the Marines in the field. His first book, *A Chaplain Looks at Vietnam*, was a defense of the war, one he later regretted.

Back in America, O'Connor finished a political science doctorate at Georgetown (he had a master's in clinical psychology). In 1972 he was appointed chaplain at the Naval Academy. While there, his niece and nephew lived with him while attending local colleges. For the sailor-priest, it was an internship in parenting. (His niece later sent him Father's Day cards.)

In 1975 Captain O'Connor was named chief of chaplains, a job that brought him all over the world. On retiring he hoped to return to a parish, but he was named a bishop for the Military Ordinariate (now the Archdiocese for Military Services), overseeing ministry to servicemen and servicewomen worldwide.

In early 1983 he was named bishop of Scranton, "a slightly bigger parish than I'd anticipated, but my roots were in Pennsylvania, I knew Scranton, and I was overjoyed." Although his stay was short, he made an impression. As a bishop, he insisted, "There can be no such thing as, 'I will not accept that assignment.' . . . We must not baby ourselves in this regard. We were ordained for the people."

In January 1984 he was named archbishop of New York, the eleventh since 1808. Lore has it that Pope John Paul II wanted "a man just like me in New York." Before O'Connor left Scranton, he commented, "I suspect I'll be going into New York as Our Lord went into Jerusalem on Palm Sunday, and there were a lot of hosannas and cheers and warm welcomes. But I try to remember what happened a few days later, you know."

He knew he would be pilloried for certain views, but "if every time the *New York Times* doesn't agree with me I . . . want to turn tail and run, I'll never be able to contribute anything to this job and to this city."

For a long time, the archbishop of New York has been regarded as the unofficial leader of the American church, and Cardinal O'Connor (so named in 1985) held forth on every topic imaginable: zoning laws, the Middle East, nuclear war, the inner city, abortion, the death penalty, poverty, racism, and gay rights. His opinions always made front-page news. While some bishops recited carefully prepared texts, Cardinal O'Connor was accused of "shooting from the hip." O'Connor responded,

> What I was doing, I have always done, and will continue to do is present the official teaching of the Church as clearly as I can. Anyone interested in the teaching of the Church can then decide whether what a candidate says accords with that teaching. Surely I have a right to make clear the teaching of the Church.

During the 1984 presidential campaign he was attacked for his stance on abortion and prochoice politicians. "I was talking about hunger, homelessness, the ill-housed, racism, and the horrors of nuclear war," he noted, "but nobody accused me of implicitly endorsing Walter Mondale." Although considered a conservative, he opposed the death penalty, excessive military spending, and unbridled capitalism.

Perhaps the area that raised the most controversy was his relationship with the gay community. At a time when AIDS patients were treated as pariahs or lepers, O'Connor quietly visited hospitals and clinics to wash and pray with them. While O'Connor condemned hate crimes he refused to stop expressing the church's position, even when activists stormed St. Patrick's Cathedral in late 1989.

Policemen and firefighters, mayors and presidents, rabbis and ministers, union leaders and teachers, to name a few—John J. O'Connor had something to say to everyone. One gay rights activist who disagreed with him greatly still considered him "a very human person." The *New York Times*, at his death, hailed him as a "a familiar and towering presence, a leader whose views and personality were forcefully injected into the great civic debates of his time, a man who considered himself a conciliator, but who never hesitated to be a combatant."

But O'Connor didn't see himself as either conciliator or combatant. Terry Golway writes, "The role he lived for . . . was that of priest and pastor." Until illness set in, he celebrated Mass every morning at St. Patrick's, heard confessions, counseled couples, and celebrated weddings. John O'Connor was always more comfortable with the average pew-sitter than with movers and shakers. In short, he never forgot his roots.

41

HELEN TRAVIS

1930–2000

I don't how to put it in words, but she did a lot, a lot, for me.
—A RESIDENT AT THE TRAVIS CENTER

"When was the last time you did crack?" the woman asks.

"One hundred twenty-seven days ago—no, 128 days ago," the man answers.

"Alright, and you went into a detox?"

"Nah, I didn't go into a detox."

"And you just totally stopped?"

"Yeah, I just totally stopped."

The woman pauses and smiles. "I love this one."

She takes a rosary out of her pocket and in an affectedly sweet voice, she says, "Good morning, how are you? Aw, it's a nice day out today. Aw, you stopped crack like that? And you prayed, and you asked Jesus, 'Please let me stop crack.' And you know what? He did!'"

Pause. "Is *that* what you were expecting?" she shouts.

"YOU KNOW WHAT, BROTHER? YOU AIN'T GETTIN' IT! 'CAUSE THAT KIND OF GIRL DON'T LIVE IN THIS HOUSE!"

No one practiced tough love like Helen Travis, better known as "Sister Helen." From 1989 until her death in 2000 she ran a halfway house in a South Bronx neighborhood plagued with poverty and addiction. What made this home unique was Helen, a widow, mother, and recovering alcoholic who lost her husband and sons to alcohol. One reporter said of her, "New York has never had a shortage of colorful characters, but even in this city of eccentrics, Sister Helen Travis is a standout."

The daughter of Irish immigrants, Helen McElroy grew up in the Bronx. For a brief period after high school, she entered the convent, but left shortly thereafter. She later married Thomas Travis, an ironworker. With two sons and a daughter, they were a hard-drinking couple who liked to frequent the many neighborhood bars.

At a certain point it stopped being fun. Thomas Travis became a full-blown alcoholic. Her sons drank and did drugs. Thomas Jr. was murdered at fifteen, his killer never brought to justice. John died of a heroin overdose at twenty-five. Her husband died of the disease. Eventually Helen stopped:

> You reach a certain point in life—it's time to shit or get off the pot. What the hell are you gonna do? You know, the party's over! And I woke up one day and said, "The party's over." Because you know that I drank. I drank enough. I drank plenty. I won't deny it. Oh yeah, I drank plenty. Seven days a week. But with some people . . . apparently I'm in this category . . . they need a crisis. And I got my crisis.

In 1988 she opened the John Thomas Travis Center on Willis Avenue and East 142nd Street, in a city-owned building where she oversaw some twenty men in various stages of recovery. "Here," she told a visitor, "it's not just the talking of 'Oh, I wanna make changes, I wanna do this.' Nah, here, it's living it. *Here* you're gonna live it. Or you're not gonna last long."

In their 2002 documentary *Sister Helen*, Rebecca Cammisa and Rob Fruchtman assumed what everyone else did: that Helen Travis really was a Sister. But longtime friend Dorothy Madden, who has run the center since Helen's death, points out that she *wasn't*. She was actually a Benedictine Oblate, a layperson who lives out the order's charism in daily life. "In the Bronx," Dorothy notes, "if you're an older woman, everybody calls you 'sister' or 'momma.'" Wearing a modified veil and a Benedictine cross was a personal choice of Helen's, a sign of her commitment to a new life. Dorothy recalls that it didn't make her very popular with church authorities, but they weren't about to stop the good things she was doing. Every week the center distributed food and clothing to over a thousand local residents. The men in the house were required to work there. They maintained the building, attended AA meetings, paid rent, and took random drug tests. "When I say 'piss,'" she shouted at one resident, "you piss!" Female guests were not permitted under any circumstances, unless they were "ninety years old and accompanied by their 110-year-old mother." The men's stays were ideally supposed to be no more than six weeks, but they could be as long as three years.

It was a tough group: addicts, pedophiles, rapists, and murderers. If they were tough, she had to be tougher. "You think only men got balls?" she shouted at one resident. "Well, women got balls, too!" As much as they loved her, some men resented her high-handedness. "Sometimes," an observer noted, "she'd reduce guys to tears." At one house meeting she kicked out Mel, a long-time resident, for his lack of hygiene. One visitor asked why she was so hard on the men. Helen answered, "Are you kidding? I was so nice in the beginning, and they walked all over me."

Despite her tough demeanor, Helen Travis could be remarkably forgiving toward some of the worst cases. Ashish, an Indian immigrant, was "the worst drinker I've ever seen." He considered Helen the mother he never had: "I don't how to put it in words, but she did a lot, a lot, for me." Over the years she kicked him out five times for drinking, but always brought him back.

"If my sons hadn't died," she admitted, "I wouldn't be here. . . . I try to do for other people's sons what I didn't do for my own. It's a second chance. . . . This house is my second chance to do it right." Helen planned to stay there as long as health permitted. In early 2000 she went to the hospital after complaining of headaches. Helen Travis died at seventy of a cerebral hemorrhage. In the entire history of Catholic New York, there's probably never been a Sister quite like her, a woman whose hard exterior covered up a deep hurt and a deeper love.

42

FATHER MYCHAL JUDGE

1933–2001

If you're looking for saintly people in New York City, he would certainly fit the bill.

—A CONTEMPORARY OF JUDGE

The photograph of his corpse being carried from Ground Zero has become a popular icon. Some call it "the American *Pietá*." The first confirmed casualty of the September 11, 2001, attacks, the Brooklyn-born priest became a national hero overnight. New York firefighters presented his helmet to John Paul II during a papal audience with all the reverence of a holy relic. In death he would receive some of the city's and the nation's highest honors. Some have even proposed his canonization.

Mychal might have found some amusement in this. His longtime friend Malachy McCourt comments, "He didn't want to be a saint. He never thought of himself as anything but a humble friar. Yet he was the ultimate servant of God and of people."

"If you're looking for saintly people in New York City," one politician commented, "he would certainly fit the bill." During a White House visit, Hilary Clinton recalled, "He lit up the White House as he lit up everywhere, as he lit up every place he ever found himself."

Long before his name was enshrined on the list of 9/11 heroes, Mychal Judge was a hero to many: to the poor, the ostracized, the sick, the addicted, the dying, and the lonely. One homeless man was quoted as saying, "He didn't stay in the sanctuary. He brought the sanctuary out to us." In the days when people with AIDS were viewed with fear, Judge took them in his arms and held them when no one else would. In a word, his biographer Michael Ford writes, Mychal "radiated love."

For many people, he *became* the father he wished he'd had. The child of Irish immigrants, he was born Robert Emmett Judge on May 11, 1933, in downtown Brooklyn. At six, he watched his father die a slow, painful death. It was a lifelong wound. "I never called anyone 'Dad,'" he later said. From early on, Robert had a deep desire to love and be loved. It was the Great Depression, and to help his mother he rode his bike over to Penn Station, where he shined shoes.

While he was there, he discovered St. Francis of Assisi Church on West Thirty-First Street, a parish famous for its morning breadlines and hearing confessions all day. It was there that he first encountered the Franciscan friars, and he liked what he saw. He, too, wanted to be a priest and work with the poor. After a year at a Catholic high school in Brooklyn, Robert transferred to the Franciscans' high school seminary in upstate New York. He would spend the next twelve years in a semicloistered environment studying for the priesthood.

In religious life he took the name Fallon Michael, which he later changed to the more Gaelic-sounding Mychal. On February 25, 1961, at Washington's Franciscan monastery, Father Fallon Michael Judge was ordained a priest. Most of the next two decades were spent in parish work and college administration. Mychal loved the post–Vatican II church. He saw it as a call to enhanced ministry—not just giving answers, but listening to people and being there for them.

At the same time, however, Mychal was wrestling with his own inner demons. He'd started drinking as a teenager. As a priest, on his day off, he hit all the bars along Third Avenue. In 1978, while was working at the Franciscans' Siena College in upstate New York, Mychal finally came to admit he had a problem, and he joined Alcoholics Anonymous. Malachy McCourt recalled, "He was a great comfort to those with troubles with the drink. He'd always say, 'You're not a bad person—you have a disease that makes you *think* you're a bad person, and it's going to fuck you up.'"

In the 1980s Mychal came back to New York when he was assigned to St. Francis in Manhattan. He seemed to know everyone from the mayor on down to the local panhandler. In his brown Franciscan robes, he was a familiar sight throughout the city. Soon he was, Ford writes, "New York's most popular Franciscan . . . a spiritualistic tour de force in the materialistic grid of New York City with as many orbits of influence as he had friends."

This was the period when AIDS first came to the public eye. One author notes, "People with the virus were both feared and ostracized in ways that are today inconceivable." Mychal "not only went close. He touched." He ministered to victims' families, sat by their bedsides, celebrated their funerals. At a time when fear and ignorance of the disease prevailed, he brought nonjudgmental love and compassion. One patient said of him, "His friendship for me was the face of God."

There's been a lot of debate about Mychal's own sexual orientation. The consensus among peers and biographers is that he was in fact gay but that he chose to live a celibate life. No one knows how long it took for him to embrace his sexuality, but over the years he became comfortable with the person he was. Fear of retribution from church authorities certainly didn't keep him from reaching out to the gay community, nor did it make him shy away from his gay friends.

Mychal never made a pretense of being a saint, as his friend and fellow Franciscan Richard Rohr commented. Tall and handsome, Mychal was admittedly vain about his appearance. By his own admission he could also be difficult to live with. There were those who resented his fame, feeling that he actively sought the limelight. If Mychal was a healer, then he was, in the words of Henri Nouwen (one of his favorite authors), a "wounded healer."

"I love being a priest," Mychal once said. "Sure, I've had my pain, my hurt . . . but I know people need me, and I need them." To be a Franciscan meant "to be today, to be this moment, to be the gospel message, bring hope and life, to preach and renew." A recovering alcoholic he may have been, but his "strongest addiction" was a "love for other people."

Part 2

CONTEMPORARY VOICES

43

Father Dave Dwyer

St. Paul the Apostle Church, Manhattan

Whatever it means to have a Catholic culture, we have to have new approaches.
—Dave Dwyer

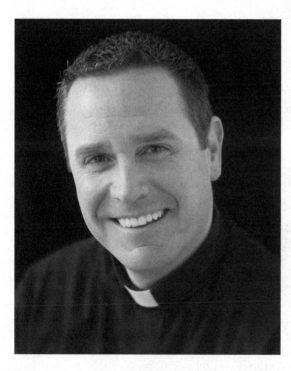

Since Isaac Hecker founded the Paulists in 1850s New York, media outreach has been a key component of their charism. A best-selling author in his own right, in 1865 Hecker founded the *Catholic World,* one of the most influential Catholic magazines of its time. During the 1920s, WLWL radio station opened at the Paulist motherhouse on West Fifty-Ninth Street. (Fulton Sheen got his start there.) For over a century Paulist Press has been a leading Catholic publisher, and the community has made successful forays into film and television. Through all these endeavors, one goal has been consistent: "to give the Word a voice."

It's no surprise, then, that the Paulists should be active with new media, maybe none more than Father Dave Dwyer. During the day, Father Dwyer is the publisher of Busted Halo.com, an online spiritual magazine for young adults. It's a full day's work in its own right, but from there he's off to host *The Busted Halo Show with Father Dave,* a three-hour call-in radio show on SiriusXM's Catholic Channel. In addition to this, he's also frequently called to speak at numerous events nationwide.

Most of this isn't really that new to Dwyer, a Long Island native who graduated from Syracuse University in 1986 with a communications degree. At Syracuse he hosted a successful radio program as "Happy Dave." Later he worked at MTV and Comedy Central, producing and directing comedy shows and meeting rising stars like Chris Rock, Adam Sandler, and Ray Romano. He also encountered the likes of Chuck Norris and William Shatner. In a recent interview, he recalled, "Yeah, you can't ask for much better than to get paid to laugh for a living."

Throughout high school and college, Dwyer also had an active faith life. During his teenage years he was in youth groups—Catholic and interdenominational. "At least since the age of fourteen," he says, "I was pretty into my faith and even pretty interested in church and religion." At Syracuse he joined the Newman Association for Catholic Students. When he asked them if there were retreat programs, he was told, "No, but why don't you take the ball and run with it?" So he did.

Dwyer's path to priesthood was by no means Augustinian. "It was never," he says, "a matter of . . . 'falling off the horse' of sex, drugs, and rock and roll from my previous career and somehow suddenly falling into the priesthood." While he worked at MTV and Comedy Channel, he was still living on Long Island, where he did Bible study, worked with teens, and formed a young adult group in his parish. But World Youth Day at Denver in 1993 proved the real turning point in Dwyer's life, which he calls a period of great "spiritual power."

In the year following WYD, he thought more about the priesthood. While he loved his job, he also wondered what God was really calling him to do. He certainly did not want "to close the door on my past and see that as some sort of dark history." As he further investigated, it seemed like the Paulists were the best fit, a media-friendly community dedicated to evangelizing the culture instead of condemning it. Over time, it made more sense, and in 1994 he left

MTV to join the Paulists. He recalls the reaction of some of his coworkers:

> Then people started "coming out of the closet." It was like we were in Russia and they had to be careful about what they said. They'd come over to me and discreetly show me a little prayer card they carry in their wallet. People were coming out as Christians, telling me, "I go to church on Sunday, too" and looking around the hall to make sure no one else heard.

Since his ordination in May 2000, Father Dave Dwyer worked as a campus minister in Texas and Colorado before coming back to New York. "There's a whole different energy and pulse here," he feels, "that's different from elsewhere." The bulk of his day is devoted to Busted Halo, which is essentially the Paulist community's outreach to young adults. Besides the online magazine and the daily podcasts, there's also retreat work and working with faith communities seeking to develop their own outreach. Since its founding in 2000 Busted Halo has received numerous awards for its work in this often-neglected field.

At night he hosts *The Busted Halo Show with Father Dave*. He also co-hosts a weekly show with New York's Cardinal Timothy Dolan. (It's hard to say who has the bigger laugh.) Located in the McGraw-Hill Building, the show is one of a hundred compressed onto two floors. (The waiting room, Dwyer notes, can be an interesting scene, with nuns in habits sitting across from strippers waiting to go on Howard Stern). Watching him in action is a rewarding experience. For three hours he answers any variety of questions, from big ("How do I become a Catholic?") to small ("What's a monsignor?") with humor, sensitivity, and compassion. His energy and his enthusiasm never seem to fail.

He draws his strength from a number of sources: the energy of the city itself, his prayer life, celebrating the sacraments, and the support of his fellow Paulists. The Paulist community, he feels, brings important gifts to the church in New York. Most important is a willingness to engage the culture on its own terms and meet people "where they're at." "Whatever it means to have a Catholic culture," he says, "we have to have new approaches." For Isaac Hecker, it was the printed word and the pulpit. For his modern-day followers, it can be a podcast, a tweet, even a Facebook posting. "In the new media," Father Dwyer comments, "you could be in a basement anywhere." But for now, he's glad to be in New York, "the modern Areopagus."

44

DR. PAMELA SHEA-BYRNES

St. John's University, Jamaica

It matters that we're Catholic, both for our Catholic and non-Catholic students. If they don't leave with a deeper connection to their own faith, we've failed.
—PAM SHEA-BYRNES

By the end of the Civil War, Brooklyn's Catholic numbers had grown rapidly, and the Vincentian community was asked by the local bishop to found a college serving the children of immigrants. Founded in seventeenth-century France by St. Vincent De Paul, the Vincentian mission is to serve the poor in numerous capacities, educational and pastoral. In September 1870 the College of St. John the Baptist opened in Brooklyn's Bedford-Stuyvesant section. Today with its central offices in Jamaica, Queens, St. John's University hosts six campuses worldwide.

For twenty-five years, Dr. Pamela Shea-Byrnes, vice president for university ministry, has worked at St. John's. "We're the parish for this campus," she notes. Its work is based on spirituality and service: serving the homeless; immersion programs abroad; the Catholic scholars program, forming future church leaders; and seminars on Vincent De Paul and the Vincentian spirit.

Just as there is a distinctly Jesuit approach to education, there is also a Vincentian approach. Anthony Dosen, a Vincentian scholar, sees their schools as having four goals:

1. Educating the poor, especially first-generation college students

2. Utilizing Catholic social teaching as a basis for its activity

3. Instilling in students a love for the poor leading to action

4. Researching the causes of poverty and ways to end it

As their founding religious communities decline in numbers, many Catholic universities seek lay leaders to keep that charism alive. At St. John's, Pam Shea-Byrnes is one of them. When she attended St. John's as an undergraduate in the 1980s, "We didn't talk a lot about being Catholic or being Vincentian." Now, however, "The concern is to carry the foundation of faith into the next generation."

A Long Island native, Pamela Shea graduated with a communications degree, intending to be a religion writer, "the next Ken Woodward." Along the way, she encountered the Vincentian charism, getting the "bug for service." After graduation she spent a year with the Vincentian Service Corps in Philadelphia, working with abused and delinquent teenage girls. It was her "conversion experience. I knew I wanted to work with young people."

For two years, she directed youth ministry in Brooklyn before being asked to work at St. John's. "It was the best 'yes' I've ever said." She earned a master's in theology and a doctorate in ministry, but her communications degree didn't fall into disuse: "It helps me craft a message and invite people to come and know Christ." She tells her students, "I pray you find a job you love as much as I love mine."

Before St. John's built dormitories, Pam visited residential life programs in other Catholic universities. It was a "beautiful experience" that convinced her that there's nowhere like St. John's, still educating the poor. In Queens, America's most diverse county, 40 percent of students fall below the poverty level. Young people from underserved communities, who never left the city, study at Rome and Paris campuses. One student told Pam, "I feel like I'm dreaming someone else's dream!"

St. John's is thoroughly New York and thoroughly global—"Catholic with a big C and a little c." It offers an "experience of the universal church, what it means to be Vincentian and Catholic." While only 50 percent of students are Catholic, she notes, "It matters that we're Catholic, both for our Catholic and non-Catholic students. If they don't leave with a deeper connection to their own faith, we've failed." Furthermore, she adds, "They've had the chance to see the power, beauty, and *possibility* of the Catholic Church in our world."

"Meeting God," she observes, "is very important for young people." The church "has such an opportunity in urban settings to evangelize, for people to see what we do, and be attracted to it." For example, twenty-three students are in the RCIA (Rite of Christian Initiation for Adults) program, where candidates are received into the Catholic Church. One student joined after seeing people leaving Mass smiling. "This," she proudly says, "is a sign of our success."

Many students come knowing little about their faith. College might be their only opportunity "to get to know Jesus Christ through the church. The stakes can be really high on a Catholic college campus. So much of what we do is being a role model for something they've never seen." Pam finds that Vincentian spirituality "really resonates with young people." Initially attracted to service, they're exposed to "the untapped piece of who we are, the spirituality, that is the foundation for it."

Last summer, she visited France with students, walking in the footsteps of St. Vincent, reflecting on the places they visited. For many, the experience "really put meat on the bones of Vincent's story. Talk about word made flesh!" Today Paris' St. Lazaire section, where the Vincentians were founded, is a poor area with many gypsies. The students talked and ate with them. There was a portrait of Vincent on a nearby building, and they shared with the poor literally "in the shadow of a saint."

Students have the opportunity for immersion experiences in Panama's Vincentian missions. For returning students, Pam does a theological reflection seminar. "Helping these young people who have had such a transformational experience," she comments, "is the best example of how our work reaches its pinnacle, forming students in service and spirituality." She finds God in so much of her work, but perhaps never more so than in this case.

"As a Catholic woman," she says, "the opportunities given me to be a faith leader on this campus—I can't tell you how amazing this experience has been! Working with priests on a pastoral plan for this institution. The church is all about those voices coming together." Today the Vincentian approach to education is more relevant than ever, calling people to work for change in society, a change rooted in a concrete experience of God's deep love. Thanks to people like Pam Shea-Byrnes and her colleagues at St. John's, that charism is alive and well.

45

BISHOP GUY SANSARICQ

St. Gregory the Great Church, Brooklyn

To reach out as best one can.

—GUY SANSARICQ

From the days of the Irish and Germans to the more recent newcomers, New York has always been a city of immigrants. Today it's home to America's largest Haitian community. Beginning in the 1970s, immigrants fleeing poverty and political unrest arrived in unprecedented numbers. Out of that dias-

pora, Brooklyn neighborhoods like Canarsie, Flatbush, and Crown Heights became centers of Haitian American life. In a population still predominantly Catholic (about 80 percent), the church plays a major role in the lives of New York's newest immigrants.

A major figure in this outreach has been Bishop Guy Sansaricq, one of the most respected figures in the Haitian American community. Almost continually since his ordination fifty-four years ago, he's ministered to Haitian immigrants around the world. Many of the major Haitian American organizations in place today are his work. Now a retired auxiliary bishop for the Brooklyn Diocese, he's currently the only Haitian member of the American hierarchy.

Born in western Haiti, Guy Sansaricq studied for the priesthood in Canada and was ordained at Port-au-Prince in 1960. After a year of parish work in Les Cayes he was sent to the Bahamas, where many Haitians had migrated for work. The bishop of Nassau needed a Haitian priest fluent in English; Father Sansaricq fit the bill. He was supposed to work only for the tourist season, but it turned into what he calls "seven years of extreme circumstances."

The people, he notes, "had a thousand problems." He "did everything." He visited prisoners, wrote letters to government officials, translated for doctors, found housing, and mediated labor disputes. He contacted the Bishops' Conference in the United States to find homes for refugees. In addition, he "ended up being a bank," sending more than $1 million back to Haitian families.

Eventually the Duvalier regime blacklisted him after a group of insurgents asked him to celebrate Mass for them. When the government found out, Sansaricq was labeled a revolutionary and banned from returning. His superiors arranged for him to study in Rome for what he calls "three happy years." When he finished school, he still couldn't return to Haiti, so he went to New York, where his two brothers lived.

He planned to work in Manhattan, but few Haitians were there. So he went to Brooklyn, where many Haitians started going in the 1950s. In 1971 he was assigned to Sacred Heart Church in Cambria Heights, where he served for twenty-two years. The parish had a few hundred Haitian parishioners, many of them doctors, lawyers, nurses, and engineers.

People, he recalls, "came to me for all sorts of services." In 1975 Sansaricq formed a committee that purchased a storefront, the nucleus of Haitian Americans United for Progress. HAUP helped immigrants with references, legal advice, employment, counseling, and housing. They also offered ESL classes. Today HAUP is a national organization.

The National Center for the Haitian Apostolate started after a meeting of local Haitian priests in the 1980s. Many refugees had been incarcerated in the Brooklyn Navy Yard, and the priests reached out to Haitian clergy in other cities. Father Silvano Tomasi, director of the Migration Office for the Bishops' Conference, asked Sansaricq to start a national organization for Haitians. The center now operates an outreach program, a newsletter, and radio program, "to reach out as best one can."

In 1993 he was named pastor of St. Jerome's in Flatbush. Once a bastion of Irish American life, it's now known as the "Haitian cathedral," a congregation numbering over a thousand families. Sansaricq founded the Kolej Pastoral (pastoral school) to form lay leaders. Haitians were "basically Catholic, but not very well educated in their faith." The three-year program, meeting in the parish school, offers classes on scripture, church teaching, and public speaking. Retreats are offered yearly, and students come from across the city. Many have become pastoral leaders, and some deacons.

Haitians, he notes, bring important gifts to the New York church. The single largest group of black Catholics, they have revived many faith communities. "Many parishes," he comments, "would have closed without them." To the liturgy, he adds, they bring a "liveliness." St. Jerome's choir, he asserts, "could sing on Broadway, could sing anywhere." Furthermore, he adds, Haitians bring a tradition of service, providing more religious vocations than any other immigrant group.

One Catholic New Yorker whom Bishop Sansaricq especially admires is Pierre Toussaint, another Haitian immigrant. He only learned about Toussaint since coming to New York. "He was," he says, "an amazing black slave in nineteenth-century New York. He was cherished by so many for his wisdom, discretion, and good manners. He must have been a man of tremendous character."

In 2006 the bishop of Brooklyn called him for what he assumed would be a routine meeting. He was told he'd been made an auxiliary bishop. It was, he recounts, "a total surprise." He adds, "I had to accept. The Haitian people wouldn't let me not accept." Now retired, he lives at St. Gregory the Great in Crown Heights. Life, he insists, hasn't changed that much. Basically, he says, "I'm a curate," celebrating Mass, running a Bible study group, and still involved in the Haitian community.

In fifty-four years of priesthood, Guy Sansaricq has served the migrant and refugee wherever the need was greatest. His work places him in the tradition of other immigrant New York pastors: John Raffeiner with the Germans, Felix Varela with the Irish, Nicholas Russo with the Italians. What he calls "extreme circumstances" shaped a ministry that continues in the organizations he's founded, the leaders he's trained, and the legacy of humble service that he continues to live.

46

MEGAN FINCHER

Catholic Worker, St. Joseph House, Manhattan

I find that the church is much more radical than we think.

—MEGAN FINCHER

Walking down East First Street to the Catholic Worker house, one notices on a building wall a sizeable painting of Dorothy Day, founder of the Catholic Worker movement. Underneath it is a quote attributed to Day: "Our problems stem from our acceptance of this filthy, rotten system."

At the end of the street a line of men and women wait for the doors of St. Joseph House to open, when food is served at the Catholic Worker. Once a poster board for urban poverty, today the neighborhood is slowly gentrifying, as the growing number of coffeehouses and baby carriages attests. But the poor haven't gone away. Megan Fincher sees them every day.

A Chicago native, Megan attended the University of Illinois at Urbana (as did Dorothy Day), where she considered entering religious life. She thinks it would have been a cloistered order. "The happiest I feel in my life," she says, "is during Mass. The Eucharist is the reason I'm a Catholic. No matter how I might disagree with certain issues, this is what keeps me in the church." Although life on a commune proved a positive experience, she missed the spiritual component, so she did some research and came across the Catholic Worker.

There she found the faith community she sought. Besides the commitment to the poor, other aspects attracted her, including a commitment to the environment. She sees this as part of the stewardship entrusted to humans. "After all," she points out, "our first vocation was to work in a garden." Pacifism, an issue that gained her attention during the Iraq War, was another important component.

Megan is one of five Catholic Workers living at St. Joseph House, along with twenty guests. They have Friday night meetings, Bible study on Wednesday, Mass on Tuesday and Thursday. Volunteers get twenty dollars a week, known as "ice cream money." Activists nationwide come through their doors. Every morning at ten, five days a week, they feed some 125 people, sometimes using leftovers of leftovers from local grocery stores. These days, Megan has gone from vegan to "free-gan"; "I eat whatever's given."

The New York Worker sponsors monthly antiwar vigils and "Shut Down

Guantánamo" demonstrations. At the latter, they stand in Union Square for an hour and a half in orange jumpsuits and black hoods. "It's interesting to hear what people are saying," she notes. They silently stand witness "for those at Guantánamo who don't have a voice." Much of Megan's energy is devoted to the monthly newspaper, writing about social justice and the environment. "Looking at Vatican documents," she says, "I find that the church is much more radical than we think—on the environment, on war, on all sorts of suffering."

The New York house faces several challenges. First are numbers; Megan's one of the youngest members. "I came here through a novena," she comments. As the neighborhood gentrifies, members ask, "Are we here because we're furthering Dorothy's sainthood, or are we staying for the movement itself?" Then there's the question of getting the message out there. The New York house, she admits, has resisted technology. The website is minimal, and the paper is still the main source of information (sold for a penny since 1933). "As a young person," Megan observes, "I understand the worth of keeping distance from technology. But I also appreciate the need for it."

But other things, she feels, shouldn't change, like the movement's personalist philosophy, which she interprets to mean, "We don't want to be an institution; otherwise, we don't know faces and names." She recalls one man who arrived covered with scars, pacing around yelling at everyone. She decided to be as compassionate as possible, she says, "and this really changed his attitude." She invited him to dinner. "We've all fallen in love with him," she adds. "He's still hard to deal with, but he's the angel in the house. He feels at home, comes every night for dinner. Still, he just is lost in his own head. Nothing you can pinpoint."

She's gotten several job offers, which she's declined. The call to the Catholic Worker, she insists, needs to be seen as "a legitimate vocation, not just something you do when you get out of college and don't know what to do." There's a "discernment process," she notes, "involved in being here." Her parents have mixed reactions: "Dad says, 'If it's God's will, you've gotta do it.' Mom says, 'You've got an M.F.A., what are you doing?'" That's not to say there aren't days she asks herself, "Are you really called to do this?" But then, she notes, "Something every day makes me feel like I'm in a holy place."

All in all, she comments, "It's very humbling work." One of the tougher parts is encountering the anger of the poor. "People," she observes, "sometimes are angry at us for serving them." But, she adds, "when I read the gospel and think of myself as Catholic, I can't hear Jesus saying, 'Feed the hungry,' and just say, 'That's nice,' and move on. It's easy to ignore what the gospel says." What sustains her is the "praying and working—the ongoing conversation—the daily encounter."

What keeps her Catholic, she says, are "two thousand years of scholarship and prophets. I want to understand the church and who I am in the church." In New York she sees hope in the young people trying to figure out what it means to be Catholic. She also gets inspiration from the older members of her community, "amazing people still passionate about their work. I can understand why Abraham lived to be 175." In her commitment to the city's least, to the Worker's founding principles, Megan Fincher shows that its message has continued relevance and will continue well into the future.

47

ED WILKINSON
Tablet, Brooklyn

In Brooklyn and Queens, we're all about neighborhoods.
   —ED WILKINSON

New York Catholics of a certain age remember the *Tablet*, Brooklyn's diocesan newspaper, as a bastion of political and religious conservatism that championed the likes of Father Coughlin and Joe McCarthy. Longtime editor Pat Scanlan once asserted there was "no such thing" as a "liberal Catholic newspaper." In the 1960s, under new leadership, the paper took a more progressive stance, opposing Vietnam and supporting women's rights. Today it's mainly concerned with doing what it has always done, chronicling the many happenings in Brooklyn, long known as a "diocese of immigrants."

At his Park Slope office, editor Ed Wilkinson oversees the weekly, as he's done for the last twenty-nine years. But today the *Tablet* is part of a larger diocesan endeavor called the De Sales Media Group. Named for the patron saint of journalists, it encompasses the paper, public information office, diocesan website, and television. "We're far from slowing down," Wilkinson notes. "We're actually growing. We see ourselves as a one-stop media organization."

Weekly topics include Mount Carmel Festivals and Guadalupe processions, Croatian Masses and Filipino prayer services, basketball championships and youth congresses. The focus is unapologetically local, celebrating Brooklyn's and Queens' unique faith communities. Once a bastion of Irish American life, now it's a champion of ethnic diversity. James Joyce's quip about Catholicism applies especially to Brooklyn: "Here comes everybody!" As one former bishop said, "The whole world is here!"

The same could be said of Ed Wilkinson's childhood neighborhood. Greenpoint, he recalls, "was a real mix": Irish, Italian, German, Slovak, Polish, and Lithuanian. Each group had its own parish. "It was basically a Catholic neighborhood," he notes. Growing up in the 1950s, one's whole life "centered around the parish and the parish school." Wilkinson still has a high regard for his grammar school teachers, the School Sisters of Notre Dame: "These ladies easily controlled a classroom of fifty to sixty kids. All they had to do was look at you."

The priests, he adds, "had at least as much influence on me as my father did." In 1961 he entered Cathedral Prep Seminary, a Brooklyn high school for young men considering the priesthood. Students had Thursdays off and attended school on Saturdays. One alumnus comments, "It was to keep us away from the girls." Wilkinson says of the education he received, "They exposed us to a whole new world of ideas. They showed us a whole new world outside of Greenpoint."

These were the years of Vatican II, which the faculty explained to the students. "It was," he says, "an opening the doors to the rest of the world." But, he adds, life was never the same thereafter: "Before, it was black-and-white. Now everything was gray." After a year in the seminary he decided he was called elsewhere, but he wasn't sure where yet. Many found the changes hard to accept. "It was a time of questioning, a topsy-turvy time. But if you stuck with it, you eventually made sense of it all. You saw there was a path to follow."

In 1970 he interviewed for a reporter's job at the *Tablet*. He soon learned the ins and outs of writing, editing, and shooting photographs. He even resurrected the defunct sports column, covering parish and high school sports at every level. Several players he covered became professional athletes, including NBA star Chris Mullin. When editor Don Zirkel retired in 1985, Bishop Francis Mugavero nominated Wilkinson to succeed him. "If you can," Mugavero told him, "keep me out of trouble. Good luck!"

As editor, Wilkinson is most proud of giving the paper a greater "local flavor. Anyone in the diocese can pick it up and find something about themselves. If there's no stories, there's photos." Moreover, he adds, "The paper reflects who we are as a diocese of immigrants." While some papers emphasize national and world news, the *Tablet* focuses on neighborhoods. "In Brooklyn and Queens," he proudly states, "we're all about neighborhoods."

He doesn't want to be anywhere but New York. He loves the busyness and the diversity. On his Brooklyn block, one finds "a snapshot of the entire city." His neighbors are Irish, Arabic, Puerto Rican, African American, and Italian. Here, he says, "You're part of a community, a neighborhood, a parish. I can't imagine living any place where people aren't living next to each other."

New York Catholics, Wilkinson feels, are a special breed unto themselves. A New York Catholic, he suggests, is someone "who's faithful to the church while able to live in a frenzied atmosphere." They can "step back from all the busyness and the activity and still see, with the eyes of faith, the hand of God in our daily lives." He likes to quote New York Cardinal Timothy Dolan, that New York is "a very holy place." At De Sales, he notes, they sponsor four days of recollection every year, "to remind us of who we are."

Local heroes include St. Frances Xavier Cabrini, friend of immigrants, and Dorothy Day, champion of New York's poor. An "overlooked figure" is Brooklyn's first bishop, John Loughlin, "who created a diocese from nothing." There's also Bishop Mugavero, "a man of Vatican II. He wasn't afraid of it. He wasn't a great orator, but he had a human touch." Then there's the parish priests, the women religious, the deacons, and the laypeople who don't make the news, the "unsung heroes on whose shoulders the church is built."

Since its founding in April 1908 the *Tablet* has gone through many changes. At one time, one scholar notes, it was essentially "an Irish newspaper," reflecting the paper's constituency at the time. Today, it might well be called "everybody's paper." Monsignor Ronald Marino, longtime director of Brooklyn's migration office, says that the diocese's "particular charism is to welcome the immigrant." Today the *Tablet* celebrates that charism, painting a picture of a proudly multicultural Catholic New York.

48

Sister Tesa Fitzgerald
Hour Children, Long Island City

God made so many different kinds of people. Why would He allow only one way to serve Him?
—Sign on a painting in Sister Tesa's office

L ocated between two of the city's largest housing projects, Hour Children was founded in Long Island City in 1986 to help incarcerated women and their children. From the outside, it looks like any other building in the area, but inside is a warm, friendly place where two cats, Romie and Richie, wander the office at will. In the waiting room, surrounded by photos, flowers, and balloons, my eyes are drawn to a framed picture with the words, "God made so many different kinds of people. Why would He allow only one way to serve Him?"

Hour Children serves in many ways. Inside the prisons, they provide legal assistance and counseling, as well as parenting classes. Outside they work to keep families united and help mothers make a fresh start; they also maintain residences for some sixty families. A success story, the program has faced many challenges through twenty-eight years, and today it is regarded as among the finest of its kind. The name "Hour" Children, founder Sister Tesa Fitzgerald says, arose because the children's lives are dictated by the hour: "the 'hour' of the mother's arrest, the 'hour' of the visit, and the 'hour' of the return."

As I sit down to interview Sister Tesa in her office, I notice a couple of things: it's a cheerful place, neat and clearly well-organized. Although her phone is constantly ringing, she never seems the least bit ruffled by the many demands on her time, including mine. And she enjoys telling a good story.

Above her desk are a series of photos and holy cards, "my saints." Some are familiar faces: St. Francis, Dorothy Day, Mother Teresa; other are relatives, friends, clients, and coworkers. She especially admires Dorothy, who got "down there with the people."

In the Fitzgerald family, Sister Tesa proudly notes, "Service was always a big thing." The daughter of Irish immigrants who worked on a Long Island estate, one brother became a social worker, another conducted retreats for prisoners, a niece and nephew joined the Peace Corps, and another nephew is studying to be a deacon. No matter how poor you were, her mother taught her, "You always helped your neighbors." Another important lesson she learned from her father was, "Be kind. It doesn't cost you anything."

At St. Joachim Parochial School in Cedarhurst and at Hempstead's Sacred Heart Academy, she found another approach to service in the Sisters of St. Joseph of Brentwood. The Sisters, she says, "were great role models," a model she wanted to emulate. At eighteen, right out of high school, she joined the community. Much of the next three decades would be spent in teaching and administration.

From Puerto Rico to South Ozone Park, from Floral Park to Flushing, Sister Tesa taught in the classroom. During the 1980s she became principal at St. Vincent de Paul in Brooklyn's Williamsburg section, back in the days before gentrification. All of her educational experiences, she notes, were by and large very positive. From there, she became curriculum coordinator for the Brooklyn Catholic Schools Office. She fully expected to spend the rest of her life in education. "By trade," she says, "I am a teacher."

A turning point occurred when a friend of Tesa's, Sister Elaine Roule, gave a talk to the Sisters' entire community. A chaplain at the Bedford Hills Correctional Facility, Sister Elaine talked about the plight of incarcerated women and their children, asking her fellow Sisters to think about ways the community might best respond to this need. Sister Tesa admits it was a topic she had never fully considered up to this point. At home she prayed over it—and what she might do to help.

Looking around for a house, she found an abandoned convent in Long Island City. In the fall of 1986 Sister Tesa and four other Sisters opened Hour Children on Twelfth Street as a residence for children whose mothers were in prison. Although the initial reception of the locals ranged from lukewarm to mildly hostile, over time Hour Children has become an integral part of the community. If she wants volunteers for some program, all she has to do is go across the street to the local bodega and she can get half a dozen men for any given project.

Hour Children has "about a million" success stories, she says. "Give me about four days, and I'll tell you." Two sisters, age thirteen, arrived "basically uneducated," unable to write, read, or add. Today, through "lots of TLC," one has a master's in social work and helps Hour Children. The other has a happy life in the Bronx with her own children. Another young woman came after her mother was deported and she was left alone in an apartment. Today, a graduate of St. Joseph's College, she teaches in the public schools. Tesa's administrative and leadership skills and her enthusiasm are all major factors in Hour Children's success. But perhaps a more significant factor, one woman notes, is that "she genuinely cares and loves us. That's what makes her special."

One educational foundation aptly describes Sister Tesa as "a pure New Yorker": a fast talker and a fast thinker who "gets things done." She loves living and working here; just going for a walk, she says, "is exciting." She loves the city's "richness" and "diversity"; it's in the people that she sees the city's real beauty. Asking about where she finds God most here, she answers, "In the life of the people I work with, in the joy and the freedom of the kids." One observer writes, "She's all business. The thing is, Sister Tesa's business is kindness."

49

FATHER JAMES MARTIN

America, Manhattan

You're always dealing with the new. They don't call it New York *for nothing.*

—JIM MARTIN

The American theologian John Courtney Murray once said that a Jesuit's job is to "explain the church to the world and the world to the church." At their Midtown Manhattan offices, the Jesuits of *America* magazine do this on a daily basis, addressing issues theological and philosophical, scientific and cultural, political and economic. For over a century, *America* has been

a major sounding board for the dialogue between religion and culture. For Father James Martin, the magazine's contributing editor, there's no better place for this dialogue to take place than in New York, the media capital of the world.

For over a decade, Martin has been associated with the magazine as writer and editor. In the mid-1990s he spent a year there as part of his Jesuit training. After his ordination he returned and has been there ever since. A frequent presence on television and radio, he's also a bestselling author, writing on topics such as the saints, Jesuit spirituality, Africa, and Ground Zero. In all his books, he says, he tries "to help people find God." His autobiography, *In Good Company,* has invited apt comparisons to Thomas Merton's *Seven Storey Mountain.*

Growing up in the Philadelphia suburbs, priesthood was the last thing Jim Martin imagined himself doing. By his own admission, his religious upbringing veered toward the lukewarm. At the University of Pennsylvania's prestigious Wharton School he studied business less from a love of the subject than because it seemed the practical thing to do. After his graduation in 1982 he moved to New York and was on the fast track to CEO.

It didn't take long, however, to find he wasn't happy with this high-pressure corporate life. He knew he was looking for something more, but he couldn't name it. One night after work he turned on the television to watch a documentary about Thomas Merton, restless young Manhattanite who found his vocation in a monastery. Merton, he recalls, was "a revelation. I thought monastic life looked so beautiful. It was like falling in love. I ran out and got all of Merton's books and asked my parish priest, who certainly didn't know me, where I could go to become like Merton, a holy person."

Within two years, Jim Martin left the corporate world to begin his basic training as a Jesuit. Over the next decade he found himself in places and in jobs he never could have imagined: cleaning hospices in Jamaica, helping start businesses in Africa, visiting prisoners in Boston. Maybe the most unlikely job of all was a writing internship with *America,* where he discovered a writer's vocation.

As a Jesuit, Jim has been all over the world, but most of his religious life has been spent in New York as priest, author, and editor. On any given day he might be working on the magazine, appearing on the *Colbert Report* (where he is honorary chaplain), discussing current events on National Public Radio, and giving an interview to CNN or the *New York Times.* In discussing religion, he notes, "I help them get the story right and they help us get the story out there immediately."

"Being a Jesuit priest in New York City," he observes, is "complicated and challenging." There's an old saying that St. Ignatius Loyola, the order's founder, "loved the big cities," where his Jesuits could reach the greatest number of people. One of the first things Ignatius did in Rome, Martin notes, was to buy a printing press. For his own interaction with the media, he says, there's no better place to be:

> In twenty minutes I can walk to the *New York Times,* CNN, or NPR. You can't do this just anywhere. Recently, for example, I did an interview with NPR on New York's newest saints. I left home at 9:45 a.m., got there at 10:15, did the interview in fifteen minutes, and was back home at 10:45. Where else can you do this? This is uniquely New York.

To be a Catholic in New York City, he observes, "means by necessity bumping up against other religions, cultures, nationalities, and socioeconomic groups. It means being forced to live one's faith in the busy, confusing modern world that is New York." Here, he adds, "You're always dealing with the new. They don't call it *New* York for nothing." Catholic New Yorkers are engaged in a unique and "active intellectual reflection on the culture, always responding to the newest happenings and being comfortable with change."

In addition, Martin contends, to be a New York Catholic is "to belong to a distinguished line of people," like Dorothy Day and Thomas Merton. Catholic New York "has produced some of the great religious figures of our time, a rich heritage." One of Martin's favorite New York sites is St. Patrick's Cathedral, whose impressive bronze front doors feature saints with a New York connection: Isaac Jogues, Frances X. Cabrini, Elizabeth Seton, and the newly canonized Kateri Tekakwitha. When he looks at it, "I see all my heroes. They say to you, 'Come in to this storied church which is the church of New York.'"

These days Jim Martin's calendar is booked far in advance. Besides his frequent media appearances, he speaks at parishes, colleges, and forums nationwide. His books are *New York Times* bestsellers, and he's already received honorary doctorates. Through it all, he remains modest and self-effacing. For Jim Martin, it's all part of living out his Jesuit vocation: furthering a positive dialogue between faith and culture in the big cities and beyond.

50

Pamela D. Hayes

Law Offices of Pamela D. Hayes, Manhattan

I have very serious problems with the hierarchy, but my faith is intact.
—Pam Hayes

In January 2002 the *Boston Globe*'s revelation of clergy sex abuse scandals rocked Catholic America to the core. At their June meeting in Dallas the bishops authorized the creation of a national review board to investigate its scope and nature. Two years later the board published its findings in a document known as the John Jay Report. Still, twelve years after Dallas, the underlying issues of trust and accountability are far from resolved, and the ramifications of the scandals are likely to be felt for decades to come.

New York attorney Pamela Hayes was one of the board's original members. Long connected with the *National Catholic Reporter*, as an assistant district attorney in Brooklyn she prosecuted sex crimes against children. "I'm the one with the technical know-how," she notes. "I know what questions to ask and what to look for." During the investigation she visited diocesan officials across the country. The experience led to her resignation and to reassessing her relationship with the church.

A prominent media commentator, she's been called a "legal powerhouse." A solo practitioner specializing in criminal defense and civil rights, she's served on numerous fundraising committees, including the finance committee for Hilary Clinton's 2008 presidential run. She attributes her fundraising prowess to her Catholic school days selling Christmas cards, stamps, and World's Finest chocolate bars. "It served me well in politics," she comments.

Pam Hayes grew up in Harlem's St. Nicholas Houses, the daughter of a Baptist father and a Catholic mother. At St. Aloysius Parochial School she was taught by the Franciscan Handmaids, an African American community. Nearby at St. Charles Borromeo parish was Father Emerson Moore, later the first black monsignor and bishop in the New York Archdiocese. Later she worked with him at the Office of Black Ministry, where he was a religious advisor.

By third grade Pam knew she wanted to be a lawyer. Her parents and the Sisters at St. Al's encouraged her. So did the Dominican Sisters at Aquinas High School in the Bronx. "Nobody said, 'You can't do this, you can't be this.' If you wanted to do something that would bring honor to the school, why not?" At Boston's Northeastern University, she graduated with honors, tutoring history and teaching dance at the campus' African American Center.

Overall, her experience in Boston was positive, except for her introduction to racism. As public schools were desegregated, racial violence erupted citywide. South Boston, a predominantly Irish Catholic community, was rife with racial incidents. The future lawyer, whose great-grandfather was Irish, was shocked at what she saw: "I never knew people could hate people like this. I couldn't believe Catholics would act like this."

After graduating from Atlanta's Emory Law School, she worked as a public defender in Elizabeth, New Jersey. Back in New York, Cardinal Terence Cooke asked her to serve on the advisory board for the Black Ministry Office. "He was a very gentle man," she recalls, "not political." On the other hand, she notes, Cooke's successor John O'Connor "*was* political, but he had so much goodness. He was a good guy, loyal to his priests, loyal to New York, loyal to the faith."

At thirty-five, a successful lawyer and a practicing Catholic, she began to question the way she had always related to her church. "I had believed all the hype, about the 'one true church.'" But now she began to address more fully her personal relationship to Christ. As a student of history, she realized that actual church practices hadn't always squared with the gospel, particularly in its treatment of women. She resolved, she recalls, "to keep my vision clear."

She recalls the initial impact of the sex abuse scandals. "When Boston hit," she recalls, "it was an epidemic. When you think 'Catholic,' you don't think 'New York.' You think 'Boston.'" When she was asked to serve on the board, she approached the job like any other case. "I saw no difference between the bishops and corporate leaders who hide stuff." At the review board's first meeting, a group of abuse victims were invited. The level of anger was stunning. "People were foaming at the mouth," she remembers.

Even more surprising was the bishops' hostility. Many wanted nothing to do with the board. At one meeting, a cardinal she admired showed up with half a dozen lawyers. *What are they hiding?* she asked herself. Another cardinal refused to allow any bishops to celebrate Mass for board members and blatantly ignored female members during questioning sessions. Still another told her (and later denied saying it), "You all are going to be the death of the Catholic Church."

"That was it for me," Pam says. "I knew they were liars." The board unraveled a culture of secrecy and denial. For her, the bishops lost credibility. And none resigned willingly, not even Robert Finn, the Kansas City bishop convicted of a misdemeanor after failing to tell authorities about a priest possessing child pornography. "He's a goddamn criminal," she says with disgust. "And nobody ever said to him, 'You've got to step down.'"

Furthermore, she felt, these men "had deep-seated issues. They have no role for us other than having babies. When they talk about how much they love Mary, I say, 'Oh, stop it!'" That was the "straw that broke the camel's back." How, she asks, "can you listen to them for anything? I mean, who *elected them*?" She resigned from the review board. Still, she says, "Once a Catholic, always a Catholic."

Pam Hayes is a special type of Catholic, a New York Catholic. "Boston for a long time was an Irish Catholic city. New York was, too, for a while, but other groups came. There's different types of Catholics here," she notes. "Although there are cultural differences, there is a more universal kind of Catholicism here. Here you're always challenged. That's what being a New York

Catholic is all about." Like many Catholics, she is excited about the election of Pope Francis in March 2013. Although her faith has been challenged, it's still there: "I have very serious problems with the hierarchy, but my faith is intact."

51

FATHER RAYMOND NOBILETTI
Transfiguration Church, Manhattan

I learned how important it was to be an instrument of God's presence and am still humbled by that privilege.
—RAY NOBILETTI

Like many New Yorkers, Father Ray Nobiletti, M.M., remembers the morning of September 11, 2001, as "a perfect fall day, cloudless and filled with bright sunshine." After celebrating the eight a.m. Mass at Transfiguration Church in Chinatown, he went around the corner to vote in the New York mayoral primary and then went back to the rectory. He planned to enjoy the rest of the day.

But when he returned he learned that a plane crashed into the World Trade Center. He got a call from a neighboring pastor asking him to come down to the site. Priests were needed for the wounded and dying.

"I was in a daze," he recalls, "while collecting the holy oil, stole, and prayer book." On the television he saw the second plane hit the towers. *How could something like this happen in New York City?* he asked himself.

As he ran toward Ground Zero, thousands ran past him evacuating the city. As he reached a triage center near the Millennium Hotel, he put on his stole:

> People just started to come to me, because they just saw a priest. It's interesting. And I think half of them, most of them, weren't even Catholic. It's just that people were so upset about what's happening, why is this happening, who's doing this, what happened to this beautiful morning we started off with?

Throughout the morning, Father Nobiletti ministered to attack victims until the South Tower collapsed. For ten or twelve minutes he was covered in debris, unable to see. When he emerged, "There was devastation all around us. . . . And like us, everything was covered with a gray-brown ash." He was looking for survivors when the North Tower collapsed. He barely escaped with his life.

Over the years, Ray Nobiletti has received numerous honors for his work as a 9/11 First Responder. Twelve years later, he's still serving Transfiguration's Chinese congregation. As a boy he'd dreamed of serving as a missionary in China, so he joined Maryknoll, the first American Catholic missionary order, after high school. Ordained in 1969, he spent fifteen years in Hong Kong before going to work in Maryknoll's central governance.

Most of Nobiletti's priesthood hasn't been overseas, but in a downtown Manhattan parish. But New York isn't foreign territory for this Brooklyn-born priest, who grew up in the Bronx and Valley Stream. The grandson of Italian immigrants, his family owned a laundry plant in the Bronx. After reading a biography of Francis X. Ford, the Maryknoll bishop who died in Communist China, he wanted to enter the order's high school seminary, but his parents persuaded him to wait a while.

In 1960, then, after graduating from Power Memorial Academy, Ray Nobiletti entered Maryknoll, officially named the Catholic Foreign Mission Society of America. After studying at their schools in Illinois, Massachusetts, and New York, he was ordained on May 24, 1969. He was given three choices of where to go: Hong Kong, Chile, and Venezuela. His first choice was Hong Kong, which he was surprised to get. Given his New York background, he knew he "wanted to be in an urban situation."

After studying Chinese he spent fifteen years in Hong Kong. While he was there he founded a parish, school, and youth center. He trained seminarians and served in various administrative roles. September 11 wasn't the first disaster he encountered. In 1972 he was involved in a Hong Kong mudslide that took seventy-two lives. "I learned," he writes, "how important it was to be an instrument of God's presence and am still humbled by that privilege." The experience served him well on the morning of September 11.

Returning home in 1984 he was elected assistant to Maryknoll's superior general. There he got to know New York cardinal John J. O'Connor, whom "I really admired. He was a hail-fellow-well-met." In early 1991, concerned over the situation in a downtown Chinese parish, O'Connor asked him, "Y'know, Ray, could you go down to Transfiguration for a few months to see what's going on?" The appointment, the priest notes, was dated April 1. "Hey," he joked with O'Connor, "what'd you do to me?"

The assignment has lasted twenty-three years, but he doesn't mind. "I'm a city-type person," he says. He sees Transfiguration as a metaphor for the city itself. Originally started as a Dutch Lutheran church, it became Episcopalian with the arrival of the English. During the 1800s, as Catholics poured into the city, it became Catholic. Later it evolved from an Irish to an Italian parish. Since the 1960s it has been a predominantly Chinese parish, with Mass celebrated in both Mandarin and Cantonese. Through it all, he notes, the parish has been a "church of immigrants."

Today, he notes, the face of Chinatown is changing as well, thanks to gentrification and the rising cost of living. Much of the Chinese population has relocated to Brooklyn and Queens. The bishop of Brooklyn, he notes, has often asked him to take over a Chinese parish in his diocese. Nobiletti hasn't ruled out the idea completely, but for now he's happy serving the people of Manhattan's Chinatown.

It's been over twenty years, and Ray Nobiletti loves being a priest in New York. Here, he says, there's "never a dull moment. You're always dealing with different people and different cultures." In New York, he contends, it's normal to have a parish serving "five or six different cultures, and we're proud of it." He sees New York as the place where "we all come together. Pastorally, you're part of a big family." In the long run, there may be no better place for a missionary to be than in this city, ever changing and ever new.

52

SISTER MARGARET MCCABE
Robert N. Davoren Center, Rikers Island

They know I care.

 —PEG MCCABE

L ocated in the East River between Queens and the Bronx, Rikers Island is New York City's main correctional facility. Known as the "world's largest penal colony," it consists of ten jails. One of them, the Robert N. Davoren Center, holds adolescent and adult male detainees headed for either court or prison. Author Jennifer Wynn sadly observes, "Even when the sun shines on Rikers, little cheer penetrates the dreary penal colony."

This past year, Sister Margaret McCabe marked two important anniversaries: her fifty-sixth anniversary as a member of a religious community, the Holy Union Sisters, and her thirtieth year as chaplain at the Davoren Center. She likes to note that she's the "only Sister who's spent half her life in jail." Rikers, she admits, can be a scary place, where a "sixteen-year-old comes in as an altar boy and leaves as a gangster." But, she says, "they don't scare me." The reason is simple: "They know I care." Sister Margaret works with inmates ages sixteen and up. She counsels them, prays with them, advocates for them, and consoles them. At prayer services, she does short reflections and prayers before distributing Communion. "I hold their hands," she says. "Nobody ever refuses their hands." She runs AA and NA groups. "The alcoholic addict," she's careful to point out, "doesn't scare me. It's the addiction that scares me."

This job could easily lead to burnout, but, she says, "I thank God every day I'm there." She lives a short distance from Rikers, in a convent in Astoria, blocks from where she grew up. To unwind, she takes walks, reads mystery novels, knits, and spends quality time with friends. She also reflects on her ministry.

Her model of ministry is "the Samaritan woman, minus the five husbands." In John's Gospel, Jesus reveals himself to the Samaritan woman, challenging her to repent and start over. Back home, she tells the townspeople, who set out in search of Jesus. "I minister," Sister Margaret adds, "not because I'm so perfect, but because I'm a sinner as well. This woman's questioning and searching for the truth, and going back to her town. The 'town slut' has a peace about her, and they all get up and follow her."

One of three daughters born to Irish immigrant parents, Margaret McCabe was raised in Astoria. She had a happy childhood: "I don't know what it's like not to be loved." At Immaculate Conception School on Twenty-Ninth Street, she encountered the Holy Union Sisters and became attracted to their way of life. In 1958, after graduating from high school, she joined the community and took vows three years later.

For sixteen years, she taught in classrooms from New Jersey to Maryland. For seven years she was a principal. As a teacher she found that boys who caused trouble for other teachers weren't a problem to her. "If you care, you can do anything. They knew I cared." She began to consider other ways to help kids in trouble. In Baltimore, she earned a master's in guidance and counseling. Of her teaching years she says, "I belonged there for the time I was there."

Her last school assignment was as principal of St. Francis De Sales School in Spanish Harlem. Until then, her educational ministry had been primarily suburban. However, she says, "I realized that color didn't make a difference; kids were kids and parents were parents." During the summers, she worked with the New York Archdiocese's prison apostolate, visiting prisoners and writing letters for them. In the process she felt increasingly drawn to this ministry. Applying to Rikers for a chaplaincy, she was initially rejected but later hired. She's been there ever since, "where I'm meant to be."

At the start, she admits, she felt overwhelmed, but she soon got over it by walking around the jail introducing herself to everyone. Most inmates, she notes, "don't have people they can talk to, or trust." She fills that gap. "I never say. 'I understand,' but I say, 'I *can* feel for how much you're hurting. Is there any way I can help?'" One inmate recalls, "She asked who I had backing me up. I said nobody. She said, 'I'll back you up.'"

She never tells an inmate "what he did is right," but neither does she "rub their nose in it. The question is, what can we do right now?" With her, inmates "feel cared for, they feel accepted, and they feel loved." One inmate said, "I don't have anyone, but I have you." And she always has a hug, because it "makes an inhumane situation human." She's there for the guards, too. "I can't smile at the inmate and growl at the officers. The officers make my job. The whole world is my parish."

When her religious superiors accompany her to the jail on a routine visit, inmates nervously ask, "You're not gonna take her away from us, are you?" For them, Sister Margaret is hope, this woman whose own hope is in "the wounded, broken, tortured Christ; Christ the prisoner; the Christ who said, 'I was in prison and you visited me.'" And she won't retire anytime soon if she can help it.

53

THOMAS MICHAEL COLUCCI

St. Joseph's Seminary, Yonkers

Why did this happen? Where is God?
—A New York firefighter at Ground Zero

For every New Yorker, September 11, 2001, was a life-changing experience, but maybe for none more so than the Ground Zero rescue workers. For Lieutenant Tom Colucci of the New York Fire Department, it led him to make a major vocational decision. Today he's studying for the priesthood at St. Joseph's Seminary in Yonkers. For most of his life Tom had considered the priesthood. "It was always a thought," he reflects. But God, he notes, had other plans for him before that.

The son of a chemist from the Bronx, Thomas Michael Colucci attended Catholic schools in Rockland County before studying at Springfield College in Massachusetts. During a college break he began seriously considering a call to the priesthood. At the time, he decided against it, but he did work in campus ministry and began praying the Liturgy of the Hours (the church's official prayer). After receiving his master's degree, he worked at John Jay College's fitness center. After a friend suggested taking the Fire Department exam, he did and was called up in February 1985.

Over the next twenty years, he worked in firehouses in the Bronx and Manhattan, reaching the rank of captain. "I loved being a fireman," he says. "I loved the camaraderie, the excitement. I knew this was it." A former marathon runner, Tom played on department football teams in the winter, softball in the spring, basketball in the summer. He still stays in touch with his former coworkers, "a great bunch of guys." Recently when he spoke about vocations at a parish, an old friend from the department was in the congregation. "A small world!" he comments.

When September 11 came, Lieutenant Colucci was stationed in Manhattan's Chelsea section. He'd just gotten off work when he got a call to come back. When he arrived at Ground Zero, the second tower had just fallen. For months, he searched through the remains of the World Trade Center. "Why did this happen?" his fellow firefighters asked. "Where is God?" "Christ is here," the seventeen-year veteran answered. "He's here in the volunteers, the workers." On his day off, Tom recalls, "I went to funerals. I knew about a hundred guys who died. Thirty or forty were real good friends."

By then, he'd decided to pursue the seminary after his retirement. But in August 2003 he was caught in a basement explosion on Eighth Avenue and West Thirty-Eighth Street. A concussion led to a blood clot on the brain, and he was placed on medical leave. He wasn't expected to survive: "They gave me last rites in the hospital." When he did recover he was placed on a desk job in Little Italy until he retired in February 2005 with twenty years on the job.

For several years prior, he'd been attracted to the monastic life, making one or two retreats a year at Mount Saviour, a Benedictine monastery in Elmira. Reading Thomas Merton was a big influence: "I think I read about twenty of his books." After retiring, he entered Mount Saviour. "Tom the fireman" (as the monks knew him) became Brother Thomas Bernadette: "They told me I could take any name. I could be Brother *Polycarp* if I wanted to." He chose the name Bernadette because of his devotion to Our Lady of Lourdes.

Mount Saviour is a purely contemplative monastery, with no outside attachments like a school or a parish. Brother Thomas's life revolved around manual work and communal prayer ("Seven times a day!" he recalls). In 2009 he was sent to St. Vincent's Archabbey in Latrobe, Pennsylvania, to study for the priesthood. The experience, he recalls, was "phenomenal." St. Vincent's included a parish as well as a monastery and a college, and this pastoral dimension of monastic life led him to think about the diocesan priesthood: "I wanted something more apostolic."

In September 2012 Tom Colucci transferred to St. Joseph's Seminary to study for the New York Archdiocese. His day begins at 6:30 a.m. with communal prayer, Mass, and classes all morning. After lunch, there are more classes, recreation, and study. The day closes with more study and night prayer. He feels like he's come home. "Now," he comments, reflecting on his return to New York, "I can see how God worked through the whole thing."

He would love to work in the city again as a priest. "The diversity," he says, "is great. There's a rich heritage here. I've been reading about our history as a church in New York, which goes way back." His heroes include his friend Father Mychal Judge. "Father Mike was a great guy," he recalls. "The guys loved him." Another person he especially admires is Father Vincent Cappodano, a Maryknoll priest who was killed while serving as a military chaplain in Vietnam. Their courage, he comments, "inspires me in my own vocation."

At heart, Tom says, "I'm a New Yorker. I want to serve the people of New York. This is where my family is. This is where my roots are. As long as I'm going to be a priest, I might as well be here."

54

Marilyn Santos

Pontifical Mission Societies in the United States, Manhattan

Bringing Don Bosco to different places.
—Marilyn Santos

One of Marilyn Santos's most prized possessions is a painting of St. John Bosco hanging on her office wall. The patron saint of youth, Don Bosco founded the Salesians in nineteenth-century Italy to serve young people. Marilyn first encountered the Salesians while teaching at Mary Help of Christians School in Greenwich Village. Since then, she's gone on to work in youth ministry at every level, from the parish on up. Today she's a nationally renowned authority with a specialization in Hispanic outreach. Wherever she's worked, her goal has been consistent: "Bringing Don Bosco to different places."

Her ministry has taken her all over the country, but since March 2012 she's been back in her native New York working at the Pontifical Mission Societies, an organization designed to coordinate missionary efforts nationwide. Besides overseas missions, there's also a need for missionaries at home, especially among youth and young adults. Working on a national platform, with networks in every diocese, Marilyn's objective is to "animate youth and young adults to be missionary disciples, to empower and form our ministers at home to reach out to other groups."

Growing up on East Twenty-Fourth Street in Manhattan, she went to Epiphany parish, where the pastor was Monsignor Harry J. Byrne, a prominent Catholic activist. There she had her "first real encounter with God." At college, she encountered a nondenominational Christian group that invited her to worship with them. She took up the offer a few times, but somehow she felt like "something was missing." Later she taught religious education at Epiphany and served on the parish Social Action Committee.

Soon Marilyn was offered a teaching position at Mary Help of Christians. Over nine years she worked with the summer camp and the parish youth ministry. It was, she recalls, a period of "so many blessings." She traveled to Ecuador with the Sisters for missionary work. The experience expanded her understanding of vocation; "we all have missionary vocations." (She also notes, "We romanticize poverty.") From teaching she served as youth minister for St. Mary's Church on Grand Street in downtown Manhattan.

As director of young adult formation in the Brooklyn Diocese, she began to coordinate youth work at a wider level; it was, she recalls, "awesome for me. It really cemented my vocation." Soon other dioceses asked her to coordinate their youth ministry. While working in Atlanta and later Metuchen, she was elected to national leadership roles. Today she is president of the

National Catholic Network de Pastoral Juvenil Hispana, better known as La Red, and serves as a consultant to the Bishops' Conference on youth issues. (She is also completing a doctorate in religious education at Fordham University.)

"My faith," Marilyn comments, "continues to grow and be open and fuller working with them." She sees in young adults a "desire, enthusiasm, a 'Holy Longing,'" adding that these gifts have often been neglected. Youth have a strong sense of justice, openness, and genuineness. ("They have a hidden radar," she says.) They want to be challenged in their faith, to give of their time and talent. While the service trips raise a lot of enthusiasm, for most young people "the humanitarian aspect takes over. This is good, but we want to show them that, as Catholics, it's not the only reason we do it."

In her ministry, Marilyn's learned the importance of meeting young people on their own terms. It's important not to condemn their culture, but to try to distinguish between what's positive and what might be potentially harmful. "Don't use the word 'secular' like it's a dirty word," she advises. "Young adults live in that world." Because of technology, she notes, they value differences in others a lot more than previous generations have. At the same time, she insists, "We need to let young people be the evangelizers. We need to see more of this. The kingdom of God begins here."

Hispanic Catholics, in particular, she contends, "are primed and ready to be evangelizers for the entire world—to be leaders, not recipients." Missionary discipleship is "automatically embedded in the way we live our faith. There is a feeling—I am baptized, I can be a missionary." There's also an openness to evangelize "and be very verbal about my faith. It's 24/7 integrated into what we are, not just relegated to Sunday service." Furthermore, she adds, deeply embedded in Hispanic culture is the notion of "servant leadership." At a function, for example, the leader introduces himself/herself as *su servidor/su servidora*.

To the New York church, Hispanic Catholics bring important gifts, especially a strong sense of community. Family, Marilyn notes, "doesn't just mean the biological—it's a lot broader."

They also "bring a vibrancy" to Catholic life, inside and outside church buildings. To newcomers they extend a welcome they didn't always get when they arrived. "For many new Latino immigrants," she points out, "they come here, and the first place they go is to the church, which they see as a connection to home, but they get the door slammed in their face. When they're welcomed, that's a gift we've brought to the church."

While her ministry has taken her to many places she couldn't have imagined, Marilyn Santos is deep at heart a New Yorker. And she loves being a Catholic New Yorker. She loves the opportunity "to be with, to pray with so many different people, to talk about faith with such a variety of people." Every now and then, she likes to go to a different parish, sit there anonymously, and feel "united with the people. This God thing, this Catholicism thing, is very loving." She sees God at work throughout this city. "Where *doesn't* he work? If we don't find God, we aren't looking well enough. In a city like this, how can you not, if you're really looking?"

55

TONY ROSSI

The Christophers, New York

We tend to complain about the culture. But if we don't engage the culture, we really don't have the right to complain about it.

—TONY ROSSI

When James Keller joined Maryknoll in 1918, his sights were set on the Chinese missions. But he proved so capable a fundraiser at home that he never got there. Over the years he thought of ways that ordinary people could "play a missionary role themselves." After World

War II he founded the Christopher movement as a way to apply gospel principles "in the market of everyday life." Today through the printed word, broadcast media, and the Internet, they still encourage men and women to make a positive difference in the world. Keller is perhaps best known for saying, "It is better to light one candle than curse the darkness."

While he was a student at St. John's University, Tony Rossi discovered a Christophers newsletter on an empty pew in his Queens parish. He liked what he read, and soon he became a regular subscriber. After completing a communications degree he applied to the Christophers "as a fluke. I took a chance." To his surprise, he was hired. He originally planned to get some experience and move on to a bigger company. Today he's been there sixteen years. He calls it a "perfect fit" that combines his personal and professional interests.

Over the years, Rossi's duties have expanded: associate producer, producer, host of the weekly radio show as well as the podcast. He also coordinates the Christopher Awards, which since 1949 have honored books, films, and individuals that "affirm the highest values of the human spirit." Past movies honored range from *The Ten Commandments* to *Apollo 13*, while individual honorees include David McCullough and Mother Dolores Hart. Father Keller, notes Rossi, believed that such awards "might encourage positive trends in popular culture."

The main emphasis of the Christophers is on sharing "the stories of people living their faith in the world," the famous and not-so-famous. The first Christopher film, a 1951 documentary titled *You Can Change the World*, was directed by Catholic director Leo McCarey, featuring Catholic stars like Bing Crosby and Loretta Young, along with non-Catholic stars like Jack Benny and William Holden. For fifty-five years, until television became too expensive, *Christopher Closeup* featured guests ranging from activist Dorothy Day to singer Betty Hutton.

From an early age Tony Rossi has been interested in all aspects of media. A native of Long Island City, he's been a movie buff for as long as he can remember. An only child, his father worked as a customs broker at John F. Kennedy Airport, while his mother worked at the Waldorf Astoria. A graduate of Catholic schools from parochial school through graduate school, he's never felt called to priesthood. It was at St. John's that he discovered his vocation.

As an undergraduate Tony got involved in St. John's own TV Club. At first, he recalls, he was "intimidated by all the equipment." But it turned out to be "the best learning experience of my life. You learned every aspect of TV that you wanted to. Imagination was the only limit." As a graduate student pursuing a master's in English, he stayed involved with the club. In May 2013 he was inducted into the St. John's TV Hall of Fame. He stayed involved with the program during his time at graduate school. "Everything I learned here," he says, "I used at the Christophers."

While technology is important, the primary focus at the Christophers is on people and their stories. "I was always a sucker for a good story," Rossi comments, "regardless of the medium in which it was told—be it television, radio, film, books, or music." For Rossi, working at the Christophers "integrates everything in my life. I'm naturally drawn to popular culture's storytelling dimension, as well as to the religious dimension."

Rossi considers himself "a writer at heart." For many years, he notes, he was reluctant about speaking in public. One Sunday morning his pastor at St. Raphael, Father Tom Pettei, suggested he become a lector in the parish. He accepted the invitation, and he's glad he did, because it "helped prepare me for future work. It was a new endeavor."

His work has taken him to places like California, where he interviewed Dom DeLuise, "possibly the funniest interview I've ever done." He's met supermodel Kathy Ireland, who talked about her prolife work. Actor Efrem Zimbalist Jr. and game-show host Monte Hall talked about their Jewish faith. Actress Maureen O'Hara asked the lighting director to "light me the way John Ford used to." Carroll O'Connor, he recalls, was "quiet and soft-spoken, nothing like Archie Bunker." All in all, Rossi has found most celebrities "willing to talk about their faith. In fact, many are happy to talk about it."

While some Catholic programs have a strong catechetical emphasis, the focus at the Christophers is evangelical. It's less about instructing people in the faith than in getting them to share about their own, and encouraging them to apply it to the world around them. The goal is to "keep a voice for God in public life." As Catholics, he points out, "We tend to complain about the culture. But if we don't engage the culture, we really don't have the right to complain about it."

New York, he feels, is "the center of the Catholic world in the U.S. It helps to have a media-friendly cardinal here who speaks the truth with love." He sees the church here as a "very vibrant church," but he doesn't see it as "liberal

or conservative—it's a little bit of both. It's a big tent of Catholicism—orthodox, liberal, you find it all." And he sees the Christophers as bringing some
important gifts to the church, locally and nationally:

> Our voice is about what's positive in the media. Providing individual
> stories of people living out their faith. Whenever you can get a story
> out there that people can relate to, we are lifting up the church in
> New York and the country. Father Keller called people to be a candle
> in the darkness.

56

ROSEMARIE PACE

Pax Christi Metro New York, Manhattan

The newness of what I was learning struck a nerve.
—ROSEMARIE PACE

Dating back to the 1830s, St. Joseph's Church on Sixth Avenue is the
oldest standing church building in the city of New York. Founded for
the city's growing Irish Catholic population, today it houses a variety of
ministries, chiefly NYU's Catholic campus ministry. On the second floor
of the rectory is the Metro New York office for Pax Christi and its director,
Rosemarie Pace, who has overseen the group's citywide operations since
2000.

Founded in Europe at the end of World War II, Pax Christi was dubbed
the "Catholic peace movement" by no less a figure than Pope Pius XII. Still,
however, probably no other program in the Catholic Church has been subject
to such misunderstanding—especially in the United States, where violence
undoubtedly plays a central role in American life. In many circles (Catholic
included), Pax Christi is mistakenly seen as a product of the liberal sixties,
just another antiwar movement. Pace, however, contends that its roots go
much deeper:

> Pax Christi's agenda, grounded in the gospel, especially the Beati-
> tudes, and in the rich body of Catholic social teaching, promotes

peace and social justice for all. As such, it is one of the most "conservative" Catholic organizations I know, not modeled after Constantine's church of the third to fourth century or a medieval monarchy, but on Jesus.

While Pax Christi is noted mainly for its antiwar activity, it deals with a wide variety of issues: workers' rights and environmental justice, poverty, racism and sexism, peace in the home itself. Members take a vow of nonviolence, striving to be peacemakers in their daily lives, pursuing "nonviolence of tongue and heart," living simply and "actively resisting evil and working nonviolently to abolish war and the causes of war from my own heart and from the face of the earth."

In Italian, pace means "peace," and Rosemarie Pace certainly exudes peace in her Greenwich Village office. But as director of Pax Christi Metro New York, she's often "juggling one hundred things at the same time": planning programs and lectures, issuing public statements, working with other faith communities, and organizing events such as the annual Good Friday Way of the Cross procession in Manhattan—an event she describes as "the most profound prayer experience I've ever had in my life."

A lifelong educator, this Queens native has taught at every level from grammar to graduate school. When Rosemarie first read about Pax Christi in a newspaper, she was a tenured professor at the Bronx's College of Mount St. Vincent. Its combination of two important issues, Catholicism and peace activism, caught her attention. After further investigation and reflection, she joined Pax Christi's Queens chapter in 1987. She really learned about Pax Christi, she says, "by being there."

As a teacher, she recalls, she was attracted to its emphasis on educating the public. Their program of study, prayer, and action further intersected with her educational work. "The newness of what I was learning," she says, "struck a nerve." More than that, she was fascinated "by the people themselves," particularly their vow of nonviolence: "Pax Christi became community for me."

In the process she found a new calling, one that built on her teaching. Increasingly drawn to the group's work, she debated whether to devote herself to it full time. "Am I crazy enough?" she asked. Switching from the college to Pax Christi, she recalls, "was an almost mystical experience. My heart said, 'Pax Christi'; my head said, 'You're crazy.'" It was on a retreat in the Canadian Rockies that she "learned to turn it all over." Listening to

David Haas's hymn "You Are Mine," she found God "saying to me, 'This is where you are.'"

In 1991 Rosemarie went to Central America with Augsburg College's Center for Global Education. It was an "eye-opening experience," she says, meeting with government officials, labor leaders, and the people themselves, whose "amazing faith and wisdom" deeply impressed her. That same year Pax Christi opposed the first war in Iraq. It was a "lonely" fight, she recalls. She also went back to school, to study at the Fordham School of Religious Education. Most of what she learned, though, was learned "on the job."

On the job, she daily addresses issues such as nuclear weapons, school shootings, and peace in the Middle East—always avoiding partisan politics and keeping focused on the issues themselves. She organizes programs on conflict resolution and forgiveness, gives talks at high schools on war and peace, and works with schools to promote issues of social justice. In addition to advocacy, she notes, "Much of what we do is education." Interfaith work is a primary focus. Pax Christi participates in local rallies against violence and religious hatred. Its peacemaker honorees include Muslim women and Jewish rabbis.

Peacemaking today, Rosemarie comments, "is a hard sell," especially in the post–9/11 era where "patriotism is so tied in with supporting wars." But she sees God's hand in the work, and it keeps her going. She sees it in the people (those "Pax Christi saints"), in the issues addressed, in the lives that experience healing—in short, "in everything." Like Thomas Merton, she sees writing as a form of prayer. In the world's media capital, in a time of increased violence and hate, Pax Christi points out another way, and Rosemarie Pace continues to work as a channel of Christ's peace, in the city and the world.

57

DEACON GREG KANDRA
Our Lady Queen of Martyrs Church, Forest Hills

You can appreciate how big the faith is by the bigness of the city itself.

—GREG KANDRA

Gone are the days when Catholic media consisted mainly of diocesan newspapers and some independent journals. With the new media, Catholics at all levels are active. Popes tweet, cardinals and bishops blog regularly, and news is online long before it "makes the papers." In *America* magazine, Deacon Greg Kandra, a professional journalist and blogger, writes, "It just might be that of all the forms of communication, the Internet is the most catholic; the Web is truly universal."

Before his ordination, Greg worked for twenty-six years in broadcast news, winning two Emmys. Later he started television's first Catholic daily news show. Today he edits *One*, a magazine for the Catholic Near East Welfare Association. A popular speaker, he's best known for his blog "The Deacon's Bench," with over five million visitors since its inception. As a deacon he ministers at Our Lady Queen of Martyrs in Forest Hills, where he and his wife, Siobhan, live.

A Maryland native and University of Maryland graduate, he worked for CBS's Washington bureau before transferring to New York, where "everything is louder, bigger, bolder. The volume is turned up on life in a different way." By his own admission a "suburban kid," he didn't fall in love with New York when he first arrived; "it kind of grew on me."

He loved the work and atmosphere at CBS. It was exciting, he says, to be "part of a dynamic operation at such an exciting time, working with such incredibly gifted people." He had, he notes, "a front-row seat in some of the greatest events in modern history." As a producer and writer, he would earn every major journalism award.

At a certain point, he reflects, "Professionally I achieved all I wanted to achieve." He wanted something more. He wasn't an active churchgoer then. "I was a journalist," he says, "before I was a serious Catholic." But he was undergoing what he calls a "maturing process, something we all go through"— thinking more seriously about his purpose in life. September 11, 2001, was the catalyst drawing him closer to his faith.

That morning, he arrived at the CBS offices just before the first tower fell. Not for three days would he get home to his wife. He adds, "I realized how impermanent everything is." In the days and weeks following 9/11, Greg attended Mass "more fervently and regularly." An important influence on his spiritual growth was the New Yorker turned Trappist monk, Thomas Merton. His father-in-law had earlier sent him a copy of Merton's autobiography, *The Seven Storey Mountain*.

Reading it on vacation, he "fell into it. I felt like he was talking directly to me." A retreat at a Trappist monastery proved "very beautiful and very haunting." There he met an English deacon who worked at BBC. "You should be a deacon," he told Greg, who was "flabbergasted. No one ever said that to me before." As a boy, he briefly considered priesthood, but this was different.

He discussed it with Siobhan, who was "a little taken aback." She suggested waiting until retirement. But over the next few weeks, "Deacons started materializing in our life. Surfing the channels, I'd come across a roundtable of deacons talking about the diaconate on the Prayer Channel. My wife had similar experiences." Finally, he talked to his pastor about applying: "It was either complete the application right away or wait two years. It was a sign to do it now."

Over the next five years he took courses in everything from scripture to moral theology. Looking back at his ordination, he says, "So much of it is a blur." He does remember kneeling in front of the bishop. "As he placed his hands on my head, I felt different, I can't explain it. Call it the Holy Spirit, call it grace."

As a deacon, he assists at three or four Masses every Sunday, preaching and distributing Communion. During the week he's at parish council meetings, instructing people who are becoming Catholic, doing wedding rehearsals, Stations of the Cross during Lent, and much more. His favorite part of being a deacon, he says, is "breaking open the Word of God to people, getting them to think of the gospel as something immediate and real in front of them."

But his most famous ministry is "The Deacon's Bench," the blog he started in 2007. In a recent interview, he explained why he began it:

> Too many blogs were skewed to people who were either very progressive or very conservative. They also tended to be strident and, often, angry. I wanted to capture the middle ground and offer a Catholic perspective that was accessible and entertaining.

Kandra stresses the unity of the church: "Madonna and Mother Angelica; Mariachi and Latin Masses; social justice and prolife Catholics. We're all Catholic, and we need to accept and appreciate all that that means." He has no agenda to promote, he insists, noting that he's taken flack from left and right. "It means I must be doing something right."

One Catholic New Yorker he admires is Fulton Sheen, a "larger-than-life character" in radio and television. An important figure today, he believes, is Cardinal Timothy Dolan, whom he considers a "transformative figure in our church. He loves the culture, he loves the people. He's like lightning in a bottle." Dolan, he believes along with many other new media Catholics, may be the "greatest evangelizer in the church today."

Deacon Greg Kandra is proud to be a New York Catholic. "You can appreciate how big the faith is," he argues, "by the bigness of the city itself." Growing up in the suburbs, he notes, many churches were built after World War II. He's impressed by "the incredible churches we have here. Churches after churches in Brooklyn that look like cathedrals are actually ordinary parishes built by people who had nothing. It's very humbling and very inspiring to be part of that today."

58

MOTHER AGNES DONOVAN

Sisters of Life, Suffern

This is a city of great saints and great sinners.
—THE MOTHER OF AGNES DONOVAN

When Dr. Agnes Donovan moved to New York City thirty years ago, her mother (a New York native) wrote her a letter welcoming her to the city. "Agnes," she wrote, "this is a city of great saints and great sinners." A Pennsylvania native, Donovan had just taken a prestigious position at Columbia University, a job she expected to hold for the rest of her life. But something unexpected happened along the way, and to the surprise of her peers, she left academia for religious life. Today as Mother Agnes, she serves as superior general of the Sisters of Life, a religious community of women founded in New York by Cardinal John J. O'Connor to care for "vulnerable human life" at its various stages, but primarily the earliest.

A native of northeastern Pennsylvania, Agnes Mary Donovan grew up in a predominantly Irish American farming community. Her father was a local, but her mother grew up in Queens. Religious life, she notes, was something she never really considered. Instead, she went on to college and graduate school. In 1985 she earned a doctorate in psychology from the University of North Carolina at Chapel Hill. Later, at the College of William and Mary, she directed the graduate program in psychology before moving to New York.

In New York, Dr. Donovan taught in the Child Development Department at Teachers College, directed Columbia's Literacy Center, and engaged in private practice. "It was wonderful teaching at Columbia," she recalls. Teachers College was a sort of "secular monastery—serious scholars, a great spirit of camaraderie, a quiet place of academic pursuit." In a recent interview, she recalled, "I was happy and thought I would be there the rest of my life. But I always knew in my heart the distinction between a career and a vocation, and I knew that I had not yet found my vocation."

Then she began to consider religious life. After making an extended retreat in 1990 she became more conscious of a religious vocation, but the how and the where still eluded her. One Sunday, as she attended Mass at St. Patrick's Cathedral, she heard Cardinal O'Connor talk about his plans to start a new women's community whose charism would be uniquely the protection and enhancement of the sacredness of human life. As she remembers it, "I contacted the chancery, one thing led to another, and that following summer I entered."

At Columbia, the reaction of her academic peers tended to be "very varied." Some considered it "a devastating waste of talent." Others asked how she could join an organization that "hurt women." But when she met with the president of the college, she got a surprisingly different reaction. After listening to her story, he looked at her and said, "You know, Agnes, in my day, we called it a gift."

On June 1, 1991, Dr. Agnes Donovan became one of eight founding members of the Sisters of Life in New York City. She remembers those early years learning how to live religious life as "confusing in the extreme." None of the original members had any previous experience as religious. Two years later she was named superior general, a position she still holds today. Looking back, she recalls,

> As for my role as superior general, I have never done anything so difficult, but delightfully difficult. It takes all of myself, and requires a total integration of heart and mind to lead and to summon the energies of women who wish to dedicate their lives to God. It has also been a tremendous challenge to become a religious at the same time one is leading a new community.

Today there are about eighty Sisters working in New York, Connecticut, Washington, DC, and Toronto. As an apostolic community, they spend about four hours of their day in prayer, both private and communal. A major focus of the community's ministry is with pregnant women, for whom they provide residences and counseling. They offer a ministry of hope and healing to women who have experienced abortions as well as retreats to build up the culture of life.

In their former lives, some Sisters were teachers, some were nurses, one was a NASA engineer, another a biochemist. What attracts young women to the community? Some of the main components Mother Agnes sees are "a dedicated communal life of prayer, a focused apostolic work, and a visible community life." Young people today, she feels, are drawn to an "authentic following of the traditions of religious life."

She has a number of heroes. Regarding Cardinal O'Connor, she feels that "we'll look back and see his greatness, much more visibly than in his lifetime." She admires Dorothy Day for her "integrity, her grittiness, her truthfulness." She sees Elizabeth Seton as a "saint for everyone: mother, wife, convert, religious." Of Pierre Toussaint, she asks, "How could you not love that quiet saint, who did so much good?"

Today in New York she sees a great spirit of generosity among people "living their faith in the service of others." The Sisters have had literally hundreds of donors and volunteers through the years. She also sees modern witnesses at work today. She especially admires Monsignor Philip Reilly, a Brooklyn priest involved in the prolife movement for several decades. Of Cardinal Dolan she says, "Praise the Lord for him who communicates the message with such joy." Through the years New York has witnessed the birth of several religious communities. The Paulists were founded in the 1850s to evangelize the American people at a time when anti-Catholicism was rampant. In 1890s Manhattan, Rose Hawthorne Lathrop founded a community to serve the sick poor. For Mother Agnes, the Sisters of Life was founded to answer the question, "What does the church do to live its proclamation that every human life is sacred?" The Sisters, she believes, "are a sign of that commitment" at every stage of life.

59

FATHER MICHAEL GREENE

Bishop Molloy Retreat House, Jamaica Estates

In a busy place like New York, many people feel anonymous and don't know their neighbors. . . . We create community for a weekend.

   —MIKE GREENE

A retreat is a chance to put aside the demands of everyday life for a while, to spend some time alone with God, to go back home spiritually renewed. Most last a weekend, some longer. Many religions (and even nonreligions) have retreats in one form or another, but the majority are under Catholic auspices. Today, there is one Catholic retreat house operating in New York City: Bishop Molloy Retreat House in Queens. Since 1924 the Passionist community has conducted hundreds of retreats there for people from all walks of life, providing an oasis of peace in the middle of a busy metropolis.

Throughout the year, a variety of weekend retreats are offered for individuals and groups, the latter organized mainly according to gender, profession, and parish. Matt Talbot retreats are offered for men and women in recovery from addiction. From Friday night through Sunday morning, a series of conferences and workshops are organized around a particular spiritual theme, along with liturgies and prayer services. Free time alone or with others is also an important part of the retreat. Father Michael Greene, a staff member and veteran retreat director, feels there's a special need for retreat houses in big cities like New York.

For most of his priesthood, Father Greene has served at the community's New York retreat houses. One of the most important gifts a retreat can offer, he contends, is a renewed sense of community. "In a busy place like New York," he notes, "many people feel anonymous and don't know their neighbors." At Bishop Molloy, "We create community for a weekend. Sometimes people just want to have a meal with somebody." When people are asked why they come there, he observes, "Ninety percent say, 'I just want to get closer to God, to be with other people who want the same thing.' The retreat gives them a different experience."

Like many cradle Catholics, Michael Greene first thought about the priesthood in parochial school. (His parents were both converts to Catholicism.) One of five children, he grew up in the Bronx and Harlem. At St. Thomas the Apostle School on West 118th Street in Harlem, he and his siblings were taught by the Sisters of the Blessed Sacrament, a community dedicated to serving African Americans. It was a positive experience, he recalls: "We were their mission; it was a special thing. They were dedicated to us." In Harlem, he adds, "The only white people we knew were the priests and the nuns."

In 1970, after graduating from Bishop Dubois High School in Harlem, he enlisted in the U.S. Navy. "I met a lot of good people there," he says. It was there that "my vocation was fostered." His interest in the Passionists began when he discovered *Sign* magazine, a Passionist publication. His chaplain was a Passionist. During a visit back home he visited their retreat house in the Bronx. Six weeks after receiving his honorable discharge, Michael Greene joined the community. He was ordained in May 1982.

His first assignment was to a Passionist parish in Baltimore. From there he did his first retreat work, at St. Gabriel's—a retreat house for youth on

Shelter Island. "They were mainly city kids," he recalls, "and Shelter Island with its ten buildings, land, beaches—was a spiritual Disneyland. Just coming over on the ferry was an experience for some of them." At the retreat house, they "had the opportunity to pray, to be quiet, to enjoy each other outside the normal school setting, and have access to the sacraments." The experience gave "the kids a chance to look back on their lives and look ahead, get straight with whatever's going on at home and at school."

After three years on Shelter Island, he was sent to Cardinal Spellman Retreat House in the Bronx. "There you dealt mainly with adults. You learn to talk adult again." Subsequent assignments brought him to Scranton, where he worked in the community's media program, and later to an African American parish in Atlanta. "The advantage of working in a parish," he says, "is that you get to know people on all sorts of levels for a long time."

Today, Father Greene is in his second assignment to Bishop Molloy. In terms of its visitors, it's one of the most diverse retreat houses he's encountered, and as such is "a reflection of the city we live in." Besides the retreats, Bishop Molloy offers many programs—for married couples and youth, for non-Catholic groups. Their days of recollection, he notes, "have standing room only."

For those who can't commit to a full weekend, there are "Dinner-to-Dinner" Retreats. But whether they stay for a night or a weekend, they get the chance to spiritually recharge, to regain a sense of balance and perspective, to take a good look at themselves, their family, friends, and business associates. "One of the great pluses of retreat work," he notes, "is that you're inviting people into your own home. When people come here, they feel at home. They're ready to go to Confession, get square with God, open their hearts. People come hungry."

"For me as a priest," Father Greene reflects, "the greatest reward is this: They come Friday one way, they leave Sunday another way. We have thirty-six hours. People can pray. They can say, 'Father, can I see you a minute?' Or they can have a meal if that's what they want. Taking people where they're at is Passionist hospitality." That may be one of the most important gifts that the Passionists can offer to the New Yorkers. "We preach Christ crucified," Father Greene says. "We stand with people in the midst of their suffering. We do Alcoholics Anonymous retreats; we work with the aged, with the physically poor, with the sick and dying. It's not just for people who got it all."

60

Paul Moses

Brooklyn College, Flatbush

Who we are contributes to the life of this city.
—Paul Moses

Many bishops lamented the outcome of the 2012 election, but few as strongly as Brooklyn's Bishop Nicholas DiMarzio, who argued that "those who voted for President Obama bear the responsibility for a step deeper in the culture of death." Writing in *Commonweal*, an independent Catholic journal, Paul Moses noted that DiMarzio himself cultivated close ties with prochoice politicians for support on other issues dear to the bishop's heart. "It's to be expected," Moses concluded, "that a bishop would weigh the pluses and minuses of the candidates in light of church teaching. Members of his flock are entitled to do the same."

This isn't the first time that Moses, a prize-winning journalist and professor of journalism, took church leaders to task. His remarks highlight the difference between a Catholic journalist and a journalist who is Catholic. Journalists working for the institutional church don't always have the same critical freedom as a writer working outside the ecclesiastical system. Over the years, Moses has written widely for secular and religious publications, ranging from the *Village Voice* to the *St. Anthony Messenger*. A former religion reporter for *Newsday*, he puts himself in the latter category.

While Moses lived in New England for several years, for him "Brooklyn is home." The Flatlands of his childhood was a predominantly Jewish and Catholic neighborhood. (Not until fifteen did he meet someone his age who was Protestant.) His father, a Jewish convert to Catholicism, worked for the Housing Authority, while his Italian American mother was a cradle Catholic. "My parents," he recalls, "were among the few liberals in the neighborhood." At Mary Queen of Heaven School, he was taught by the Sparkill Dominicans, a strict conservative order. "In some ways," he says, "it was sort of a throwback education. But it was offset by the influence at home."

At Nazareth High School in East Flatbush, he had a richer experience.

The teachers, mostly Xaverian Brothers, were very progressive. "It was a tremendous time," he recalls. "The teachers were young. Many of them went on to impressive careers. The place was filled with the spirit of Vatican II." There he became active with the Cursillo, a retreat movement he considers "a transforming experience. You can study all you want, but when you feel something about your Catholic faith, it brings the teachings to life."

It was during the retreats that Paul met his wife, Maureen. For the last seven years, they've worked with engaged couples in the Brooklyn Diocese. "That's our ministry," he says. Over the years they've served as Eucharistic ministers and catechists, and Paul has served as president of the parish council.

After graduating from Brooklyn College in 1975 Moses studied creative writing at the University of Massachusetts. From there he went into journalism and, after a stint with the Associated Press, joined the staff of *Newsday*, sharing a Pulitzer Prize for spot reporting. He served as city editor and, before leaving in 2001, was the national religion writer.

He then returned to Brooklyn College to teach journalism. His most recent book, *The Saint and the Sultan*—which covers Francis of Assisi's attempt to bring peace to the Middle East during the Crusades—has been praised for promoting interreligious dialogue in a post–9/11 world.

It's hard to say there's any one such thing as a "Catholic New Yorker," Moses feels, because the community is so diverse. Still, he believes, the influence of the Irish shouldn't be underestimated. Here, he argues, "Irish and Catholic go together." He sees their legacy most present in the penchant for service in the church, in the police and fire departments, and in service professions. In many ways, he contends, other ethnic groups such as the Italians have become "Hibernicized" through their involvement in the church. (Paul is currently working on a book covering Irish-Italian relations in the city.)

Because Catholics form close to a religious majority, Moses says, "Who we are contributes to the life of this city. Catholics are part of the fabric of life in New York City." In the period directly following September 11, 2001, he recalls "one Catholic funeral after another." He notes the proliferation of candles and statues on city streets, of prayers posted publicly on street corners. He cites religious imagery in Bruce Springsteen's song "The Rising." "In this time of greatest need," he adds, "you see the Catholic nature of the city."

There's also the Catholic ethos, which places a high emphasis on the common good. A good example of this ethos in action is the late Frank Mac-chiarola's "life of service." A product of Brooklyn Catholic schools, Macchi-arola "brought Catholic values into the civic life of the community" as New York City schools chancellor, dean of the Yeshiva University Law School, and president of St. Francis College. Other examples of this ethos in action in-clude Edward McGlynn, the nineteenth-century social activist priest; Catho-lic Worker founder Dorothy Day; and Brooklyn bishop Francis J. Mugavero.

Moses contends that through the influence of people like Frank Mac-chiarola, the Catholic ethos has influenced the public school system. Suc-cessful public schools, for example, have been picking up certain Catholic school values, such as discipline, order, and even uniforms. Furthermore, he contends, the Catholic style of education attends to the whole student, rather than just looking for short-term results. Public school teachers and princi-pals who are Catholic, he feels, bring these values to the table.

While he's not uncritical of the church and its leadership, Paul Moses likes being a New York Catholic—"There's an enormous tradition behind us. I don't want to sound triumphalistic, but I feel proud of my city and my re-ligion." He's proud of the rich legacy of service, not just to Catholics, but to all New Yorkers. He's proud of the commitment to social justice. Catholics, he feels, shouldn't underestimate the difference they make in the life of the city, nor the extent of their contribution to the common good: past, present, and future.

61

ROSANJELA BATISTA

Cristo Rey High School, Harlem

Knowing you made an impact—that's the difference.

—ROSA BATISTA

Every year seems to bring worse news for Catholic schools. Since 2001, almost two thousand have closed nationwide. Empty buildings stand testament to a once powerful educational system. But out of the ashes a phoenix is rising. A new, successful model has arrived, where students from low-income families receive a quality college-prep education. It started in 1996, when some Chicago Jesuits turned an abandoned parochial school into Cristo Rey High School for disadvantaged urban youth. Today there are twenty-five schools nationwide, all named for the first.

In 2004 New York's Cristo Rey High School opened in Harlem as a collaboration between the Jesuits, the Christian Brothers, and the Holy Child Sisters. Tuition is kept low (two thousand dollars a year) through the Corporate Work Study Program, where students work one day a week at some of New York's most prestigious companies. The companies pay toward the student's tuition, while the rest of the money is made through fundraising. One hundred percent of graduates are accepted to college. Jesuit Father Joe Parkes, the school's president, comments, "It's one thing to talk about social justice. It's another thing to get up off your ass and do something about it."

Rosanjela Batista's cousin belonged to the school's first graduating class. She "fell into" Cristo Rey, she says, by accident. As she was completing a graduate degree in mathematics, a friend teaching at Cristo Rey went on sabbatical. "Could you take over my classes?" she asked Rosa. Originally Rosa said no, but she reconsidered. "What she saw," she reflects, "I don't know. It was quite an honor for her to think of me." She's been teaching math to juniors and seniors ever since, with no plans of leaving.

An only child, Rosa Batista grew up in Alphabet City, a neighborhood that's undergone significant gentrification. "Oh my God," she comments, "the changes are astronomical!" She still lives there with her mother. "If you work at a Catholic school, you kind of have to." As a child, she attended Holy Child School and Notre Dame, both in Greenwich Village. Like her Cristo Rey students, she was the first in her family to go to college.

Life at Villanova University was a unique experience. "I learned a lot," she says, "and I taught a lot." Many of her classmates came from affluent suburban families. "When I told people I was from New York," she recalls, "they assumed I meant Long Island." When she said she was from Alphabet City, they asked, "Do you hear people shooting outside your window?" "Not since the 1980s," she responded. Later she founded the Latin American Student Organization: "'Let's see if we can diversify Villanova,' I said."

After graduation, she went back to New York, taking a teaching job at her alma mater. It wasn't an experience that captured her imagination, and she went on to graduate school at St. John's. Then the invitation to Cristo Rey came. Eventually, she says, she "fell in love with the work, especially the impact we have each day." Today, her first students have graduated college. "They come back to visit," she notes with a happy pride. "Knowing you made an impact—that's the difference."

The Jesuit notion of *Cura Personalis* (personal care) plays an important role. Students here "are anything but a number." Every morning, Principal Bill Ford greets each student by name at the door. "It shocks the kids," Rosa observes, "how he knows all their names. On day one, when the freshmen walk through the door, we know who they are." Furthermore, she adds, "Our students look to us to see what a role model is. It's hard on us to have to always live up to it."

Students at Cristo Rey are not referred to as freshman or seniors, but rather by the year of their college graduation. Rosa comments, "Here it's not, 'Am I going to college?' It's, 'You are going to college.' We're not here to see you fail." The school's reputation has already grown: "People say about Cristo Rey, 'Oh, everybody goes to college there.'" For most students, no one in their family went to college. "It's the norm," Rosa says. "But if you're going to be a student here, you need to see there's a different future for you."

Regarding the work program, Rosa sees the students excited about their internships. "They're doing real work," she notes. "People on the 6 train know that they're Cristo Rey students by how they're dressed going down to Wall Street." They work at banks, law firms, and hospitals. "They come back to Cristo Rey and say, 'That's what I want to be doing.' Sometimes they say, 'This is definitely not what I want to do!'" At Cristo Rey, she proudly observes, "They're practically equipped for the world."

For Rosa Batista, the best part about teaching at Cristo Rey is "seeing a child grow into a true adult, able to hold an adult conversation." Furthermore, she adds, "I love being here, I love this model, and I love what we do for the kids." She adds, "*They* make a difference in *our* lives every day." There may not be as many Jesuits in classrooms as there used to be, but it's clear that *Cura Personalis* is alive and well at Cristo Rey New York, thanks to teachers like Rosa Batista.

62

Brother Tyrone Davis

Office of Black Ministry, Archdiocese of New York

The people of the ministry, the welcoming of the stranger, in the struggling of the longtime faithful Catholic, the confused convert, and the sometimes bewildered outsider. . . . We have to be at the tables.
—Tyrone Davis

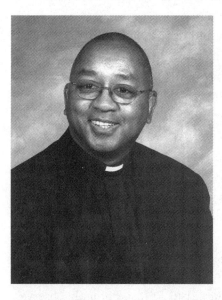

On the outside, 1011 First Avenue, the headquarters for the Roman Catholic Archdiocese of New York, looks like any other corporate building on New York's Upper East Side. Dating back to 1973 it houses a parish church, a girls' high school, and a myriad of offices from the archdiocesan newspaper to the cardinal's office. My appointment brings me to the sixteenth floor, where Brother Tyrone Davis, a member of the Congregation of Christian Brothers, has directed the Office of Black Ministry for the last nineteen years.

A trained lawyer and educator, Brother Tyrone notes that the office's title is not "Office of Black Catholics," or "Black Catholic Ministry," but simply "Office of Black Ministry." Its purpose is to assist *all* persons of African descent, regardless of creed. Hence it is both ecumenical and service oriented. At a recent dinner sponsored by the office, the chairpersons were a black Protestant and his Jewish Ethiopian wife. Honorees included a Filipino priest and a Jewish benefactor of the program. All this, Davis notes, is rooted in the Catholic understanding of community.

That sense of community directed a fifth-grader toward Catholicism. Catholicism, Davis notes, was an "ominous presence" in 1960s Newark. Growing up near Blessed Sacrament Church on Van Ness Place, he decided he wanted to be part of it (especially the parish drum and bugle corps). Knocking on the rectory door, the priest advised him to consult his family first. His mother's immediate reaction was, "What did you do this time, boy?" But he became a Catholic and transferred to Blessed Sacrament School.

At Newark's Essex Catholic High School, Tyrone Davis first encountered the Christian Brothers (traditionally known as the *Irish* Christian Brothers, as opposed to the De La Salle Christian Brothers). Back then he had no interest in joining the predominantly white community. He was, however, close to the school's only black brother, one of his "most passionate teachers." This was the era of the Newark riots, a time when the young man was "struggling" with his own Catholicism. Majoring in education at Ohio's Case Western Reserve University, he felt himself moving further away from the Catholic Church.

After several years in the Cleveland public schools, Davis took a teaching job at a local Catholic school. Middle school was a far different experience from earlier jobs, and it turned out to be the "most kick-butt year" of his career. "Part of the recipe that brought me back to the Catholic Church," he recalls, was prayer. To get through a tough day, he found himself going to Mass each morning, saying, "Lord, I need your help today." At the same time, he found a great experience of Christian fellowship in the black Catholic community.

Soon he began exploring a religious vocation. "I felt the Lord was calling me to ministry." He moved back east to join the Christian Brothers, teaching at their schools in New Jersey and Staten Island. He eventually became vice principal of his alma mater. At night he earned a law degree from Seton Hall, and for several years he worked in the Brooklyn district attorney's office. Law, he notes, was another form of ministry, a "justice ministry." Representing the people for him was more than just winning a case. It was a matter of "doing justice."

But he felt called to do something more, and around this time a priest friend suggested applying for directorship of the archdiocese's Black Ministry Office. He frankly admits he didn't relish the idea of working for Cardinal John O'Connor, whom he considered "too much of a politician." Still he took the job, and over time his relationship with O'Connor developed into mutual respect. Over time, he came to "deeply love" the cardinal, whose passing "was a great personal loss."

It's turned out to be the longest job he's ever held. One of the main reasons, he notes, is that his ministry is constantly changing. It's "life-giving," he says. What was originally considered an outreach specifically for African American and Caribbean Catholics has developed into a ministry involving the entire black community. His first Black History Month Mass was strictly in English. "Now, it's multilingual, multinational, and *black.*"

In recent years, he notes, the office has been reaching out to the Eritrean community. For twenty-five years, Davis notes, the number of Eritrean Catholics in the tristate area has been slowly growing. At home they had their own priests and their own liturgical rite. For years, they have had to worship here without the benefit of either, although this situation is slowly changing. The Eritreans, he contends, embody a major trait of the black Catholic community, its "uncommon faithfulness."

People from all walks of life call the office nationwide with "every conceivable need": information, referrals, financial advice, homework assignments, even finding a spouse. "People realize the role of the church in New York," Davis observes, and in some ways the office serves as a sort of clearinghouse for black Catholic life in America. After all, he points out, New York is "the national diocese."

One Catholic New Yorker Davis especially admires is Pierre Toussaint, the Haitian-born layman whose canonization cause is under way. (The office sponsors a scholarship and dinner in his name.) He sees in Pierre a committed believer who used all the means in his power to build up God's kingdom in New York, a man unafraid to question the larger evils of his day. He also sees a link between Pierre and the office's interfaith work: "Pierre couldn't imagine himself excluding anyone because of their religion."

For Brother Tyrone Davis, the black Catholic experience is the story of a people's deep-seated faithfulness, the journey of a people of service, active in ministry. He sees God most closely in "the people of the ministry, the welcoming of the stranger, in the struggling of the longtime faithful Catholic, the confused convert, and the sometimes bewildered outsider . . . We have to be at the tables." More than anything, their experience highlights the very meaning of the word *catholic*: "universal."

63

Peter Quinn

Hastings-on-Hudson

It's easy to be Catholic here, in a great metropolitan city, the city that runs the world.
— Peter Quinn

Since its release in 1994, Peter Quinn's *Banished Children of Eve*, a historical novel of nineteenth-century New York, has been hailed as one of the best fictional renditions of urban immigrant life. For those seeking to better understand the era and its people, one can do no better than this epic account of the 1863 New York City draft riots. A fourth-generation Irish American from the Bronx whose ancestors fled the Great Famine in 1840s Ireland, Quinn wrote the novel as a way to better understand his own roots: Irish, Catholic, and New York.

Growing up in the postwar Bronx, the center of his world was St. Raymond's, the oldest parish in the Bronx, a veritable Irish megachurch. "We were more Catholic than anything else," he recalls. "That's what it meant to be Irish in the Bronx: identification with your parish, your school, knowing you were Irish but not knowing much about it." It was a world nobody thought would ever change, yet change it did. After a year as a VISTA volunteer, Quinn returned to the Bronx in 1970 to find his childhood world gone: "The neighborhoods went away. The church changed, the city changed." He concluded, "I've got to go back and find out something about it."

Quinn's Bronx roots run deep. In 1847 his great-great-grandparents married in Our Lady of Mercy Church (now the Fordham University Campus Church). His father, Peter A. Quinn, served for twenty-five years as a judge in city and state courts. A daily communicant and devout Democrat, he stressed loyalty to both. "Belief in the Democratic Party," Peter recalls, "was ingrained in me as a child." But loyalty to the church didn't rule out criticism. His father, for example, felt Cardinal Spellman tended to favor the Republicans.

As a boy he remembers young Father John Flynn praising the work of a Protestant minister named Martin Luther King (complimenting Protestant clergy wasn't common in 1959). Flynn became a much-loved inner-city pastor and activist. In eighth grade, invited to consider entering a high school seminary, he thought, *How could I not be honored at the thought of God calling me to be a priest?* But his father nixed the idea, insisting that fourteen-year-olds had no real idea of a calling.

Instead he attended Manhattan Prep, a Bronx high school run by the Christian Brothers, whom he credits with teaching "me how to think for myself" and giving "me my skill as a writer." In the fall of 1962, at the start of the Second Vatican Council, he recalls one of his teachers, a Brother Patrick, telling the students, "Don't get any delusions. This isn't going to change anything."

But it did. In 1967 at Manhattan College, he stopped attending Mass. After briefly teaching Catholic school, he became a court officer in the Bronx, a job he would hate "more with each passing day." In the long run, though, it gave him a fuller appreciation of what his own immigrant ancestors' experience must have been like. "History took on flesh and blood in ways it never had before."

As a graduate student at Fordham, Quinn studied Irish history, but he decided against an academic career. His studies, however, "gave me a fuller appreciation of the complexity and richness of Catholic culture and thought." His first published article, in the Jesuits' *America* magazine, led to his being hired as a speechwriter for Governor Hugh Carey. (Quinn helped write Mario Cuomo's famous speech at Notre Dame in 1984, in which the governor discussed abortion and his Catholic faith.) Later he went to Time Warner as a speechwriter, "a corporate prose monger."

While he was there, *Banished Children of Eve* was published to popular and critical acclaim. Reflecting on his Irish roots, he once said, "We didn't know that much about ourselves." Writing the book was a way to find out. Earlier he had considered writing a sweeping social history of the Irish immigrants and to tell their story in novel form. In response to one critic's charge that the book "lacked a central character," Quinn responded, "The central character is New York. The city touches, transforms, transfixes everyone who comes in contact with it—enriches, debases, exalts, crushes, renews—so that, one way or another, no one comes away unchanged."

By its very nature, Peter Quinn contends, New York City "is Catholic, it's universal. It's part of the universal experience that includes everyone." From the start, he notes, "You're aware of other people. Even as you're living in your own culture, you're still aware that yours is not the only culture." For example, he argues, if New York is the capital of Catholic America, it's also the Jewish capital in America, and it's the capital of gay America. "It's easy," he maintains, "to be Catholic here, in a great metropolitan city, the city that runs the world."

Peter Quinn is a New York Catholic, a Catholic who thinks of New York as "my country." Today, he feels the church has none of the "suffocating insularity" of earlier days. "While they listen to their bishops and priests," he writes, laypeople "weigh other opinions and make up their own minds. No encyclical, fiat, or anathema will change that." While the days of crowded rectories and convents are over, perhaps never to return, Quinn doesn't fear a mass exodus from the church. Instead, he contends, younger people "will continue to practice the Catholic faith, although in more syncretic and free-spirited ways than their grandparents."

64

PETER FORTUNATE VALLONE SR.
Former New York City Council Speaker, Astoria, Queens
A Catholic should be a perennial optimist.
—PETER VALLONE

Catholicism is best found in its neighborhood parishes (in New York City, there are nearly four hundred), and New York is above all a city of neighborhoods. Ask a New York Catholic of a certain age, "Where do you live?" and he or she names the parish. Peter Vallone is a child of a New York parish.

When Immaculate Conception Church was erected on Ditmars Boulevard and Twenty-Ninth Street after World War I, much of Astoria was still untouched farmland. But things were changing, as subways and bridges brought newcomers seeking to leave overcrowded Manhattan. To former tenement dwellers, Queens must have seemed idyllic. The parish's small but growing congregation, composed of many recent immigrants, included a young lawyer, Charles Vallone; his wife, Leah; and their two sons, Charles Jr. and Peter.

Growing up in the shadow of the Hell Gate Bridge, Peter Vallone's childhood was a happy one. In a day when ecumenism was suspect he grew up in a household that prized diversity. "This 'melting pot' ideal," he writes, "was more than just words for my father." Every year Charles Vallone led Brotherhood Day parades up Ditmars Boulevard with a minister and rabbi. As they passed Immaculate Conception, the pastor shouted, "Vallone, you should be ashamed of yourself. You are going to be excommunicated!" Peter recalls, "Dad would merely tip his hat in respect and keep marching—and never missed Mass on Sunday." Today he still serves as a lector and Eucharistic minister in the parish.

When Peter was thirteen, his mother was diagnosed with cancer. Sister John Alicia, his religion teacher, told him not to worry. His mother would be alright. "Peter," she said, "I want you to say the rosary every day, and go to Mass as often as possible." His mother recovered. "Sixty-five years later," he comments, "I still go to Mass every day, and say the rosary." He sees it as a major source of his strength.

Peter Fortunate Vallone (named for his Sicilian immigrant grandfather) still lives in Astoria, not far from the apartment where he was raised. Like his father, he practices law on Thirty-First Street, just downstairs from the N train. But his reputation extends far beyond there. A speaker of the city council under three mayors, he's held political office for twenty-seven years. One scholar writes that he has "secured a place in New York City history—it is hard to imagine the city without him."

Public service was also stressed at home. Peter studied at Fordham Law School, but he didn't go into politics right away. In the early 1960s he wanted to run for the state senate, but his father warned him it wasn't time yet. "I love you, son," he said, but he was still voting for his opponent. "Electoral luck," Vallone writes in his memoir, came his way in 1974 when he was elected to the city council, where he made his political mark.

In 1990 he was elected as the council's first Speaker, the second highest official after the mayor. Among many accomplishments, he's been praised for helping create the council, promoting accountability, balancing the budget, and keeping the city's streets safe. Fully familiar with government at every level, he's earned the respect of friends and opponents, often serving as a bridge between them. Adept at handling all kinds of requests, he once helped Mother Teresa:

> On one occasion she held my hand and said, "Mr. Speaker, I need help in Vietnam—" when her assistant politely cut her off. "Mother, he is the Speaker of the City of New York, not Mr. Gingrich of the United States Congress." "Oh, yes," Mother Teresa replied. "Mr. Speaker, I need three parking spaces in front of this convent." "Well, Mother," I said, "*that* I could help you with!"

Politics, one politician told a young Vallone, is "the science of government." His experience has been "anything but." It's a means to an end, about getting things done. Peter Vallone gets things done. But for him, it's about more. He's fond of quoting the prophet Micah: "All that God requires of you is to do the right thing, to love goodness, and to walk humbly with your God" (Micah 6:6–8).

Being a Catholic politician today is no easy task, but he sees freedom as one of the best things about Catholicism. Rather than prolife or prochoice, he considers himself proconscience. God, he comments, doesn't ask us to judge other people's conscience. On hot-button issues like abortion and gay marriage, he insists on respecting the conscience of others and their right to exercise that conscience. This philosophy has helped "immeasurably" working with those holding different views.

Occasionally, it's put him in hot water with religious leaders. Brooklyn Bishop Thomas Daily, a leading abortion opponent, chided his proconscience stance, suggesting instead "correct conscience." Vallone replied, "I'm not in the business of condemnation. I leave that to God. I took an oath to obey and enforce the law to the best of my ability." He considers himself prolife "in the larger sense," meeting the needs of the poor and disadvantaged at all stages of life.

One person he admires is the late Cardinal John J. O'Connor, "a giant in life," for his humor and his integrity. "The only thing that I can say," he writes, "is that I loved the guy." At one gathering, O'Connor joked, "If I see Peter

Vallone one more time that would make three times in three days, and I'll have to make him a monsignor." Another hero is Father Mychal Judge, whose loss Vallone still mourns. Others include the teachers who formed him, and perhaps most of all, his own father.

"A Catholic," Peter Vallone writes, "should be a perennial optimist." He exudes optimism, cheer, and goodwill as he practices law down the block from the Judge Charles J. Vallone School. He and his wife of fifty-four years still live in the same house where his sons were raised. He remains the model of a lawyer and public servant, a neighborhood son to the end.

65

Sister Ann Marie Young

Visitation Monastery, Bay Ridge, Brooklyn

We're not perfect, but we're happy.
   —Ann Marie Young

A monastery isn't an institution normally associated with urban life, but New York City has no fewer than four. The oldest, Visitation Monastery, was founded in downtown Brooklyn in September 1855. Today it stands on eight acres of land in Bay Ridge, which the Sisters purchased in 1903. In addition to living a life of prayer and contemplation, the Visitation Sisters also run a successful girls' academy. The Sisters' chapel, an impressive church in its own right, has become an object of local veneration. Throughout the year women make retreats at the monastery, looking for time away from the busyness of city life.

Today the monastery is home to sixteen Sisters, ranging in age from fifty to ninety-one. No one has been there longer than Sister Ann MarieYoung, a member of the community for sixty-seven years. ("My last name is getting harder and harder to live up to," she laughs.) At eighty-seven, confined to a wheelchair, she still teaches religion to fifth-graders. "By the time they get to sixth grade," she comments, "they're different people." When she started teaching, Ita Ford was in the fourth grade. "She was a beautiful person," Sister

Ann Marie recalls, "full of tricks. She had everything, gave everything. She learned to live Jesus and love Jesus."

From early on, Ann Marie Young was drawn to religious life, but monastic life was something she never considered. Growing up in the Whitestone section of Queens, she was one of six children born to a Swedish German father and an Irish mother. After her father was seriously injured on a construction job, she went to work at Met Life to help support the family. Still, she always planned to enter the convent one day.

For a long time, Ann Marie set her sights on the Dominican Sisters, who taught her in grammar school and high school. But she began to take an interest in monastic life after reading a book on the subject from the New York Public Library. Her spiritual director referred her to the Visitation Sisters in Brooklyn, and she entered in 1947 with nine other women. Her sister accompanied her on the trip to Brooklyn. At the time, she recalls, "I was scared to go all the way to Brooklyn—Brooklyn had a bad name. And I'm an ardent Yankees fan."

Founded in seventeenth-century France, the Visitation community is primarily contemplative with an apostolic dimension in teaching. (Because schools and convents are physically attached, the rule of enclosure is not violated.) Since 1799 some twenty-two convents have been founded nationwide. "For my first thirty years," Sister Ann Marie notes, "we didn't go anywhere." After the rules were modified in the 1970s, she earned a library science degree at the Pratt Institute, serving as school librarian for thirty-one years.

Sister Ann Marie sees the monastery as "a place where people who really love God and want to serve him come together. We're not perfect, but we're happy." ("I couldn't stand a person who was perfect," she adds.) Recently, when one of the Sisters appeared on a television show, she was asked, "You mean there's a place in Brooklyn where you have peace and quiet?" The Sisters are there, she feels, for three groups: "Ourselves, our students, and the women who come here on retreat."

"We believe in prayer," Sister Ann Marie simply puts it. "Our prayer is meant to sustain people in the world." The monastery bulletin board, she notes, is covered with prayer requests from people all over the city, even the country. "You wouldn't believe it if you saw it." But they do more than pray. Every week, Sister Ann Marie calls a single mother who just lost her job, giving her counsel and comfort. "You don't know what talking to you means to me," the woman tells her. Many others come to visit her monthly, even weekly, to visit her, talk to her, and maybe gain a little of this peace that the monastery exudes. New York City needs monasteries, she insists. "It's an oasis of peace and prayer in this busy city."

The monastery day begins with wakeup at 5:30 a.m., and the Sisters are in their choir stalls by six-thirty. ("Nobody in the neighborhood ever complains about the bells," she says.) At seven they recite the Divine Office, the official prayer of the church, and Mass is at eight, followed by breakfast. For some, teaching takes up their morning duties, and another session of communal prayer precedes lunch. The afternoon, she notes, is "pretty quiet. You can stay in the choir and pray."

At 4 p.m., the Blessed Sacrament is exposed on the altar, which she calls "the second highlight of the day after Mass." Evening prayer at five is followed by dinner, then recreation. "We have a lot of Scrabble players. If you could see our recreation sometimes . . ." Bedtime is at 8:30 p.m., but she doesn't always go to sleep right away. "I like to do puzzles," she says.

The last few years have seen a number of new postulants. "We've been very fortunate," Sister Ann Marie comments. To anyone considering the monastery, she says, "You have to love prayer. If you don't love prayer, you won't stay here very long. You have to love God very much and be sure it's what you want." A monastery, she contends, is not a dark, gloomy place. "I tried writing a poem about this once," she says. "A monastery is like a light in the darkness. When Our Lord looks down, he sees this light in the darkness." "It's a joyful place," she adds. "We get joy out of seeing others happy."

66

MATTHEW SCHILLER

Catholic New York, Manhattan

As Catholic New Yorkers, we have all have two things in common: faith and geography. Everything else is up for grabs.

 —MATT SCHILLER

New York is heir to a rich tradition of Catholic journalism. Home to magazines such as the *Catholic World, America,* and *Commonweal,* the city became a national center for Catholic opinion. During the mid-twentieth century, even local diocesan newspapers like the *Catholic News* and the *Brooklyn Tablet* achieved a nationwide circulation. Today *Catholic New York,* the New York archdiocesan paper, has the largest circulation of any diocesan publication.

These days Matt Schiller, the paper's publisher, commutes from his home in northern New Jersey, but he still considers himself a New Yorker at heart, having grown up and worked here all his life. Since graduating from St. John's University in 1973 he's worked as business manager and publisher for both the *Tablet* and *Catholic New York.* "I'm proud of the fact that I've worked for two great Catholic newspapers," he says.

Born in Jersey City, the son of an insurance salesman and a Catholic school teacher, Schiller grew up in Queens' Briarwood section, a neighborhood he calls a "real mix" of ethnicities. It was a positive experience, he recalls. "Growing up there taught me about respecting people before you made any decisions about them." He also notes that he's walked to every school he ever attended: Our Lady of the Cenacle Parochial School, Archbishop Molloy High School, and St. John's University.

At Our Lady of the Cenacle, Schiller recounts, the Sisters of Charity of Halifax provided "a great sense of the faith." At Molloy, the Marist Brothers provided "a great sense of service"; through their projects and community service programs, they "put faith in action." At St. John's, the Vincentian Fathers had "a great heritage starting in Brooklyn and a rich tradition of serving the poor." There he studied business and became interested in communications, beginning with the *Tablet* after his graduation in 1973.

As a publisher, Schiller's job is to "pay for the paper, find ways to pay for it, and make sure that the paper is well produced and distributed." He's a big believer in high circulation as a way to get the paper into the hands of the greatest number of people. Schiller sees the Catholic press's purpose as "giving the people a Catholic voice, helping them to put things in perspective, and teaching people." "As a Catholic press," he feels, "we failed to adequately prepare people for the aftermath of Vatican II. What did people not know about Vatican II?"

Schiller sees much to celebrate in New York Catholicism. "Every single group is represented here," he notes. "As Catholic New Yorkers, we have all have two things in common: faith and geography. Everything else is up for grabs." In visiting places like Arkansas, for example, he sees a Catholic minority on the defensive ("The idea of one Catholic per square mile is amazing to me!") In South Dakota, where his father now lives, there's a homogeneity to the Catholicism there; most Catholics have a similar educational and socioeconomic background. Here, Schiller comments, "The world isn't something outside us—we're Haitian, Spanish, Filipino. Here there's always an energy—it's always so welcoming."

He loves the history surrounding St. Patrick's Cathedral on Fifth Avenue. Recently, his father and stepmother visited St. Pat's. Until then, the largest church she'd ever seen was the cathedral at Sioux Falls. She couldn't believe the size of the cathedral. "It's as close to Vatican City as you'll find in the U.S.," Schiller observes. At the side altars, "I always find something different: an icon, different saints you never knew." By his own admission, he's "a huge fan of crypts, and St. Pat's has one of the greatest: Cardinal Cooke, Archbishop Hughes, Pierre Toussaint, Fulton Sheen, and so many others. The stark sense of the presence of our forebears are there."

In the world today, Schiller sees a "tremendous need for service." For him, the church is "a shining example of service." The Catholic press, he points out, tells the story of so many service organizations asking for help, volunteers, and food. "Who else will do it, if not us?" he asks. He sees this "positive message" as a "counterbalance to the problems we've had since 2002. We're flawed, we have people who haven't done the right thing. But, still, look at what we do accomplish."

Among the many Catholic New Yorkers Schiller admires, he places *Tablet* editor Ed Wilkinson near the top. No one, he feels, has "has their finger on the pulse of the church in Brooklyn and Queens like he does." From Brooklyn bishop Francis Mugavero, he "learned how to treat people with compassion, respect, and firmness. Mugavero was always pastoral. He saw what the church could do in tough times." He'll always drop everything for Monsignor Matthew Foley, a longtime inner-city pastor in pregentrification Williamsburg. Among historical figures he admires New York archbishop John Hughes and his "great vision for the church. He saw where things are and where things need to be."

Once a New Yorker, always a New Yorker. Matt Schiller loves many things about the city: the sports, the exhilaration, the faith of the people. The qualities he admires most in New Yorkers are their forthrightness, their acceptance of newcomers, and their resilience. In New York, the Catholic press is alive and well, seeking to "bring the good news (capital and small 'g')" to as many of them as possible. He likes to quote Bishop Mugavero, who once said of the Catholic Church, "We're like the gas company. Our pipes are in the ground and we're not going anywhere."

67

Rudy Vargas IV

Field Consultant, University of Notre Dame, Alliance for Catholic Education (ACE) Consulting

To walk into a welcoming group of people embracing you, that is church.

—*Rudy Vargas*

Hispanics have always been part of New York City history, but only in recent decades did they arrive in any sizeable numbers. Today New York's Hispanic/Latino population hails from all corners of the Western Hemisphere, with the majority coming from Mexico. Local church outreach dates back to 1902, when Our Lady of Guadalupe Church was founded on West Fourteenth Street for Spanish-speaking Catholics. By the 1950s, the number of city parishes offering Spanish increased noticeably, to the point where today it's rare to find a parish not offering Spanish Masses.

Rudy Vargas IV has tremendous admiration for those early pioneers who pushed for Spanish Masses in an Anglo church and refused to be consigned to the basement. "If we're upstairs at the altars," he comments, "it's because of them." They were *en la lucha* (in the struggle). But *lucha* means more than just "struggle"; more specifically, it means a fight for what's right and just, keeping an eye on that or losing your Catholicism.

Since his teenage years Rudy has been involved in that struggle. Born in Brooklyn's East New York section, he was baptized in St. Peter's Church on Hicks Street, a parish providing services for Spanish-speaking Catholics throughout Brooklyn. Early on he became involved in St. Agnes Church, Carroll Gardens, whose Spanish community, he recalls, "nurtured me in my faith."

Nearly all of those early leaders belonged to the Cursillo movement, a retreat program introduced from Spain in the 1940s. Its influence on the Hispanic/Latino community cannot be underestimated, Vargas contends. Literally meaning "little path," it provides a life-changing encounter with the person of Christ. What happens after the retreat is almost as important. How does it influence the Cursillista participation in the struggle?

At sixteen, Rudy was attending Automotive High School, planning to become an auto body worker, when he attended a Jornada retreat. Literally a "journey" in the Christian life, the Jornada is a Cursillo for young people. He met people from all walks of life, most of whom he still sees today. "For the first time in my life," he recalls, "in the presence of the Blessed Sacrament with a group of peers sharing the Jornada, I opened up to the Lord." It was a transforming moment, "educating me about who Jesus is, a real person, coming into contact with that person."

It was, he recalls, "a life-changing moment for me. To come out of that experience, to walk into a welcoming group of people embracing you, that is church." The memory of that experience still sustains Rudy. He knew now that he wanted to work with people. After college he went to work for Aspira, a New York educational agency. All the while he continued to participate in the Jornada, which he sees as "so important in the life of young people."

In 1985 Rudy got a call from his friend Monsignor (now Bishop) Octavio Cisneros, inviting him to help coordinate the Brooklyn Diocese's Spanish-speaking apostolate. Over the next ten years, he learned to work with clergy in a spirit of "complementarity," respecting the gifts that each brings to the table. This spirit of "mutual appreciation," he says, "energizes and nurtures my work within the church." Many of these priests are more than coworkers, he notes; they're *compadres*.

He started a leadership program titled Enlace (to link), which nominated two representatives from each Spanish-speaking parish and ministry. In 1992 as the five hundredth anniversary of Columbus's arrival was celebrated, the Hispanic Ministry Office (so renamed in 1991) collected parish histories from over ninety Brooklyn and Queens parishes. At St. John's University, over four thousand Hispanic/Latinos attended a conference offering programs on church, youth, and culture. It was a huge success, he recalls, one that "shattered a lot of stereotypes of Hispanics."

In 1995 Rudy assumed leadership of the Bronx's Center for Catholic Lay Leadership. By then he'd earned a graduate degree in pastoral leadership from Fordham. At the center he designed a program named Called Forth to Be Sent Forth, based on the experience of the Samaritan woman in John's Gospel. Like the Samaritan woman, participants first encounter the person of Jesus, and then they bring that experience to others, inspiring them to go and personally encounter Jesus for themselves.

After seven years in the Bronx, Rudy joined the Northeast Hispanic Catholic Center (NHCC) in Manhattan as executive director. The NHCC advised and supported Hispanic ministry directors in thirty-four dioceses while helping other dioceses start one. It also created a summer institute at a seminary in Connecticut and helped prepare for the first National Hispanic Youth Ministry Encounter held at the University of Notre Dame in 2006. Many participants, Rudy notes, have become leaders in the Hispanic Catholic community.

Notre Dame was looking for a consultant in connection with their campaign to promote Catholic schools in the Hispanic community. In 2010, then, Rudy entered a new stage of ministry. Only 3 percent of the Hispanic population, he notes, currently send their children to Catholic schools. Notre Dame has committed to raise this another 3 percent by 2020. "Education," Rudy says, "has always been very central to me, and I value it tremendously."

Today he works with twenty-six Catholic schools from Poughkeepsie to Staten Island. He organized the Madrinas (godmothers) program. Godmothers, he points out, are highly consulted figures in the Hispanic family. In each school, the principal identifies two school mothers to seek out families interested in Catholic education. When the Madrinas program began, within a few months the Madrinas had made contact with over two hundred families.

The Madrinas' initial outreach paved the way for the creation of a Madrinas scholarship to provide financial assistance for new families who had decided to place their child in a Catholic school recruited by a Madrina. This scholarship was initiated by Dr. Timothy McNiff, superintendent of schools in the Archdiocese of New York.

Rudy Vargas's own heroes, in addition to his parents, his wife, and Dr. Martin Luther King Jr., include husband-and-wife scholar-activists Anthony Stevens and Anna Maria Stevens-Arroyo; internationally renowned theologian Virgilio Elizondo; local leaders like the late Eddie Kalbfleisch and Encarnación Padilla de Armas; former coworkers like Bishop Rene Valero in Brooklyn; and Mario Paredes and Carmen Castro at the NHCC. "These are the people," he says, "who nurture me with their prophetic leadership, their ability to stand against things that prevent people (in particular, Hispanic/Latinos) from participating in the life and mission of the church." Along with them, he remains steadfast *en la lucha*, still faithful in the journey.

68

FATHER GREGORY C. CHISHOLM

St. Charles Borromeo Church, Harlem

God has been very kind, and has been teaching me with each different change.

—GREG CHISHOLM

Harlem is a neighborhood known for its beautiful churches. Among the most impressive is a Gothic structure on West 141st Street, St. Charles Borromeo Church. Called the "Cathedral of Harlem," it was built to serve a growing Irish population. By the 1920s, however, the Irish had moved out as the community became African American. Over the years, St. Charles has had a series of dynamic pastors, white and black, who have worked hard to strengthen and affirm its rich African American Catholic identity and heritage.

Father Greg Chisholm, S.J., has served as pastor since the summer of 2011, the first Jesuit pastor. A native son, he grew up in nearby St. Mark the Evangelist parish on West 138th Street. His mother and father also grew up in Harlem. He's the third generation taught by Sisters of the Blessed Sacrament. He and his father had the same third-grade teacher at St. Mark's, Miss Northcroft, the only black faculty member. She brought African American culture to the students in a way the white Sisters couldn't. Father Chisholm was first exposed to gospel music in her classroom.

Although most of Harlem wasn't Catholic, Greg Chisholm grew up assuming the world was black and Catholic. As a choir member he was picked to sing at St. Patrick's Cathedral, where he also served Mass. He remembers serving Mass for Monsignor Terence Cooke, whom he describes as "the most focused man I've ever met, very kind, very religious." He also got to see priestly ordinations. By around age ten or eleven, he says, he knew he wanted to be a priest: "I was infected by the priesthood as a boy."

While attending Manhattan College Prep in the Bronx, Greg's parish priest—Father (now Monsignor) John Meehan—made a strong impression. He recalls the priest as being "committed—committed to Harlem—committed to the people—committed to the young men of the parish—committed to me." (Now retired, Monsignor Meehan returned to St. Charles after Father Chisholm invited him back.)

For Greg's father, priesthood wasn't an option. A New York policeman, he believed in one university, MIT. ("He may have wanted to go there himself," Chisholm speculates.) Greg himself wasn't naïve about the prospects for a young black man in the church of the 1960s. "One would have to have had a healthy dose of naiveté to join the church then," he comments. At MIT, he earned bachelor's and master's degrees in engineering, staying in Boston after graduation with a good job and a good salary.

During his father's illness he transferred briefly to New Jersey. Following his father's death in 1975 he began exploring the idea of priesthood again, first considering the New York Archdiocese. A priest friend suggested looking at the Jesuits, given his academic background. He waited awhile, but by twenty-eight, he says, "I couldn't get the idea out of my mind." Finally, in 1980 Greg Chisholm entered the New England Province of the Society of Jesus.

As part of his training, he returned to MIT for his doctorate. In retrospect he feels, "I probably should have discouraged the Society from sending me on for my Ph.D." After several years teaching engineering at the University of Detroit, he realized he wasn't "turned on by teaching. I was turned on by families, communities, faith, issues of blackness." In time he convinced his religious superiors to assign him to parish work in Los Angeles. Eventually he became pastor of Holy Name of Jesus parish in South Central Los Angeles.

He loved working there, "an enthusiastic congregation, great music ministry." In St. Mark's, his home parish, most parishioners were from either the Deep South or the Caribbean, and they tended to be converts. In South Central, however, many of the black parishioners were cradle Catholics from Texas or Louisiana; "Catholicism was all they knew." After seven years at Holy Name, Father Chisholm was named pastor of St. Patrick's Church in Oakland, where the congregation was half African American and half Hispanic.

After five years at St. Patrick's, he got a call from the New York Archdiocese, asking if he'd consider taking over St. Charles Borromeo. His Jesuit superiors thought it would be a good idea. ("I suspect they may have wanted to keep a Jesuit presence in Harlem," he suggests.) He decided to accept the position, and he is currently one of two Jesuits working in the neighborhood.

Being a black Catholic in this city, he feels, is an "odd experience." Perhaps less than other cities where he has ministered, Father Chisholm feels that the city's Catholic leadership is less reflective of the people it serves. He recalls, for example, attending a recent Rite of Election for new Catholics at St. Patrick's Cathedral. The congregation, he notes, was "a celebration of ethnicity." On the altar, however, he feels that this was not entirely the case.

Still, he believes, African American Catholics bring very special gifts to the church of New York. For one, he contends, they bring "an exuberance to the liturgy. African Americans demand praise in the liturgy." Music and preaching have a high priority. "The involvement of the entire person with the Divine is something that many nonblack churches have not been able to achieve. Black Catholic churches do that." At St. Charles, many parishioners travel from as far away as Long Island and New Jersey to attend this "unique experience of liturgy."

He loves being home again after so many years. New York, he observes, "is an extremely exciting city, more exciting than any other city I have been in, except perhaps London." After fourteen years in California, he got used to the weather. His greatest shock, he jokes, was "coming back to a place where there are genuine seasons." He now lives within walking distance of his childhood home. As engineer, teacher, and priest, he comments, "God has been very kind, and has been teaching me with each different change."

69

BROTHER MICHAEL FRANCIS GROGAN
Sacred Heart Church, Bronx

Are we really reaching out to the people Christ wants us to reach?

—MIKE GROGAN

Since the 1960s, the Bronx's Highbridge section has been a neighborhood struggling with gangs, drugs, and crippling poverty. The name comes from the Aqueduct Bridge, the city's oldest, which connected the borough to Manhattan in 1848. For decades the area was a mainly Irish and Jewish enclave. Today's residents are predominantly Puerto Rican and African American, concentrated in apartment buildings and housing projects. "It's a pretty tough neighborhood," observes Brother Michael Grogan, youth minister at Sacred Heart Church on Shakespeare Avenue, "but I couldn't imagine being anywhere else."

For nearly two decades, Michael Francis Grogan has worked in the South Bronx with troubled youth. What began as high school volunteer work developed into a full-time ministry to dropouts and homeless teens, drug addicts and drug dealers, prisoners, ex-cons and gang members. His day consists of praying with them, talking to their families, and feeding them. He encourages them to volunteer as well. He visits them in jail. And he lives with them, "completely dependent on Providence."

Brother Michael grew up on Long Island, but his parents met in the Bronx, at the Lavelle School for the Blind on Paulding Avenue. (He and his four siblings are all legally blind.) Growing up on Long Island, he had little contact with poverty, drugs, or gangs. His interest in religion was lukewarm, until at fourteen he attended Youth 2000, a metropolitan gathering of young Catholics. During the weekend he seemed to hear God saying, "Keep your eyes focused on me and you will see clearly." He wasn't cured physically, but he gained a life-changing insight into the purpose of his own life.

On weekends he volunteered with the Capuchin Friars of the Renewal, a newly established wing of the Franciscans. "I was getting a taste of the Bronx," he recalls. After graduating high school in 1997 he briefly attended St. John's University, but recalls, "My heart was really with the poor." Several times a week he commuted from Seaford to 145th Street in the Bronx, teaching religious education at St. Rita's School. Here he also met Mother Teresa's Missionaries of Charity, who worked around the corner. All his students were expelled from other religion classes. He loved it. "God gave me a gift to work with kids," he says. Soon other students were trying to get into his class. "It's hard to say what happens," he reflects. "All I can say is I was aware of my own poverty, I could relate to their poverty, and bring love to it." God, he contends, "took the most unlikely person—a blind white guy from the suburbs—and said, 'They'll never see you coming.'" Two years later, he moved to the Bronx, working as a custodian and running prayer meetings. The first members were Bloods, drug dealers, and ex-cons—"really tough guys." He never felt unsafe. The rosary part didn't work initially, but the pizza went over well. And, surprisingly, they came back. "They seemed to like the socializing, sitting around, laughing, talking." The prayer part caught on, too. The numbers grew. Something else happened; he realized he wanted "to do this 24/7."

He quit his job to live with the poor, trusting Providence. Three days later, a stranger asked him, "Could you use five thousand dollars?" He comments, "That is completely Providence. I was floored." Others brought food and supplies. Living on Arthur Avenue he started prayer groups, distributed food, taught religion, and brought people back to church. He met homeless teens, discovering that not all stories have a happy ending: "Sometimes kids are so badly damaged. It's not always going to work out like you hope."

Searching for a "tougher neighborhood," he moved first to 175th Street and University Avenue, and then to 165th and Woodycrest. One night he saw some of his kids lined upright against the wall after the police raided their building. "They yelled, 'Hey, Mike!' The cops were like, 'Who's this white guy?'" He held prayer meetings, worked with delinquents and families, and got them to volunteer with the Missionaries of Charity on 146th Street. "These toughest of tough kids," he notes, "loved the nuns."

Along the way, he's learned some things about ministry: "Jesus says, 'Love one another,' not 'Change one another.' *He* does the changing." Sometimes he feels like Mary at the foot of the cross, "helpless in the midst of suffering." He's learned to let people make mistakes and not take it personally. Most of all, he's learned not to give unsolicited advice. One teen told him, "I'm gonna rob someone." "Don't call me from Rikers," he answered. "I won't pick up." ("But I do," he adds.)

Today Michael Grogan is Brother Michael, having taken religious vows. Walking through the neighborhood in his robes, everyone greets him and he greets everyone. One of the problems with the church today, he feels, is that there's "a lot of fear. We talk a lot about the poor, but we're afraid of them. We don't like it when they show up. We really have to start being the Body of Christ." It's important to look past externals, especially with youth: "If you get close enough, you see the wall they put up around them is made of Styrofoam. It comes down easily."

"If we have the fullness of truth," he asks, "then why are people going to the Pentecostals? Because they focus on Jesus's person. We've got everything and we're losing." He's reminded of the little boy who, when the priest announced the end of Mass, shouted, "Thank God!" "Most people feel like that," Brother Michael suggests. A major problem, he insists, is that Catholics stress doctrine without covering the personal relationship component. "Doctrine without a personal relationship to the Lord," he points out, "doesn't work. It's like soup mix without the water, dry by itself." In short, he asks, "Are we really reaching out to the people Christ wants us to reach?"

70

Monsignor Gerald Ryan

St. Luke's Church, Bronx

Being in the presence of the Lord's people brings such a feeling of comfort and joy.

—Gerry Ryan

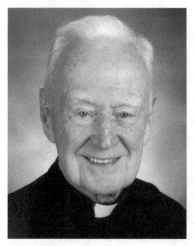

M ott Haven in the South Bronx is an area with a rich history. What began as a country estate for the elite became an industrial center attracting recent immigrants. For decades Mott Haven was a major Irish enclave, until Puerto Rican immigration increased in the 1960s. Today, Puerto Ricans are the old-timers, and newcomers are primarily Mexican and Dominican. One of the neighborhood's few constants is St. Luke's Church on East 138th Street, and Monsignor Gerald Ryan, its pastor for the last forty-six years.

Father Ryan (as he prefers to be called) has lived in the Bronx for all but six years. Since his ordination in 1945 he's served in two parishes: St. Anthony of Padua on East 166th Street and St. Luke's. For decades, he's celebrated Mass only in Spanish. At ninety-two, he's the city's oldest serving priest, with no intention of retiring. "I don't think they know what to do with me," he says frankly of church leadership.

He's known as the "mayor of 138th Street. " For many locals, Ryan is a sign of hope; he's always there for them. "When I walk down the street," he says, "I'm always amazed at how many stop me to say hello, young and old." In the rectory office, a long line of people wait for advice, counseling, or simply to pray with him. Waiting for my appointment I asked the parish secretary, "Have you known him long?" "Yeah," she answered, "since my family moved here. He's like my dad."

Ryan's entire ministry has been in minority parishes, usually as the area's only white person. But he's never felt unsafe, which he attributes to his mother's example. An Irish immigrant in Harlem, her closest friends were African American and Jewish. "I grew up," he says, "with the idea that you don't shut out people because of their color or their religion."

Growing up in Pelham Bay, then a rural area, priesthood was an idea he just "grew up with. I never thought of anything else." In 1933 he entered Cathedral Prep Seminary, a Manhattan high school for young men considering the priesthood. After studying at St. Joseph's Seminary in Yonkers he was ordained by Archbishop Francis J. Spellman.

He was supposed to be sent to Cardinal Hayes High School in the Bronx, but plans changed and he went to St. Anthony of Padua in Morrisania. Founded for German Catholics, by the end of World War II the neighborhood was predominantly black. Although Ryan had little previous contact with African Americans, he says his time there was "one of the great experiences of my life."

For over twenty years, he was active in the African American community. (Such priests were known as "black priests.") He became increasingly conscious of the privations that blacks experienced. By the early 1960s he noticed "something was buzzing." In 1963 he accompanied parishioners and priests to the March on Washington, where he heard Martin Luther King deliver his famed "I Have a Dream" speech. "We were all hypnotized," he recalls.

In March 1965 Ryan and twenty other New York priests marched with King in Selma. Before the march, King met with the Catholic priests, thanking them for their help. Walking across the Pettus Bridge, they faced "rednecks armed with billies, ready to give us a crup on the head." Hundreds of people were yelling and shaking their fists, he recalls, when local girls began shrieking and cheering at the sight of singer Harry Belafonte marching.

In 1966 Father Ryan was made pastor of St. Luke's, an old-time Irish parish that was becoming Puerto Rican. This was the era of white flight, when old-timers fled the city in droves. As the Bronx became a national synonym for urban decay, one parishioner recalls that Ryan "encouraged the people, 'Stay in the Bronx, rebuild the Bronx.'" Through the fires of the seventies, the drug epidemics of the eighties and nineties, in the face of continuing violence and poverty, he was among those who never gave up on the borough or the people.

He's also ministered at the Bronx House of Detention. "Inmates," he notes, "are the easiest people to preach to. They're naturally religious." He's fought for better housing, created a community center, and participated in the Cursillo movement (a Spanish-speaking retreat program). He still leads a weekly discussion group for local youth where they can share their issues. "I come off as tough," he says, "but I really love them."

As a young priest, he recalls, he never said Jesus's name, only "the Lord." To do otherwise, he thought, was too familiar. Today, however, he does say the name of Jesus, whom he sees as friend, brother, and beloved confidant. He wants to help others realize that

Jesus is as close to you as you are to yourselves; you're part of him and he's part of you; he wants to be part of your life. He wants you to feel intimate with him, laugh with him, cry with him. The greatest thing I can do is to make you understand that relationship with Jesus. The challenge of faith is to believe that.

In 1995, the fiftieth anniversary of his ordination, Ryan was named a monsignor, a title he only uses for formal occasions. Now in his sixty-seventh year of priesthood, he has no desire to leave Mott Haven. It's here that he finds God. "Being in the presence of the Lord's people," he says, brings "such a feeling of comfort and joy": "I suppose everything good in us is an expression of Jesus: preaching to people, talking to people, offering Mass with people. You're one of them in your piety, sharing the presence of the Lord."

At ninety-two, he's not finished yet. He's still learning, still growing in his love of God and God's people, still loving parish work, still loving the Bronx and its people. And if he has his way, New York's oldest working priest won't be going anywhere anytime soon.

Note: As this book was going to print, Monsignor Ryan died at age ninety-three. He had worked as a priest in the Bronx for sixty-eight uninterrupted years.

71

Monsignor Patrick McCahill

St. Elizabeth of Hungary Church, Manhattan

Something special happens here.

—Pat McCahill

St. Elizabeth of Hungary Church was founded on the Upper East Side in the 1890s to serve a growing Slovakian population, but today it serves a far different purpose. Since the summer of 1980, when Cardinal Terence Cooke designated it New York's parish for deaf Catholics, Monsignor Pat Mc-Cahill has been serving their needs as pastor. Very few priests in the metropolitan area have a knowledge of American Sign Language (ASL), and today he's *the* priest involved in deaf ministry in the City of New York. It's a big task, but one he clearly welcomes.

People get involved in deaf ministry for a variety of reasons: some because of their own disability, others because they have a deaf relative. Most start early, knowing it was their calling. Not so with Monsignor McCahill (he prefers to be called Father). He was, by his own admission, a "latecomer." During his junior year of college at St. Joseph's Seminary in Yonkers, a seminarian spoke to his class about taking a course in ASL. McCahill wasn't interested, but a classmate put him up to it. And since his ordination in 1968, it's become a second vocation. "You get better at it over time," he says with characteristic modesty.

There's a difference between an interpreted Mass and a Mass that's actually celebrated in ASL, as it is at St. Elizabeth's. People come from all over the city, even the state. Virginia McNamara, a teacher at St. Joseph's School for the Deaf in the Bronx, notes that while other churches provide services for the deaf, they don't have offer this unique opportunity for the deaf to be full participants in the liturgy.

There's no voice used in a deaf Mass. Because it's not an exact transliteration from English, the priest has to multitask. As he reads from the Missal in English, he has to translate those words in his head in order to convey the message to people who use a language with a grammar and structure vastly different from English. What makes it different is this: In ASL, the language is conveyed through the hands, and a great deal of the grammar comes through facial expressions. So your whole body is really involved in communicating this way. As Father McCahill puts it,

> You get very physically involved—saying the words and gesturing. Your whole self goes into it. In preaching, you act everything out. It's like what the Jesuits call "composition of place," but you're doing it all yourself. You have to act out and portray what Jesus was like. You have to act out all that to give a certain sense to the people. By the end of Sunday, I'm tired.

At St. Elizabeth's, the deaf serve in every aspect of the liturgy—as lectors and altar servers. There's a signing choir that's performed for popes. McNamara notes that McCahill "enables deaf people to have the same access to Mass and to the church as a community that any hearing Catholic has as a right. He invites people to the Church (with a capital C), not just to come to church (with a small c)."

"Something special happens here," McCahill comments. There's a strong sense of community among the deaf, which he appreciates greatly. "I've learned more about community from them," he says, "than from hearing people." They also have the opportunity to gather as a community at the parish hall; outside, he observes, "the deaf have to deal with a world that doesn't understand them." McNamara says, "It's a place where they can get together and just spend time communicating with one another in their own language. It's a place where they're the majority. They're not the minority."

In addition to celebrating Mass at St. Elizabeth's, McCahill often travels around the city serving the needs of deaf Catholics: celebrating their weddings, baptisms, and funerals. St. Elizabeth's offers all the programs that hearing parishes do, from Marriage Encounter to religious instruction. McCahill also conducts periodic retreats conducted entirely in ASL over a weekend. "New York City can be quite a lonesome place," he says, and that can be especially true for the deaf. Without Monsignor Pat McCahill, many of these opportunities—sacramental and otherwise—wouldn't be possible for New York's deaf Catholics. "It's a family," he notes.

72

Martin Scorsese
Film Director

You don't make up for your sins in the church. You do it in the streets. You do it at home. The rest is bullshit and you know it.
      —Mean Streets (1973)

When Charles and Catherine Scorsese moved to Corona, Queens, in the early 1940s, it was still a fairly unsettled area offering yards, trees, and parks, things notably lacking in the Lower East Side of their youth. Their younger son, Martin Charles, born November 17, 1942, spent his early childhood there in what seemed an idyllic setting replete with trees. But circumstances, economic and otherwise, forced the family's return to Little Italy, to the apartment where Charlie was born. It proved a defining moment in Martin's life.

"Grassy backyards," Vincent LoBrutto writes, were replaced with "concrete tenements, asphalt, constant noise, and potential danger." It was, Scorsese told critic Richard Schickel, "pretty rough . . . [a] lot of everybody living on top of each other . . . a Sicilian village re-created on the Lower East Side." In his 1974 documentary *Italianamerican,* he recalled, "Elizabeth Street was mainly Sicilian, as were my grandparents, and here the people had their own regulation and laws. We didn't care about the government, or politicians or the police: we felt we were right in our ways." There was a code on the streets, of the streets, different from what he learned in church.

It was a neighborhood in the fullest sense. Catherine recalled that people left their doors open, settled fights among one another, and kept an eye on the kids. If you didn't like supper, Charlie recalled, you could eat with the neighbors. Everyone "looked out" for one another. In biographer Martin Miliora's words, the triune pillars of that community were "family, street, and church." You identified yourself by parish. You weren't from the Lower East Side; you were from Old St. Patrick's Cathedral.

But there was a dark side, too; it was "working class, but also criminal class." Scorsese grew up in what he calls "an atmosphere of fear . . . It could be terrifying in your own backyard." These were the original "mean streets" he later chronicled onscreen. "In the middle of the night," he adds, "you could hear all kinds of fights and violence. . . . There were some tough guys around." He recalls one neighborhood gangster in particular who "was a killer, a real killer. But he was a very nice man—to me."

A sickly child, Scorsese was known in the neighborhood as "Marty Pills" for his medication. ("I wasn't tough," he says. His father said he was "a different kind of kid.") All his life, writes Schickel, there has been "a longing for some kind of transcendence," which he found in the church and the movies. "My whole life," Scorsese reflects, "has been movies and religion. That's it. Nothing else." "You had faith when you went into the church. And you had faith when you went into the movie theater, too. In their own way, they provided the only place where there was some hope."

In Old St. Patrick's, he "became fascinated by the rituals of the Mass." Holy Week, the days leading up to Easter Sunday, made a strong impression on him:

For me Holy Week was a very powerful time. It was even more dramatic than Christmas. The rituals were dramatic. The liturgies were beautiful. The Stations of the Cross were very dramatic. This colored my whole sense of God.

In his study of Scorsese, *Gangster Priest*, Robert Casillo writes, "As an altar boy Scorsese found in Catholic icons and rituals a theatrical spectacle he likens to that of cinema." (He didn't last very long; he had trouble getting up for 7:00 a.m. Mass.) Peter Boyle, who appeared in *Taxi Driver* (and a former Christian Brother), adds, "And if Marty spent a lot of time in the movies as a kid, he also spent a lot of time in church. They're both big and dark, and they're full of mystery, and the rites of purification and of life and death are acted out in the same way."

For a while, Scorsese seriously considered the priesthood, studying briefly in Manhattan's Cathedral Prep Seminary. "My first impulse," he looks back, "was to go to the priesthood. It was overwhelming. Especially if you were a kid who couldn't become a member of organized crime." In retrospect, he reflects, "Maybe it wasn't really a serious vocation after all." He would find his real vocation behind a camera, first as a student at New York University, and later as a director of some of his era's most significant films: *Mean Streets* (1973), *Taxi Driver* (1976), *Raging Bull* (1980), and *Goodfellas* (1990). In 1975 he told an interviewer, "I'm going to die behind a camera."

"My movies," Steven Spielberg says, "are whispers. Marty's movies are shouts." Although best known for gangster movies, Scorsese's output has included romance: *Alice Doesn't Live Here Anymore* (1974); musicals: *New York, New York* (1977); black comedy: *The King of Comedy* (1982); the elegantly structured *The Age of Innocence* (1993). Throughout his work, one critic notes, "His concern with matters of belief is nearly always present" in themes of guilt and redemption, faith and doubt, sin and forgiveness. Harvey Keitel's Charlie, DeNiro's Travis Bickle, and Ray Liotta's Henry Hill all struggle with these issues, with varying results.

As Scorsese grew older, he became disenchanted with the institutional church, calling himself a "lapsed Roman Catholic." But, he adds, "I am a Roman Catholic—there's no way out of it." Author Martin Miliora notes, though, that his work displays what he calls "a passion for the Christ-figure and Jesus' message of love, compassion, and forgiveness," never more so than in his adaptation of Nikos Kazantzakis's novel *The Last Temptation*. In the long run, Scorsese discovered his real vocation outside the cloister, as a true priest, a mediator between God and humanity:

> You gotta live amongst the people and change life that way or help people reach salvation in the street . . . [which] could mean Hollywood. . . . It's like a religious vocation. . . . Mine was harder. I had to do it in the street. I had to do it in Hollywood.

73

JIMMY FALLON

Host, *Tonight Show*, New York

A little song, a little dance, a little seltzer in your pants.
—QUOTE FROM FALLON'S HIGH SCHOOL YEARBOOK

With the return of the *Tonight Show* to New York, the city becomes once more the capital of late-night television. As one reporter noted, it was "a victory for New York in the coastal battles [with Los Angeles] . . . and which city has the right to think of itself as the TV capital of America (and, let's face it, the world)." If that is the case, then the new king of late night is one James Thomas Fallon, an affable, likeable character whose message is "Fun. 'Have fun' is my message. Be silly. You're allowed to be silly. There's nothing wrong with it."

Fallon's former boss at *Saturday Night Live*, Lorne Michaels, calls him "the closest to Carson that I've seen of this generation." Close friend and former coanchor Tina Fey says of Fallon, "It can't be learned, but he definitely has it." From young to old, Fey adds, "He just charms people. He's like a nice kid who's playful and always excited to see you." In a recent *Vanity Fair* article, John Heilpern wrote of the star, "Late-night star Jimmy Fallon is the strangest kind of talk-show host: a happy one."

Fallon, it's been said, is "truly living his wildest dreams": hosting, singing, dancing, rapping, impersonating. His performing career, he says, began at an early age, doing James Cagney impersonations at age two. ("I grew up in an Irish Catholic family," he says, "and I think they force you to watch every

James Cagney movie.") As a child he and his sister would reenact their favorite scenes from *Saturday Night Live*, which their parents taped for them. At family gatherings, he recalls,

> They would have parties and they would sing, you know, have a microphone set up with a reel to reel and some speakers and just—everyone would sing songs. Even though we weren't famous, you know, we were a performing family pretty much.

Jim Fallon's job led the family to leave Brooklyn—where he and his wife, Gloria, met at a block party—for Saugerties in upstate New York. There young Jimmy (the third generation of his family to be so named) attended Catholic parochial school, played and performed, and nurtured his dream of one day going on *SNL*. But in church he had his first real taste of performing, as an altar boy at St. Mary's parish.

Serving the 6:45 a.m. Mass, which his grandfather attended daily, "gave me the performance bug," Fallon recalls. It was his

> first experience on stage . . . You're on stage next to the priest. "I'm a co-star." I have no lines but I ring bells. I ring bells and I swing the incense around. And you know, you are performing. You enter through a curtain, you exit through the—I mean you're backstage. I mean, have you ever seen backstage behind an altar? It's kind of fascinating. So I think it was my first taste of show business—or acting or something.

Fallon's first experience of Catholicism, then, was a positive one, as he recalled in an interview with NPR: "I just, I loved the church. I loved the idea of it. I loved the smell of the incense. I loved the feeling you get when you left church. I loved like how this priest can make people feel this good. I just thought it was—I loved the whole idea of it."

For a while, he says, he even thought about being a priest: "If you did weddings and funerals. You'd get like five bucks. And so I go, 'Okay, I can make money, too.' I go, 'This could be a good deal for me.' I thought I had the calling."

The real call came, quite literally, during his senior year of college. At the College of Saint Rose in Albany, Fallon had studied communications, leaving fifteen credits shy of a degree (which he received in 2009, along with an honorary doctorate) to pursue a comic's life. After a few years on the circuit, he joined the cast of *SNL* in 1998. After making a number of films he began hosting *Late Night with Jimmy Fallon* in March 2009. Four years later, in April 2013 the *Tonight Show* announced that at the end of the 2014 Winter Olympics, Fallon would succeed host Jay Leno in the most coveted position in the world of late-night television.

By his own admission, Jimmy Fallon has had the "luck of the Irish." But he also has something more. One observer notes his "kind of comedic energy that's pretty rare . . . There's a wit and smartness to his comedic sensibility. He's a young Robin Williams." He's also been described as "one of the happiest people in television." He's a "joyful, easy, breezy" person whose specialty is making people smile. "Everybody looks so much better when they smile," Fallon says. In this sense, then, he found his real vocation in front of a different audience: bringing joy to others.

74

Sister Mary Lanning

Founder, Yes!Solutions, Harlem

God was asking more of me as I prayed.
  —Mary Lanning

By the late 1960s, the Bronx had become a by-word for urban decay, and nowhere was this more true than in the Hunts Point section. There on a hill, Corpus Christi, New York City's second Catholic monastery, had been built in 1889, a place where Dominican nuns lived a cloistered life devoted to prayer. But they weren't immune to the changes going on outside their walls: drugs, death, gangs, prostitution, abandoned children, burning buildings, and more.

From that hill in the Bronx, Sister Mary Lanning heard the gunshots. She saw the smoke. With the stained-glass windows opened on hot summer nights, she could hear the children's cries from the nearby Spofford Juvenile Center: "I wanna come and stay with you, get me outta here." One morning, the nuns found outside their gates Stevie, the ten-year-old altar boy who served their morning Mass, sobbing in the corner because his friend had been killed. On another morning they found a neighborhood prostitute's corpse on fire inside their garbage can.

A Long Island native, the daughter of Irish immigrants, Mary had entered the monastery thirteen years earlier. It was a life she loved. But one summer night, she found herself saying a prayer (a prayer she still says): "Give us courage to let go of the good things we've been doing so that we see the things we need to do." Her next breath, she recalls, was, "Oh, God, no. I had to let go of the good I was doing to be able to see what I still needed to do."

Not long thereafter, Mary Lanning left Corpus Christi. In doing so, she says, she discovered "the real essence of the vows." Poverty, she contends, "isn't a virtue, nor an economic bracket. It means letting go of everything you have and everything you are." After leaving the monastery, she entered the business world.

Today she works in the insurance industry, where she is one of the most respected lobbyists in the field. Her company ML&G Associates ("Mary Lanning & God") has been described as "an effective advocate and mediator for her insurance industry clients." She attributes her success to her communications skills, her writing ability, and her grasp of the basic industry concepts. ("Nobody's born understanding insurance," she adds.)

At the same time, Mary renewed her religious vows as a member of the Sisters for Christian Community (SFCC), which she describes as a "call to do things differently." Founded in 1970, members live their religious commitment in the world in a variety of roles. As one insurance executive notes, Mary "works so hard in the secular world in order to support her good works, and not for personal gain." Another colleague comments, "I have never met anyone who has the unaffected instinct, drive, and ability to care for people in need, whether the homeless, the dying, the grieving." It's been said she puts in a "thirty-six-hour-day" (she says she's still trying to fit in the thirty-seventh). She's also a highly regarded advocate for New York City's poor and disadvantaged: "I live two lives at least—I continue to do everything that I can for anyone who is suffering loss and a broken heart." Her Harlem-based Yes!Solutions, is a grassroots service organization composed entirely of volunteers, "neighbor to neighbor." It receives no government funding. Lanning comments, "I just want people to know that if they want to do something for somebody, I can help them find the person and the way."

Yes! volunteers reach out to the elderly, the poor, the homeless, the unemployed, and the grieving. With the help of her many friends (including business colleagues), they bring food, clothing, and furniture to the poor;

mentor teens; comfort the lonely; and much more. Their motto is, "We create hope—in the most unlikely circumstances." Every year at Thanksgiving they feed over a thousand people, a tradition that started years ago on top of a car outside Lanning's Harlem apartment. Yes!, she says, "hears the unspoken cry, 'Doesn't anybody give a damn?'"

One colleague calls her "New York's very own Mother Teresa," but she has no interest in media coverage, which she sees as a form of exploiting the disadvantaged. If people hear her story and it makes them cry, she asks, "What's been changed but a wet tissue?" She firmly insists that "other people's poverty, pain, and embarrassment is not a spectator sport."

At seventy-five, Mary Lanning shows no signs of slowing down. After work, she visits people in need all over the city. Among her many deeds, she counsels the grieving, helps people find jobs, and comforts the dying ("I'm most myself in hospice work," she says. "It's no-holds-barred.") People know to come to her for help. She cherishes the name by which she's known on the street: "that woman Mary."

"People," she asserts, "have a right to look to us for hope." Today Mary Lanning lives a far different life than what she might have envisioned during her years in the monastery. But she's never turned her back on those years, which she loved deeply. Rather, she sees the course of her life as a natural progression, an answer to a call that developed more fully as the years went by. To put it simply, she says, "God was asking more of me as I prayed."

75

REGIS PHILBIN
Entertainer
I try to pay back.
—REGIS PHILBIN

They say you can take the kid out of the Bronx, but you can't take the Bronx out of the kid. No single person embodies this adage quite like Regis Philbin, a man who literally thrives on cameras and crowds. (*The Guinness Book of*

World Records lists him as having spent more time in front of a camera than any other human being.) And he never seems to tire of it. The reason, according to longtime co-host Kathie Lee Gifford, is that Regis is "still a kid and he's still a fan."

Regis Philbin was born on August 25, 1931. He was named for the elite Jesuit boys' high school on the Upper East Side that his father, a former boxer and Marine who specialized in labor relations, attended. His mother Filomena was the daughter of Italian immigrants. They were, he writes, a "typical New York City couple."

After a short time in Brooklyn, the family moved to the Van Nest section of the Bronx, to a house owned by Regis's great-aunt. In his memoir *I'm Only One Man!,* he writes:

> It was a humble life, I guess. But you want to know what? I never noticed. I loved it. I loved everything about it. And all these years later, I still love the city.

Van Nest was the kind of Bronx neighborhood where everybody knew everybody else, everybody looked out for everybody else, and where kids played stickball in the streets while their parents hung out on the stoops. The Catholics identified themselves by their parish rather than their neighborhood, Our Lady of Solace on Morris Park Avenue.

"It was a happy time," Philbin recalls, one that strongly influenced his comedic style:

> It was in the forties and fifties. People laughed in those days. We had a wonderful time. There was no drug culture. And there was no television, really, in those days. And so we just relied on each for whatever amusing situations came up.

Another major influence was the radio. As a boy, Regis listened regularly to WNEW's nightly programs: "Every night at 9:30, Bing Crosby would have a half hour of songs. I thought he was my friend after a while." (A highlight of Philbin's own career would be when he sang "Pennies from Heaven" to the legendary crooner on *The Joey Bishop Show.*)

It would be a while, however, before he pursued his dream "to entertain people." At Cardinal Hayes High School in the Bronx, a boys' high school whose alumni would include George Carlin and Martin Scorsese, he wasn't active in the school's theatrical productions. At Hayes, he writes, "I was a mediocre student and did absolutely nothing that would point toward the career I eventually found." Over the years, Philbin has been one of the school's most active and generous alumni. He cites the religious and "disciplinarian" influence that served him well in life. "I try to pay back," he says.

In the fall of 1949, Regis encountered one of the great loves of his life: the University of Notre Dame, located on what he calls "those God-kissed pastures of South Bend, Indiana." To this day, he writes, "For me, the opening of Notre Dame football is when my new year begins." He studied sociology, played on the tennis team, and enrolled in Navy ROTC. Still, he avoided pursuing his real love:

> We had a radio station in those days, and a television station came in, too. I went to the station. I wanted to knock on the door to apply for a job sweeping the floors, anything. Just get acquainted with the business. I couldn't do it.

After two years as a Navy officer based in San Diego, Philbin decided to pursue his dream. The ensuing decades would find him working in California as a page for the *Tonight Show*, a television writer, announcer, editor, sidekick for Joey Bishop before finding his real niche as a host for talk shows. By the early 1980s, Philbin decided to move back to his native New York as a morning show host. From there he would move to into the ranks of pop-culture icons.

In the years since he returned to New York, Regis has won three Daytime Emmy Awards and a Lifetime Achievement Award. He's been inducted into both the Television Hall of Fame and the National Association of Broadcasters Hall of Fame. He even has a star on the Hollywood Walk of Fame. The street where he grew up, Cruger Avenue, has been renamed Regis Philbin Avenue ("I love that guy!" he comments on seeing the sign for the first time.)

Although critics have denigrated what *TIME* called his "cornball zeal," there's no doubt that Regis Philbin continues to have enormous appeal even in semi-retirement. (It's doubtful he could ever truly fully retire.) At eighty-three, Philbin remains the quintessential New York Irish Catholic raconteur: loving the crowd, loving the camera, loving the act of storytelling. In short, he's still a kid from the Bronx who's never lost his sense of awe.

76

MARY HIGGINS CLARK
Author

An Irish Storyteller from the Bronx.
—SELF DESCRIBED

She's known as the "Queen of Suspense," and her forty-two novels have sold close to a hundred million copies in the United States alone. She's been the recipient of over a dozen honorary doctorates. She's received the highest awards the Catholic Church can bestow on a layperson, and she's also been named to the Irish American Hall of Fame. Mary Higgins Clark describes herself simply as "an Irish storyteller from the Bronx."

Mary Theresa Eleanor Higgins Clark was born on Christmas Eve 1927 in the Pelham section of the Bronx to a father from Roscommon and a first-generation Irish-American mother. A talented child, she wrote poetry and plays and won acting awards. Luke Higgins owned a pub, and until his early death when Mary was eleven, the family lived in comparative middle-class comfort. Thereafter, Nora Higgins took in boarders at their Tenbroeck Avenue house to make ends meet.

Things were tight. Her mother, along with the nuns at the Bronx's Villa Maria Academy, encouraged her writing. Although she considered an acting career, she opted instead for secretarial school to help support the family. After three years at an advertising agency, she became a stewardess for Pan American Airlines, traveling around the world before marrying Warren Clark in December 1949.

While she was raising five children, Higgins Clark began writing in earnest. Despite numerous rejections, she stuck with it and in 1956 she received one hundred dollars for a story in the Catholic magazine *Extension*. After Warren's early death in 1964, she made a decision to support her family through her writing. As she told a friend, "Me having hysterics isn't going to change anything."

Her faith got her through some tough times. It was, she told one interviewer, "absolutely essential . . . You have to realize that there is a plan for all of this and there is a reason." She wrote radio scripts before turning to books. Every morning from five to seven she would write before the children got up. Her son Warren later recalled, "Virtually every morning we would wake up to the sound of the typewriter going downstairs."

Her first novel, published in 1968, was *Mount Vernon Love Story*—a fictionalized account of George Washington, which, she says, "was remaindered as it came off the press." Her real talent emerged as she switched to mystery novels. Her first bestseller, *Where Are the Children?* has gone through seventy-five printings since its publication in 1975. It proved to be a turning point in her career as a writer.

She also went back to school, enrolling at Fordham University's Lincoln Center campus. Although she originally intended to major in English, she switched to philosophy after taking a course on C. S. Lewis. She found the major "helpful in writing" because, she contends, "there is a lot of psychology in philosophy." In 1979, she graduated *summa cum laude* from Fordham. (A decade later, she spoke at the school's commencement.)

"Once you pick up a Higgins Clark novel," journalist Patricia Harty warns, "it's impossible to put it down . . . until you've found out who done it, and often as not, it's not who you think it is." Unlike many of her peers, she doesn't rely on sex and violence to get her point across. Instead, she insists, "I think I can achieve suspense using the anticipation and the imagination of the reader."

Higgins Clark traces much of her success to her Irish roots. Her earliest memories include her mother and aunts regaling one another with story after story across the dining room table over a pot of tea. The Irish, she insists, are "natural storytellers." And readers agree that she certainly tells a good story.

Although she's not usually thought of as a Catholic novelist per se, Mary Higgins Clark's Catholicism does influence her work. "My Catholicism," she says, "is very much a basis for the way I live and think." Discussing her novels, she comments,

> In my books a sense of justice prevails and the world seems a little bit calmer. The bad are punished, the good—after a series of trials—at least have the promise of a bright future. They have the hope of living happily. That's what I try to give my readers.

In this sense, then, Higgins Clark qualifies as a Catholic writer, an Irish storyteller of the highest order, and a Bronx kid who "did good."

RECOMMENDED READING

Barthel, Joan. *American Saint: The Life of Elizabeth Seton.* Thomas Dunne Books, 2014.

Bell, Stephen. *Rebel, Priest and Prophet: A Biography of Dr. Edward McGlynn.* Kessinger, 2007.

Blantz, Thomas E. *George N. Shuster: On the Side of Truth.* University of Notre Dame Press, 1993.

Boardman, Anne C. *Such Love Is Seldom Seen: A Biography of Mother Mary Walsh, O.P.* Harper, 1950.

Burton, Katherine. *Children's Shepherd: The Story of John Christopher Drumgoole.* P. J. Kenedy & Sons, 1954.

Davis, Cyprian. *The History of Black Catholics in the United States.* Crossroad, 1995.

Duffy, Francis P. *Father Duffy's Story: A Tale of Humor and Heroism, of Life and Death with the Fighting Sixty-Ninth.* George H. Doran Company, 1919.

Duquin, Lorene Hanley. *They Called Her the Baroness: The Life of Catherine De Hueck Doherty.* Alba House, 1995.

Estevez, Felipe J. *Felix Varela: Letters to Elpidio.* Paulist Press, 1989.

Farrelly, M. Natalena. *Thomas Francis Meehan (1854–1942): A Memoir.* United States Catholic Historical Society, 1944.

"Father Nicholas Russo, S.J." *Woodstock Letters* 31 (1902): 281.

Fisher, James T. *On the Irish Waterfront: The Crusader, the Movie, and the Soul of the Port of New York.* Cornell University Press, 2009.

Ford, Michael. *Father Mychal Judge: An Authentic American Hero.* Paulist Press, 2002.

Gannon, Robert I. *The Cardinal Spellman Story.* Doubleday, 1963.

Golway, Terry, ed. *Catholics in New York: Society, Culture, and Politics, 1808–1946.* Fordham University Press, 2008.

———. *Full of Grace: An Oral Biography of John Cardinal O'Connor.* Atria Books, 2002.

Groeschel, Benedict J., and Terrence L. Weber. *Thy Will Be Done: A Spiritual Portrait of Terence Cardinal Cooke.* Alba House, 1990.

Guilday, Peter. *John Gilmary Shea: Father of American Catholic History.* United States Catholic Historical Society, 1926.

Hentoff, Nat. *John Cardinal O'Connor: At the Storm Center of a Changing American Catholic Church.* Scribner, 1988.

Howes, Marjorie. *Colonial Crossings: Figures in Irish Literary History.* Field Day Publications, 2006.

Jervis, Paul W. *Quintessential Priest: The Life of Father Bernard J. Quinn.* Editions du Signe, 2005.

Jones, Arthur. *Pierre Toussaint: A Biography.* Doubleday, 2003.

Kearney, G. R. *More Than a Dream: The Cristo Rey Story—How One School's Vision Is Changing the World.* Loyola Press, 2008.

Kwitchen, Mary Augustine. *James Alphonsus McMaster: A Study in American Thought.* Kessinger, 2010.

Malone, Sylvester L., ed. *Memorial of the Golden Jubilee of the Rev. Sylvester Malone.* Privately printed, 1895.

Martin, James, S.J. *In Good Company: The Fast Track from the Corporate World to Poverty, Chastity, and Obedience.* Sheed and Ward, 2010.

McNamara, Patrick J. *The Tablet: The First Hundred Years.* The Tablet Publishing Company, 2008.

McNamara, Patrick J., Joseph W. Coen, and Peter I. Vaccari. *Diocese of Immigrants: The Brooklyn Catholic Experience, 1853–2003.* Editions du Signe, 2009.

Miller, Julie. *Abandoned: Foundlings in Nineteenth-Century New York City.* New York University Press, 2008.

Miller, William L. *Dorothy Day: A Biography.* Macmillan, 1982.

Mitchell, James H. *Golden Jubilee Celebration of the Rt. Rev. John Loughlin, First Bishop of Brooklyn.* The Golden Jubilee Committee, 1891.

Mott, Michael. *The Seven Mountains of Thomas Merton.* Mariner Books, 1993.

O'Brien, David J. *Isaac Hecker: An American Catholic.* Paulist Press, 1992.

O'Grady, John. *Levi Silliman Ives: Pioneer in Catholic Charities.* Catholic University of America Press, 1933.

Phelan, Thomas P. *Thomas Dongan: Colonial Governor of New York.* Kessinger, 2008.

Reeves, Thomas C. *America's Bishop: The Life and Times of Fulton J. Sheen.* Encounter Books, 2002.

Shaw, Richard. *Dagger John: The Unquiet Life and Times of Archbishop John Hughes of New York.* Paulist Press, 1977.

Shelley, Thomas J. *History of the Archdiocese of New York.* Editions du Signe, 2008.

Sheed, Wilfrid. *Frank and Maisie: A Memoir with Parents.* Touchstone, 1986.

Slayton, Robert. *Empire Statesman: The Rise and Redemption of Al Smith.* Free Press, 2007.

Sullivan, Mary Louise. *Mother Cabrini: Italian Immigrant of the Century.* Center for Migration Studies, 1992.

Walsh, James J. "Doctor Jedediah Vincent Huntington and the Oxford Movement in America." *Records of the American Catholic Historical Society of Philadelphia* 16 (1905): 241–67.

Index of Profiles

211

PHOTOGRAPHY CREDITS

Thomas Dongan (Author's Collection); St. Elizabeth Seton (Author's Collection); Venerable Pierre Toussaint (Courtesy of the Office of Black Ministry, Archdiocese of New York); John Hughes (Author's Collection); Johann Raffeiner (Courtesy of the *Tablet*); Sylvester Malone (Author's Collection); Levi Silliman Ives (Author's Collection); John Loughlin (Courtesy of the *Tablet*); John Gilmary Shea (Author's Collection); John Drumgoole (Author's Collection); Sister Irene Fitzgibbon (Author's Collection); Sister Mary Walsh (Courtesy of *Catholic New York*); St. Frances Xavier Cabrini (Author's Collection); Alfred E. Smith (Courtesy of the *Tablet*); Francis P. Duffy (Author's Collection); Patrick Scanlan (Courtesy of the *Tablet*); Mother Theodore Williams (Courtesy of the Franciscan Handmaids of Mary); Servant of God Dorothy Day (Courtesy of Maryknoll Mission Archives); Bishop Francis X. Ford (Courtesy of Maryknoll Mission Archives); Catherine De Hueck Doherty (Courtesy of Madonna House Publications); Frank Sheed and Maisie Ward (Courtesy of Orbis Books); Thomas Merton (Courtesy of Orbis Books); Francis J. Spellman (Courtesy of the Archives of the Archdiocese of New York); Venerable Fulton J. Sheen (Courtesy of the Archives of the Archdiocese of New York); John Corridan (Author's Collection); Terence J. Cooke (Courtesy of the Archives of the Archdiocese of New York); Bryan Karvelis (Courtesy of the *Tablet*); John J. O'Connor (Courtesy of the Archives of the Archdiocese of New York); David Dwyer (Courtesy of Father David Dwyer, C.S.P.); Pamela Shea-Byrnes (Courtesy of Pamela Shea-Byrnes); Guy Sansaricq (Courtesy of the *Tablet*); Megan Fincher (Courtesy of Megan Fincher); Ed Wilkinson (Courtesy of the *Tablet*); James Martin (Courtesy of *America Magazine*); Pamela D. Hayes (Courtesy of Pamela D. Hayes); Father Raymond Nobiletti (Maryknoll Mission Archives, photographer: Gulnara Samoilova);Thomas Colucci (Courtesy of Catholic New York); Tony Rossi (Courtesy of the Christophers); Rosemarie Pace (Courtesy of Pax Christi Metro); Greg Kandra (Courtesy of Niranjan Fernando); Mother Agnes Donovan (Courtesy of the Sisters of Life); Michael Greene (Courtesy of Bishop Molloy Retreat House); Tyrone Davis (Courtesy of the Office of Black Ministry, Archdiocese of New York); Peter Quinn (Courtesy of Peter Quinn); Matthew Schiller (Courtesy of *Catholic New York*); Gregory Chisholm (Courtesy of St. Charles Borromeo Church); Gerald Ryan (Courtesy of St. Luke's Church); Regis Philbin (Courtesy of Chris Sheridan); Mary Higgins Clark (Courtesy of Catholic New York)